Bush Hat, Black Tie

Also by Howard R. Simpson

The Paratroopers of the French Foreign Legion (1997)
Someone Else's War (1995)
Dien Bien Phu: The Epic Battle America Forgot (1994)
Tiger in the Barbed Wire (1992)
Cogan's Case (1992)
A Very Large Consulate (1988)
A Gathering of Gunmen (1987)
Junior Year Abroad (1986)
The Jumpmaster (1984)
The Obelisk Conspiracy (1975)
Rendezvous off Newport (1973)
The Three-Day Alliance (1971)
Assignment for a Mercenary (1965)
To a Silent Valley (1961)

Bush Hat, Black Tie
Adventures of a Foreign Service Officer

Howard R. Simpson

An ADST-DACOR Diplomats and Diplomacy Book

Brassey's

WASHINGTON • LONDON

Editorial Offices:
22883 Quicksilver Drive
Dulles, VA 20166

Order Department:
P.O. Box 960
Herndon, VA 20172

Brassey's books are available at special discounts for bulk purchases for sales promotions, premiums, fund-raising, or educational use.

Library of Congress Cataloging-in-Publication Data

Simpson, Howard R., 1925–
    Bush hat, black tie : adventures of a foreign service officer /
Howard R. Simpson.
        p.   cm.
    "An ADST-DACOR Diplomats and Diplomacy Book"
    Includes index.
    ISBN 1-57488-154-X
    1. Simpson, Howard R., 1925–   . 2. United States. Foreign
Service—Officials and employees—Biography. I. Title.
E840.8.S545S56   1998
327.73'0092—dc21
[B]   98-19498
                                                        CIP

Designed by Pen & Palette Unlimited

First Edition

10 9 8 7 6 5 4 3 2 1

Printed in the United States of America

To the memory of my Foreign Service colleagues: Lee Brady, George Hellyer, Ed Stansbury, Everett "Dixie" Reese, Jack Andrews, John "Blackjack" Pickering, Arnold Ehrlich, Jack Hedges, and the late Lt. Col. Lucien E. "Black Luigi" Conein of the CIA.

Contents

Foreword

The ADST-DACOR Diplomats and Diplomacy Series

For more than 220 years, extraordinary men and women have represented the United States abroad under all kinds of circumstances. What they did and how and why they did it remain little known to their compatriots. In 1995, the Association for Diplomatic Studies and Training (ADST) and Diplomatic and Consular Officers, Retired (DACOR) created a book series to increase public knowledge and appreciation of the involvement of American diplomats in world history. The series seeks to demystify diplomacy by telling the story of those who have conducted our foreign relations, as they saw them and lived them.

Howard R. Simpson, now a much-published novelist and writer on defense matters, specialized in public affairs in various roles from 1951 to 1979. During the Franco-Vietminh war, he was in turn a decorated U.S. Information Agency correspondent, a psychological warfare operative, and press adviser to Premier Ngo Dinh Diem. Later, in the Foreign Service, he returned to Saigon after postings in Nigeria and France to serve as adviser to Prime Minister Nguyen Khanh. From these experiences came his 1992 book *Tiger in the Barbed Wire: An American in Vietnam, 1952–1991* and his 1994

Dien Bien Phu: The Epic Battle America Forgot. Other assignments included Canberra, Algiers, Marseille (as consul general), Paris, the Naval War College, the State Department, and the University of South Carolina.

In this fifteenth book, Howard Simpson offers a lively narrative of his Foreign Service experiences as a witness to the end of the colonial era and a frontline practitioner of public diplomacy during the Cold War.

Edward M. Rowell, President, ADST

Joan M. Clark, President, DACOR

Preface

My entry into the U.S. Foreign Service was unforeseen and unplanned. It would be no exaggeration to say it just happened. After experiencing World War II service in Europe as a young soldier, I'd studied journalism and art—including a year at the Académie Julian in Paris—under the provisions of the GI Bill. After four years of study, I'd managed to emerge with no degree. I had, however, learned a lot about life, developed a working knowledge of French, achieved an understanding of the basics of journalism, and learned to wield a pen and brush with a certain competence.

After a few months as a copy boy—the classic route into journalism in the 1950s—I had become a staff artist for the old San Francisco *Call Bulletin*, a Hearst newspaper. I had also begun to produce regular book and film reviews to remind the editors that my professional interests were not limited to art.

It was a wild period, a "Front Page" existence in a good newspaper town. The city room was wreathed in cigar smoke, typewriters and telex machines clattered, editors kept bottles of whiskey in their desks, and one of the *Call's* columnists, Ed "Cobie" Coblentz, wore a homburg and spats and carried a Malacca cane. It was somehow comforting to know that Mark Twain and Robert Louis Stevenson had been contributors to the *Call Bulletin* when the West was still semiwild. Once the paper was put to bed we often walked to San Francisco's North Beach district for a bit of bar crawling followed by momentous

Italian dinners washed down with generous glasses of jug red from the Napa valley.

I had found a small studio in the aged, red brick building on upper Montgomery Street, nicknamed the "Monkey Block" by the early residents of San Francisco's bohemia. When the fog dissipated you could see the ghostly outline of Coit Tower from my window.

I'd fit easily into the "City." My grandfather Simpson, a first generation American of Scots ancestry and original '49er, had sailed around the Horn from New York to make his fortune in the California goldfields. After a few months of pick and shovel work with little result, he'd returned to San Francisco to open one of the first pharmacies on what was then known as the "Barbary Coast."

My grandfather Profumo had left Genoa to establish an Italian delicatessen in North Beach. His side of the family introduced me to the enjoyment of good food, exuberance, and the cult of *la famiglia* above all.

When I walked out the door of the Monkey Block, I could smell the distinctive odors of San Francisco's Embarcadero: roasting coffee from the Folgers installation; rich, melted chocolate from the Ghiradelli plant; and acidy coconut pulp from the copra docks. Closer to home, the fragrance of minestrone issued from the Iron Pot restaurant across the street. The often-raided Black Cat bar, with its weird, multisexed clientele, was nearby. The dark and mysterious Li-Po tavern in Chinatown, Henri Lenoir's artsy Vesuvio Cafe, Lawrence Ferlinghetti's City Lights Bookshop—home of the "beats"—and La Tosca, famous for its brandy capuccinos and juke box of Italian operas, were a few blocks away.

Some of the women artists and writers in the neighborhood were desirable and free-living. An attractive woman from one of the temples of commerce on Montgomery Street appeared to find my semibohemian lifestyle a welcome contrast to that of her buttoned-down male colleagues.

It should have been an ideal situation for a 25-year-old bachelor. But it wasn't. I quickly learned that newspaper staff artists spent most of their time retouching photos and arguing with the photographers who took them. Producing the rare cartoon or illustration was an exception. Observing my colleagues in the art department, I noted that those approaching retirement age had occupied the same desks, worn the same green eye shades, done the same daily tasks, and followed the same routines for many years. It was not an inspiring prospect.

My memories of World War II were still vivid, and, as a student, I had observed the Marshall Plan in full swing in France. Now the Korean War was filling the front pages, the United States had become a major international power... and I was tied to an ink-stained desk at the *Call Bulletin.*

One night, listening to a late news bulletin, I heard the breathless narration of a war correspondent making a combat jump with an American parachute unit in Korea. He was a member of the U.S. Information Service (USIS), the information branch of the State Department. I made a foggy mental note of this unknown organization and thought no more about it.

Weeks later, a police reporter dropped a page-3 article on my desk. "You like to travel," he said, "here's your chance." I put aside my cigar and read that the State Department was recruiting journalists to serve overseas with USIS and that an officer would soon be visiting San Francisco to interview interested candidates. Applicants were asked to contact a specific number at the federal building to make an appointment. I made that call and it changed my life.

I entered the Foreign Service at the bottom of the ladder in 1951 and retired as a senior officer in 1979. My overseas assignments took me to French Indochina, Nigeria, Australia, Algeria, and, on several occasions, both Vietnam and France. My domestic assignments included a short stint in the State Department; graduation from the School of Naval Warfare at the Naval War College in Newport, Rhode Island; an additional year there as a faculty adviser and consultant to the president; and a period as a diplomat in residence at the University of South Carolina.

This book is not a month-by-month diary record of my Foreign Service career. Instead, I have attempted, when possible, to link the narrative to situations, events, and happenings. I hope it will provide a better understanding of life as it was in the diplomatic service during the decolonization period and the Cold War. This was a period when the old, traditional Foreign Service, with its preponderance of Ivy League, eastern seaboard officers, was leavened with a large intake of World War II veterans from various states and differing backgrounds. These newcomers, myself included, had already faced hard reality overseas. I like to think we brought a welcome nonconformism and unique humor to the profession of diplomacy. Having survived a war, we were not likely to be cowed by petty administrative tyrants or the pompous poseurs who occasionally dominated a diplomatic mission.

Some of the newcomers could never quite make the adjustment from wartime hell-raising to the diplomatic life, but the presence of those who did contributed to more flexible and realistic operational procedures.

Although the passing of time often tends to blur specific memories and dates, the events in this book are factual and, I trust, untainted by political correctness. Some names have been changed to protect the guilty.

I believe most Foreign Service veterans would agree that few other professions offer such a variety of interesting, adventurous, and—at times—dangerous assignments. My only advice to those now entering the ranks would be: Beware of creeping bureaucracy, don't take yourself too seriously, and enjoy your new career.

One further note: One of my previously published books, *Tiger in the Barbed Wire*, detailed my experiences in Indochina during both the French and American conflicts there. The references to those periods in this volume have therefore been condensed.

Acknowledgments

I would like to thank the Freedom of Information and Privacy Act Section of the U.S. Information Agency for its cooperation in providing me with a copy of my personnel file. This was of considerable help in matching dates to assignments.

I am indebted to Bob Guldin, the editor of the *Foreign Service Journal*, for allowing me to excerpt material from some of my previously published articles in that magazine.

Thanks also to Ambassador William L. Eagleton Jr., who straightened me out on facts and dates relative to our service in Algeria; to Thomas W. Branigar, archivist of the Dwight D. Eisenhower Library in Abilene, Kansas, for his prompt and detailed response to my query on President Eisenhower's 1959 arrival in Toulon; and to Marylin D. Curtis, director of library functions of the Redwood Library and Atheneum in Newport, Rhode Island, who clarified the history and location of General Rochambeau's statue in that city.

My wife deserves special credit for recalling people and incidents during our life on the diplomatic circuit and for continually reminding me that I was dealing with fact and not plying my trade as a novelist.

Finally, my appreciation to all those, of many nationalities, with whom I worked in the Foreign Service. Without realizing it, they too have contributed to the publication of this book. I hope they will find it truthful as well as entertaining.

1

From Foggy Bottom to Vietnam

Tonkin Delta, near Nam Dinh, November 1952. The two dead Vietnamese officers are already in their closed coffins in the bullet-pocked, deserted pagoda. It has been raining all day, and water dripping from the shattered tile roof has discolored the light wood of the coffins. There isn't much to do except stand there dumbly, bush hat in hand, remembering how we had shared a lunch of chicken and rice two days earlier. They had been very young and in good spirits. I turn toward the door.

"Tirés comme des lapins!" ("Shot like rabbits!") a French officer murmurs, lighting a cigarette, "not enough training, not enough experience."

I look out on the delta with its flat, gray expanse of damp paddies, scattered villages, bamboo stands, and muddy dikes, musing on what brought me there. I was far from my desk in the art department of the San Francisco *Call Bulletin*. It had all come together in Washington, D.C.

"It is *most* important that you arrange to have your calling cards printed before departing for your posts."

The protocol officer lecturing on diplomatic etiquette at the State Department's Foreign Service Institute (FSI) in November 1951 was impeccably turned out in a gray suit, white shirt, and rep tie with collar clip. Everything about him shouted Brooks Brothers. He'd then proceeded to explain how diplomatic calls on our "superiors" were to be handled and lingered on the niceties of leaving a card with a folded corner in the event the person was not at home. I think that's what he was saying. In truth, I'd lost interest and wasn't really listening. If this is what the State Department considered important, I was beginning to have doubts about my new career.

I'd arrived in Washington, D.C., one evening in the late fall of 1951 to join the Foreign Service as an information specialist. An early snowfall had dusted the streets, filling the fading light with translucent crystals. The cab ride from National Airport past the floodlit monuments, broad avenues, and statues had been an impressive introduction to the nation's capital.

I'd lodged temporarily at the Roger Smith Hotel, a short walk from the White House and across the street from 1776 Pennsylvania Avenue, the USIS building and headquarters for President Harry S Truman's "Campaign of Truth." This was a euphemism for regearing America's propaganda capabilities to fill the demands of the Cold War. The Office of War Information (OWI), responsible for the U.S. government's worldwide information operations during World War II, had been abolished in 1945, and its reduced functions had been turned over to the Department of State.

Now, to explain U.S. policies to the world and counter "Soviet lies," the propaganda attacks of the Iron Curtain countries, Communist China, and North Korea, the U.S. Information and Education (USIE) branch of the department was expanding. Although this entity was officially known as the U.S. Information Service (USIS) overseas, the same nomenclature was generally used in Washington.

Our incoming group of recruits had been formally greeted in the staid halls of New State, but most of our time was spent in the old brick pile of the Foreign Service Institute attending lectures, learning Foreign Service basics, and being tested in whatever skills we had to offer. We were a mixed bag: some former journalists—print, radio, and film—a few OWI retreads, some professorial types specializing in exotic languages or foreign cultures, and some earnest librarians, both male and female.

Watching these heterogeneous colleagues fit into their new official positions, I pondered the task of the FBI agents and State Department security officers charged with obtaining our security clearances. Not that we were particular risks, but the clearance process must have taken the investigators into wholly unfamiliar environments. My own Confidential clearance document, dated August 14, 1951, and addressed to the chief of Foreign Service Personnel, is now unclassified. At one time it had six attachments: four FBI reports, one State Department security report (domestic), and one State Department security report (Paris).

Under "Remarks," the drafting officer had placed an X in one of the six explanatory categories. It reads, "Investigation reveals personnel information you may desire to review prior to appointment." I will never know what this note refers to, but I would guess it probably covered my wild student days in Paris or my bohemian lifestyle in San Francisco. The last penned note on the memo was undoubtedly instrumental in opening the doors to a new career. "Favorable," it reads and is signed, "Alden." Whoever Alden is or wherever he may be today, he merits my thanks.

My low rank meant that my assigned courses included the use of the one-time pad—the basic tool of coding and decoding—and a disastrous few days trying to improve my typing skills. These were followed by a formal written French examination that I barely passed.

As our short introductory course at the FSI drew to a close, our group spent a lot of time speculating on the possible locations of our first assignments. We had also learned some basic truths about the State Department. We were all in the same organization, but there was a considerable difference between the personnel, working methods, and outlook of the department and of USIS.

The sounds were muted in the long halls of the department, the personnel were conservatively dressed, and the secretaries seemed impersonal and their bosses aloof. It soon became apparent that the word "information" was a red flag to some of the department's senior officers. They were at home in their quiet, traditional world of hand-drafted diplomatic notes, classified material, dispatches, telegrams, and courier-borne pouches. Information programs, particularly if managed by OWI veterans and newly recruited newsmen, were often viewed as beyond the pale of diplomatic activity and as possible threats to the department's goals and procedures. Some career Foreign Service officers looked down on USIS as an upstart propaganda organization, a loose cannon, and joked among themselves that USIS was pronounced

4 Bush Hat, Black Tie

"useless." I was too busy with my training schedule to analyze these attitudes, but I had the uneasy premonition they extended to the field.

This was a heady period in Washington. The United States was filling a new, participatory role as a major international power, and members of the Foreign Service were destined to be among its leading players. There was a definite buzz in the corridors of power, and it transmitted itself downward to the rank and file. Nothing seemed impossible. This can-do attitude contained a certain naïveté, a definite hazard in dealing with the real world of postwar political-military truths.

Rumor had it that the USIS personnel office decided our overseas assignments by throwing darts at a large map of the world. It made a good story. The assignment list appeared in the Foreign Service lounge just before Christmas. One colleague told me he'd drawn wartime Seoul, another was headed for Rome. I hurried to read the notice, optimistically expecting to return to Paris. The USIS staff there was expanding, I spoke the language, I'd been there during the liberation and as an art student, and I knew the territory. It seemed a natural. That dream faded when I found my name on the list.

"Howard R. Simpson—Saigon, Vietnam, French Indochina." Stunned, I tried to muster some instant knowledge by replaying the memory of black and white newsreel footage: French troops trudging through thick mud near a burning village; Vietminh guerrillas raising their starred flag over a captured French outpost. Hell, a full-scale war was going on in Vietnam!

I tried to concentrate on the good news. Saigon, because of health conditions and other "risks," was rated a hardship post. This meant a welcome 25 percent addition to my base pay.

Halfway through the briefings on my first assignment I found a message in my mail slot. The chief of USIS Saigon was passing through Washington on his way back to the post and would like to see me before his departure. A meeting was quickly arranged. Lee Brady, an OWI veteran and the officer who had originally interviewed me as a job candidate at the Fairmont Hotel in San Francisco, greeted me with a wry smile, welcomed me to his staff, and gave me some personal tips on life in Saigon. He warned me about the steamy heat of the tropics and recommended I bring at least two light suits. Shorts and knee socks would be acceptable for daytime wear in the office, but a white dinner jacket and black tie would be needed for formal occasions. This gave me pause. I had not even considered the acquisition of formal attire. Brady must have seen my frown.

"If the director of Vietnam Presse invites you to a formal dinner," he explained, "you don't want to run around Saigon looking for a tailor." It was a reasonable comment, but a black tie soirée didn't fit my image of Indochina at war.

I was about to leave Brady's temporary office when he remembered a last bit of information. "Oh," he said, "I've arranged for you to have a week's consultation at the American Embassy in Paris on your way to Saigon."

Only three years had passed since I'd finished my art studies in Paris, and I was eager to see Montparnasse again. The USIS officer behind a huge desk at the embassy looked blank when I explained my presence. He examined my orders as if they'd been drafted on Mars, shrugged, and sent me to the embassy's political section.

My interlocutor there had never been to Indochina. He hesitantly referred to a briefing paper he'd produced from his filing cabinet. The entire process took no more than 20 minutes and left me with the impression that the embassy would not be unhappy if France's Indochina colonies, with all their problems, were to disappear overnight. After stopping by the travel office to confirm my onward voyage, I returned to USIS.

"Look," the embarrassed officer admitted, "we have no program planned for you. You're on your way to Saigon. Why don't you enjoy your few days in Paris. Give me your number and we'll call if anything comes up."

A week of freedom in Paris! It was as if someone had presented me with a belated Christmas gift. I turned down the offer of a room in an embassy-favored hotel on the Right Bank and returned to the Hôtel de Blois on the rue Vavin in the heart of Montparnasse, a *hôtel de passe* where I'd occupied a garret room as an art student. My old friends, including *madame la concierge* of the Hôtel de Blois; Adrien, the former Foreign Legionnaire and owner of the nightclub Chez Adrien; *madame la patronne* of the Café Kosmos; and the "professional women" who worked the quartier, were nonplussed at my appearance. A beardless, necktie-wearing "Sim-son" in a three-piece suit and shined shoes—and with money in his pocket! It was almost too much for them to contemplate.

My week in Paris went fast. So did the money. There were no calls from the embassy, but twinges of conscience did force me to carry out my own informal consultation. I sat on the enclosed terrace of the Café Select each morning over an ice-cold Perrier and a black coffee, scouring three or four French dailies for news and editorial comment on Indochina. Although the editorials split along established party lines, it was obvious that France's Asian war had become even more unpopular. Certain phrases leapt from the pages: *sale guerre* (dirty war), *nos pertes* (our losses), *embuscade* (ambush) and *nos morts* (our dead). These were just part of the daily lexicon of violence and loss being absorbed by the French public. It was somehow surreal to sit comfortably on a café terrace in Paris knowing that I'd soon be entering that same environment for a period of at least two years.

Saigon welcomed newcomers with sledgehammer heat, bright colors, and pungent, unfamiliar odors. Wide avenues ran between the walled colonial villas, their porticos festooned with bougainvillea, their grounds shaded with broad-leafed banana, whispy tamarind, and brilliant flame trees. The busy streets were alive with small Renault taxis, cyclos, and bicycles. The café terraces were enclosed with antigrenade mesh and filled with stout *colons* in white suits sipping pastis, off-duty officers, and groups of Foreign Legionnaires on leave from their upcountry units.

And the women! The slim, graceful Vietnamese in their silk ao dais, black hair cascading down their backs, walked on clacking sandals, their conical, woven hats held at an angle to shade them from the hot sun. Their sudden laughter tinkled like delicate chimes. Young Chinese women in high-collared cheong-sams slit to the knee moved like oriental princesses through the crowds, followed by their betel-chewing amahs laden with full shopping baskets. Chic, mixed-blood métis of incredible beauty sipped lemonade on the café terraces that were frequented by young French army officers in their tropical whites.

The still Saigon air carried the sweetness of exotic flowers, the richness of black tobacco, the scent of various perfumes, whiffs of draft beer and spilled wine from the cafés, the mixed redolence of European and Asian cooking, the rich beef or chicken broth of the street vendors' *soupe Saigonnaise* or *Pho*, with their acid bite of *nuoc mam*, or the aura of crushed garlic rising from the *Aïoli* sauce served to the Corsican entrepreneurs on the terrace of the Hotel Continental. The rare breeze from the Saigon River brought with it the heated miasma of the nearby mangrove swamps and the salt tang of the not-too-distant sea.

At night the French artillery on the city's outskirts began its harassment and interdiction fire, the sound carrying to downtown Saigon as a series of thumps, a reminder that the war was real and not far away.

In addition to my original assignments as legation press officer and U.S. representative on the Franco-Vietnamese Psychological Warfare Committee, I was appointed official USIS war correspondent, complete with bush hat, shoulder tab, and concealed Colt. The latter was not an affectation but a reflection of the type of war I was to cover. This included a general disregard for the Geneva Convention and the likelihood that a captured "imperialist American propagandist" would have either an extremely uncomfortable captivity or a short life span. Regardless, American military aid was pouring into Indochina, and it was my job to report on its actual use in the field. My travels would take me throughout Vietnam and into Cambodia and Laos.

Phnom Penh, Cambodia, April 1952. The two armies faced each other on the dusty field in front of the royal palace. Bright overhead lights caught the gold, scarlet, and blue of the soldiers' uniforms and glinted on the polished metal of their unsharpened swords and lances. The nervous, decorated royal elephants shifted in place, blowing, trumpeting, and swaying their huge, gray heads. They moved a few steps backwards and forwards, unused to the hammered metal of their makeshift battle armor and the weight of the overcrowded howdahs on their backs. Beyond the lights the flowing band of the wide Mekong provided a dark backdrop to the spectacle.

Prince Norodom Sihanouk, our host for the evening, was beaming down on the scene, a reenactment of a centuries-old victory of his Khmer ancestors over the Vietnamese. His chubby face shone with excitement and his high-pitched voice could be heard over the Cambodian music of the court orchestra as he enthusiastically explained a historical point to a Western ambassador.

I'd been summoned from the encampment of a Cambodian parachute battalion at Pursat, near the great lake of Tonle Sap, to represent Lee Brady at this gala evening. The prince, the essence of ebullient bonhomie, greeted me with a double-handed handshake as if encountering an old friend after a long absence.

The orchestra stopped playing, and musicians in the ranks of the opposing armies set up a terrific din of drums, trumpets, and cymbals. A signal was given, and the armies launched themselves at each other, colorful battle flags fluttering over the howdahs, the foot soldiers shouting as they ran alongside the rushing, flap-eared elephants.

The scene shifted from historical pageant to dangerous reality as the assault waves came together with an earthshaking shock. Howdahs flew into the air, loosened by the jolt of contact, shedding their human cargos. Elephants shied from the noise and the shouting soldiers who, in their excitement and desire to please the prince, were trading real blows with their dulled weapons.

The field was now a shambles. Both armies were indistinguishably mixed and were more intent on gathering the injured than finishing the spectacle. Mahouts were chasing their errant mounts. The confused beasts were doing their best to shed their off-kilter battle armor and were not being too careful where they placed their heavy feet. Litter bearers, wearing red cross brassards, trotted onto the field to carry off the injured. The prince was ecstatic, leading the applause and nodding his approval, obviously pleased that the Khmers had, once again, been victorious.

We were all led to a sumptuous buffet on candlelit tables stretching along the marble floor of the palace's open terrace. A British diplomat accepted a cognac-soda from a white-jacketed waiter and suggested I do the same.

"We have hours of Cambodian dancing ahead of us," he confided grimly. "You'll need a few of these."

"Sounds interesting," I ventured.

The Brit said nothing for a moment, sipping his drink.

"Like watching varnish dry," he finally murmured.

Nasan, Northwest Vietnam, December 1952. The outgoing friendly fire was shaking the collapsible metal desks and sending cascades of loose soil onto the earthen floor of the damp command dugout. The barrage was too regular and rapid to be a simple harassing fire. Coughs and catches in the electric generator were causing the light to fade periodically. The radio operator cursed the constant static that filled the limited space like the hissing of cicadas. None of the headquarters staff were wearing helmets. They worked with their overlays and field telephones bareheaded, wearing the soft *calot*, overseas cap, in the colors of their regiments, or the omnipresent Anzac-type bush hat.

I moved to the sandbagged dugout entrance and pushed aside the heavy flap of treated canvas. I could see red and green tracers cutting into the night and the distant flash of exploding 105mm shells behind the black outline of the hills. The Vietminh 308th and 312th Divisions were out there somewhere, perhaps preparing another assault on the French fortifications like that of November 30 that had cost them over 400 dead. Or they might be miles away, returning to their mountain redoubt for reinforcements, resupply, and rest.

"*Hé, là, l'Amerloque!*" the one-eyed parachute general shouted from his map table. "Stand clear of that entry! Do you want to catch a piece of shrapnel?"

Vientiane, Laos, April 1953. The Foreign Legion BMC *(bordel militaire de campagne)* was located near the sleepy administrative capital of Laos. My host, a huge Legion captain, pulled his jeep to a stop outside the stilted thatched hut, returned the salute of the sentry, and led me up the wobbly bamboo ladder. His job was to inspect the official bordello for enlisted legionnaires. The manager was a short, middle-aged Chinese woman with a moonlike face. Her black hair was pulled tightly back in a bun, and her gold tooth glinted when she deigned to smile from her station behind the small bar. The shaky hut, with its floor of woven mats and four alcoves with straw-filled mattresses and thin doors, was her domain. The slim, giggling Laotian prostitutes in blue and red shifts embroidered with gold thread were her staff.

We'd been driving through heat and dust. It took two Tiger beers to clear our throats. While we'd been drinking, a Legion customer enjoying himself in one of the cubicles had set the whole hut swaying with his efforts.

Then trouble arrived. Three parachutists from a colonial battalion had been drinking somewhere else and had bulled their way past the sentry. Now, ignoring the presence of the Legion officer, they were shouting for cognac.

The captain stepped forward. "You have no business here," he told them. "This is Legion territory."

One of the paras, a short man with a crude blue tattoo, lifted his tanned forearm in a defiant *bras d'honneur.* "This for the Legion!" he growled, exhaling the odor of cognac.

Emerging from his cubicle and fastening his belt, the requited Legionnaire took his place beside the captain. The manager and her girls withdrew to the far end of the hut. I moved to the window, hoping to summon the sentry, but his back was turned as if he was unaware of the situation.

"Leave now," the captain recommended, "and there'll be no problem."

"Ta gueule!" the para responded, "Shut up!" Thus ended all hope for a peaceful settlement. The captain's right fist slammed into the para's jaw with a powerful thud, throwing the man's head back. A second blow came down like a hammer, just below the para's left ear, and he fell backward onto the unsteady flooring. There was a loud crack, a swishing sound, and he disappeared from sight.

We all moved forward to peer down through the newly made hole in the floor. The para was lying on his back, unconscious, under a pile of shredded matting and split bamboo. The sentry, torn from his reverie, was bending over the man, trying to rouse him.

It was a ludicrous scene, a still from a Chaplin classic. I'm not sure who laughed first but we all joined in—the captain, the Legionnaire, the paras, and myself. Even the manager chuckled, holding her hand over her mouth. The Laotian girls giggled as they gathered up shards from a broken glass. The chastened paras withdrew to revive and carry off their comrade while I ordered two more beers.

Tay Ninh, South Vietnam, November 1953. The rococo Cao Dai temple blazed with light despite the military curfew. I had been to visit the Cao Dai once before, but this time I'd been invited to spend the night. At least 200 worshippers were kneeling on the polished tile floor before the raised altar and the huge blue ball studded with stars and an all-seeing eye. Brightly painted plaster snakes curled around the temple's thick support columns, and the wide arches on both sides were open to the night and the chirp of crickets. The chanting was continual and monotonous. The priests and monks maintained a baritone bass, the nuns' voices rose higher. To the Western ear the chant seemed a rhythmic repetition of "nga, nga, nga." The sudden loud bong of a gong followed by a diminishing series of gong taps marked changes in the service and the priest's movements.

Earlier, the monk who had greeted me at the portico and indicated that I should remove my shoes had explained that Jesus, Buddha, Victor Hugo, Sun Yat-sen, and Joan of Arc were all saints of the Cao Dai religion. A wall mural at the temple's entrance depicted these saints—with Victor Hugo in the full regalia of a French académician—in a heavenly setting. The monk also informed me that Winston Churchill, once he died, would be a prime candidate for canonization.

Watching the ceremony from a high, interior balcony, I noted the mustard- and khaki-colored uniforms that formed a separate block of worshippers near the rear of the temple. These hard-faced, lean troops were members of the 17,000-strong army loyal to the Cao Dai "pope." Trained and equipped by the Japanese occupiers during World War II, they were now fighting the Vietminh under the tutelage of French military intelligence.

The religious service lasted for two hours before we adjourned to the monks' quarters for a vegetarian meal. I was the only Westerner among the shaven-headed monks and three officers of the Cao Dai army. The refectory resembled a military mess. One wall was hung with framed photos commemorating the Japanese–Cao Dai alliance. Serious-looking Japanese and Cao Dai officers in bellicose poses stared at the camera, clutching samurai swords or binoculars.

The meal was delicious. A vegetable broth spiced with lemon grass was followed by various dishes, including rice with bamboo shoots and a vegetable paté for dipping in soy sauce. We drank green tea and bottles of French mineral water that were on the table. Young male acolytes provided the service, their straw sandals sliding over the tiles. The monks applied themselves to the filled bowls, chopsticks clicking, and paused only to urge more food on me.

My visit had been planned as an orientation effort and an attempt to make a working psywar (psychological warfare) contact with one of Vietnam's leading anti-Communist, religious-military sects. Although the monks were polite and smiled often, the Cao Dai officers were unsmiling and appeared unfriendly. Was it because only eight short years had passed since we had defeated their Japanese allies? Unlikely. It was more probable that they were reflecting the attitude of their French intelligence mentors and advisers.

Although U.S. military aid was supporting the French war effort and we were supposedly allied against the communist domination of Southeast Asia, there was considerable French mistrust of American intentions in Indochina. French intelligence operatives were particularly suspicious of what they saw as a probable "Anglo-Saxon" (read "U.S.") attempt to take over their prize colony and last productive foothold in the Far East. The fact that no French officers appeared at the dinner table while I was a guest of the Cao Dai was a minor reflection of this attitude.

Later, after a monk lighted an anti-mosquito coil in my cell-like room and left a glass of coconut milk for me, I tried to sleep on the hard, thin mattress. A woman laughed in the halls and I heard some movement. Recalling the obvious attractiveness of some of the Cao Dai nuns, I wondered whether the monks were required to take a vow of celibacy.

A major personal event occurred in Saigon during late 1953. I fell in love with Mary Alice Turner, a newly arrived secretary at the U.S. Mutual Security Mission. We'd met for the first time on the terrace of the Hotel Continental. I was unaware that this was a landmark in my life, but her lively green eyes, her laugh, her personality, and her figure combined to enthrall me. I was not alone. Other men appreciated these attributes, and there were rivals.

Following a long period of persistent courting, we became lovers. We were regulars at the terrace bar of the Hotel Majestic, where Jean, the pianist, greeted our arrival with his rendition of Charles Trenet's *"Que reste-t'il?"* We danced the pasa-doble in the seedy ambiance of le Tour d'Ivoire. We dined at l'Amiral, the restaurant rendezvous of the French paras; a Vietnamese restaurant offering ten different beef dishes in one meal; and Le Papillon, a shady Corsican establishment where Yvonne, the attractive métis manager, thoroughly approved of Mary Alice and told me I'd be a fool not to marry her.

The months passed. USIS moved out of the State Department to become the independent U.S. Information Agency (USIA). Although the State Department would continue to make and direct policy, USIA would have more operational autonomy. Most USIS officers welcomed the move.

After covering additional military operations, including the opening phase of the battle of Dien Bien Phu, my two-year tour of duty was up. I was ordered on home leave, but George Hellyer, my new boss, a pipe-puffing ex-Marine captain who had served with Ord Wingate's Chindits in Burma, lobbied me to return for an additional year. A promotion and an American assistant would be part of the agreement. At the same moment *Time* magazine offered me a stringer position in Saigon.

These proposals called for important decisions, but none of them were as important as a decision to propose marriage. I did inform *Time* that I'd decided to remain with USIA and return to Saigon. But I was still waffling on marriage.

Mary Alice and I spent a week together in Hong Kong. We drank at the Foreign Correspondent's Club, lunched at the Parisian Grill and dined at brightly lit, tile-walled Cantonese and Szechuan restaurants in Kowloon. Over dinner at Gaddi's in the Peninsula Hotel on the eve of my departure, I told Mary Alice my feelings for her were "serious" but I still didn't broach the question. I boarded the SS *President Wilson* for San Francisco, and she flew back to Saigon.

Finally, after a long sea voyage and a week among the redwoods of northern California, I proposed by cable. We were reunited in San Francisco, married in Las Vegas, and honeymooned in Carmel and Paris. Hellyer had arranged a week's consultation in Paris. This time no one even attempted to brief me.

The additional year in Saigon proved a whirlwind of important events and happenings. Many French officials and military officers, withdrawing from Indochina after their defeat at Dien Bien Phu, had become actively anti-American. The American embassy, with the help of Col. Edward G. Lansdale and his CIA team, was supporting the installation of Ngo Dinh Diem as Vietnam's first independent prime minister. I was finally able to wear my black tie to a palace function while acting as a press adviser to Diem. The director of Vietnam Presse never did invite me to a formal dinner.

I was then sent north to evacuate USIS personnel from Hanoi and cover the arrival in the city of General Giap's Vietminh forces. I returned to Saigon to learn that Mary Alice and I were going to have our first child. Meanwhile, the Binh Xuyen river pirates and the religious-military sects, the Cao Dao and Hoa Hao, were planning a revolt with the assistance of French military intelligence. The outbreak of fighting on March 28, 1955, coincided with the birth of our daughter, Shawn.

Her mother went into labor at the Clinique St. Paul to the accompaniment of exploding mortar rounds and hissing tracers. It didn't make things easier to know my name had been printed on the Binh Xuyen "death list." Later, when I came under direct, aimed fire from a Binh Xuyen position, it dawned on me with a special clarity that I was now a married man with a family.

With the revolt finally crushed and the sect armies scattered, we faced a new trial. I suffered a sudden high fever, which was diagnosed as infectious hepatitis. I was evacuated to the Air Force hospital at Clark Field in the Philippines, leaving Mary Alice and our newborn in an isolated Saigon villa with no security. Her courage and resourcefulness during this period set the norm for other rough spots that lay ahead.

Weeks later, I returned to Saigon cured, much thinner, and under doctor's orders to avoid alcohol for six months. I'd also had enough of government service. The promised promotion had not come through, and fissures of corruption and strong-arm totalitarianism were already appearing in the Diem regime. Three long years in Vietnam—the war, the tensions, and the illness—had drained me.

Daydreams in the hospital had produced a workable fantasy. I would leave USIA. Buoyed by my severance pay and Mary Alice's life insurance refund, the three of us would seek a quiet haven on some low-rent island in the sun. There I would write a novel revealing the *true* story of Indochina.

Our harbor-front villa in Puerto Andraitz, northwest of Palma de Mallorca, was the perfect location for relaxation after three years in Saigon. A rental of $35 a month seemed more than fair for the two-bedroom villa and the rowboat that went with it. The sun was constant in September and October 1955. It glistened on the bay as the small, high-prowed fishing boats chugged out to sea each morning and back-lit them as they rolled home in the late afternoon.

We'd sailed on the old French liner *la Marseillaise* from Saigon via Singapore, Colombo, Djibouti, the Suez Canal, and Port Said to Marseille. Our 14-day voyage had echoes of Evelyn Waugh's *Scoop*, complete with shipboard bores, untidy, thumb-in-the-mayonnaise waiters, backed-up plumbing, and the insufferable heat of the Red Sea.

In Colombo my wife bought me a sandalwood box of "Havana" cigars. They proved to be wormholed. Thin spirals of fetid smoke rose from each hole as they were lit. I put them aside as perfect end-of-voyage tips for the unsmiling, somnolent waiters and cabin staff. At Djibouti we hired an open taxi to visit the dung-spattered camel market on the edge of the desert. It was the closest I ever came to sun stroke. The town's bars were sub-Bogart, with creaking overhead fans and turbaned vendors selling wide-bladed spears. In Port Said, an Egyptian bartender bilked me out of some cash with the old egg-in-the-glass game.

Being on the wagon did not improve my disposition. I suppose sitting through lunch and dinner without sampling the gratis bottles of red and white wine on the table was a character-building exercise. The sommelier, accustomed to serving colonials with acute *mal au foie*, poured my Vittel as if it was a rare Bordeaux. From Marseille we'd flown to Palma de Mallorca, where an American expatriate in the real estate trade had found us the villa in Puerto Andraitz.

The small port, with its clear blue water, was surrounded by rocky hills studded with pine, olive, and almond trees. The village was tranquil and self-contained. Only the occasional Guardia Civil presence reminded us that this was Franco's Spain, but the uniformed individuals seemed as easygoing as the villagers were and paid scant attention to the presence of foreigners.

A letter from Theodore Streibert, the director of USIA, was awaiting me in Puerto Andraitz. He had "reluctantly" accepted my resignation. A handwritten note at the bottom of the page expressed the hope I would return to the agency after I had gotten the year in Majorca "out of my system." He concluded by stating "we will be glad to have you back at any time." A second missive from George Hellyer informed me that I was to receive USIA's highest honor, the Distinguished Service Award (medal), for my Indochina service and asked where the citation and medal should be sent. I suggested the USIS office at the consulate general in Barcelona as the most convenient solution.

I began work on my Indochina novel at 9:00 each morning with the intention of working at least until noon. But I was often sidetracked, concentrating on travel articles in the hope of bringing in a little cash. The mail was due on the 11:00 A.M. bus from Palma. There was a constant temptation to stroll into the village for the mail pickup. This would be followed by a glass or two of Tio Pepe at the Bodega Tor (a Spanish medico had conveniently declared me recovered from the hepatitis). After a heavy lunch prepared by Eugenia, our part-time helper, I found it hard to concentrate and often succumbed to the local custom of siesta.

The novel, needless to say, was progressing very slowly. There was always some distraction—a gleaming new yacht tacking into the harbor; an invitation to a local *matanza*, or pig-slaughtering, culminating with a communal feast of pork stew swimming in olive oil; or a bus trip into Palma for a taste of big city life. Jaime Porcel, a stout, aging villager kept us supplied with eggs and with wood for the cooking range and fireplace. He had worked in California during the Depression. His repertoire of tales from his time as a hotel chef in Fresno had the ring of Steinbeck.

"Each Sunday," he loved to relate, "we serve roast turkey with gravy. Only it is never turkey. Pork was cheaper. So they say, 'Jaime, slice pork thin and cover with gravy.' No one complained."

Picking up my USIA decoration in Barcelona was an anticlimax. On arrival at the consulate, we were left to cool our heels in the waiting room. When a secretary finally ushered us into the USIS office, the public affairs officer seemed unsure of our purpose. A dim light bulb of recognition flicked on when I explained the situation. He shuffled through his desk drawer, retrieved a large official envelope containing the citation and medal and handed it to me. That was it. I was receiving the agency's highest honor, but there were no congratulations, no photographer, not even a glass of wine for a toast. I suppose I expected too much. If I'd been so set on a proper presentation, I should have made my way to Washington for the ceremony. I left the consulate in a dark mood. We strolled down the Ramblas in bright sunshine, past the brilliant colors of the flower stalls, and regained our humor over a champagne lunch at a busy Barcelona bistro.

The cold arrived in November, and we had to rely on our smoky fireplace for heat. We were unaware that the worst Majorcan winter in 30 years was upon us. The snow fell silently in the dead of night. By noon the next day, few residents had ventured from their homes. The white mantle covering the village streets remained pristine. Separate footprints, like animal tracks, finally appeared. Most of them led to the village bodegón (tavern) with its warm fire and hot rum.

We learned to tolerate the cold, but the next letter to arrive from Washington dealt us a body blow. The Internal Revenue Service was claiming a considerable amount in back taxes on my 25-percent hardship allowance. In our precarious financial situation this meant reducing our stay in Majorca from one year to six months.

There was more bad news in store for us. Picking up a *Newsweek* in Palma, I read an enthusiastic review of Graham Greene's *Quiet*

American. The plot and many of the characters were uncomfortably close to my own. I hurriedly reread the six short chapters I'd produced. There were a few acceptable flashes of description and some passable dialogue, but I had to admit the chapters were not publishable. Luckily, I still held government travel vouchers to our home leave destination of San Francisco. Once there I would have to find a new job.

Sausalito is a small slice of paradise on San Francisco Bay. When the cool fog shrouds the Golden Gate Bridge and obscures the view from Nob Hill, most of Sausalito is likely to be bathed in sunshine. But there is one sector of the town that must have been cursed by the local Indian god of wind and storm. "Hurricane Gulch" is a steep hillside ravine and natural funnel that sucks in the wind and cold air from the Pacific as if through a straw and propels them downward toward the bayside waterfront. Rents were understandably cheaper along the gulch. That is where we found an apartment with a view of the bay.

I then set out to establish myself as a freelance writer and illustrator. I sold a few pieces to Stanleigh Arnold, the Sunday editor of the San Francisco *Chronicle.* Pierre Salinger, then the West Coast editor of *Colliers* magazine, tried to place one of my articles on Indochina. His New York office turned thumbs down. Few Americans were interested in that far-off place. I spoke on Vietnam at the San Francisco Press Club, but most of the audience was there to hear my cospeaker, a local boxing referee. I took the same talk to the Sacramento Chamber of Commerce with much the same result. While there, I opened a show of my Vietnam combat sketches at the Sacramento Public Library and tried a voice test for a newscasting job with the radio station owned by the Sacramento *Bee.* That particular media career was not to be.

My freelancing was bringing in a pittance, and I began to beat the pavement in search of a steady job. My interview in a posh advertising agency was a disaster. The pile rugs seemed ankle deep; the female secretaries were dressed in conservative skirts, sweaters, and pearls; Vivaldi's *Four Seasons* was piped in by Muzak; and the air-conditioned, sterile offices were done in pale pastels. The interviewer had an attack of the vapors when I entered his office smoking a cigar. He spent more time glancing at his watch than he did looking at my portfolio.

Then my luck changed. I'd done a full-page, illustrated article on San Francisco Bay sailing for the Sunday *Chronicle.* Shortly thereafter, I was asked to join the staff of the Sunday *Chronicle*'s "This World" section. "This World" was a condensed copy of the *Time* magazine format, presenting the week's international and national news in short, pithy articles. I went to work as a writer and was soon producing self-illustrated features. It was an ideal newspaper job. Our small team worked 40 hours in four days. We then had Friday, Saturday, and Sunday off.

After two months of riding the bus across the Golden Gate Bridge to San Francisco, the twin afflictions of itchy feet and wanderlust set in. I was enjoying some of the most beautiful vistas in the United States, but the weekly monotony of commuting and churning out endless words for tomorrow's fish wrapper had become a frustrating routine.

One evening, after putting our daughter to bed and enjoying a pleasant meal, we were gazing at the distant lights of the Bay Bridge and listening to the groan of the hollow-voiced fog horns.

"I've been thinking . . . ," I said tentatively, clearing my throat.

"About going back to the agency?" my wife replied.

"Yes."

"So have I."

"It won't be easy," I warned, thinking of the probable reaction of the personnel office.

"Let's do it," my wife volunteered. We toasted the decision with the last of our duty-free cognac.

There was a long silence at the Washington end of the line while George Hellyer tried to digest what I'd said. He was now the deputy director of USIA for East Asia and the Pacific. My call had caught him off guard.

"You what?" he demanded.

"I want to rejoin the agency," I told him, "come back into the fold." Then I dropped my bombshell. "But only as a grade 4 officer." This would constitute a four-grade jump from my parting grade of 8.

It was indeed a true test of friendship. I tried to make it easier by reminding George of the director's promise that I'd be welcomed back "at any time." I also recalled the lack of a promised promotion after I'd returned to Vietnam. I brought up the Distinguished Service Award by thanking him for his part in drafting the citation. Finally, after a few well-chosen swear words, he agreed to talk with the director and with personnel—in that order. But he warned me it would take time.

It took approximately three weeks before he was on the line again.

Somehow, he had argued my case successfully and pushed my promotion through personnel. They had agreed on a jump to grade 5 but no further. God knows what he'd told them about the importance of my work at the *Chronicle*.

Hellyer warned me that there were those in the agency who were *not* happy about the circumstances of my return. The unhappy ones did manage a small victory. Unable to keep me from returning with a three-grade jump, they made sure I was offered a limited choice of hardship posts.

The entire security clearance procedure had to be reactivated before I could return to Washington. One hot, muggy weekend in Sausalito a stranger appeared on our porch and knocked on the screen door. He was wiping his hatband and sweating heavily when I answered his knock.

"Yes?" I said, opening the door.

"Look," he told me, "I'm an FBI agent." He paused to produce his ID card. "I've been all over this damn town trying to interview your friends for your security clearance. Can you point me in the right direction, and can I have a glass of water?"

He had his glass of water. I then drove him to the homes of my friends and remained outside in the car while he carried out his interviews.

On arrival in Washington, we rented a small studio apartment not far from the agency. One fateful evening I brought two post reports home. These detailed descriptions of Foreign Service posts, designed as basic information for the department, newly assigned officers, and official visitors, covered everything from housing to health hazards. Drafted by officers on the spot, the reports were also used to determine a post's qualification for hardship status. A carefully phrased report, touching on endemic diseases, tribal banditry, and the high rate of dysentery could ensure a hefty addition to the paychecks of American staffers.

The reports that Mary Alice and I studied until late that night described Katmandu, Nepal, and Lagos, Nigeria, the two hardship posts offered as choices by the office of personnel. Our final decision would have to take into account the health and welfare of Shawn, our Saigon-born daughter.

The drafter of the Katmandu post report had been a genius whose talented pen ensured a hardship rating. Newly assigned personnel were warned of the high rate of tuberculosis, various intestinal worms, and VD. They were advised to bring "rat traps and Coleman lanterns" and it was suggested that orders for kitchen staples be placed with various international shipping companies before departure from the United States.

Lagos, on the contrary, sounded like a tropical paradise. The Ikoyi, Island, and Motorboat Clubs were open to diplomats; and cricket, tennis, water skiing, and sailing were available for the sports-minded. Wide, palm-shaded sand beaches looked out on the Bight of Benin, and, if the heat became unbearable, a week's leave in the mountains of the nearby British Cameroons would provide relief. It crossed my mind that, if this was all true, why was Lagos a hardship post? The same report had recommended evening wear of calf-high "mosquito boots and long skirts" for the ladies. We found that curious, but I didn't have time to quibble. Rat traps and Coleman lanterns in Katmandu! That was definitely not for us. We chose Lagos, and the West African desk fed me into the orientation process. We had experienced the end of colonialism in Indochina. Now a different twilight of empire performance had begun in early 1957, and our front row seats were waiting.

I was to be the information officer at the U.S. consulate general in Lagos. I received a commission signed by President Eisenhower and John Foster Dulles, the secretary of state. It granted me my first diplomatic title of consul and requested "Her Majesty, Queen of the United Kingdom of Great Britain and Northern Ireland and of her other Realms and Territories, Head of the Commonwealth" to order her officials to allow me, among other things, to "enjoy and exercise" my mission "without molestation or trouble."

My cramming period on Nigeria had been limited. I'd learned that one of Africa's largest British colonies was a kaleidoscope of 250 distinct ethnic and linguistic groups and that the Hausa and Fulani were the dominant tribes in the Muslim north and the Yoruba and Ibo the majority in the Christian and animist south.

I was also witnessing a slow but sure change in Washington thinking. Prior to World War II the State Department's African policies had depended to a great extent on the world role of the colonizing powers and their importance to the United States.

Suddenly, with decolonization and independence becoming a reality, American diplomacy was facing a "new Africa." That phrase had become a rallying cry for an equally new breed of Foreign Service

African specialists who had great hopes for the development of an independent, peaceful, and prosperous African continent.

The vacuum created by the withdrawing colonial nations posed a major challenge to the antagonists of the Cold War. Washington, Moscow, and, to a lesser extent, Peking were maneuvering to be ready with economic and military aid, assistance, and advice on everything from well drilling to factory construction.

Independence for Nigeria was tentatively set for 1960. At that point our consulate general in Lagos would expand to become an embassy. Meanwhile, our task would include explaining U.S. foreign policy to Nigeria's leaders through personal contact and written material, establishing working contacts and planting articles with the Nigerian media, facilitating the placement of Nigerian university students in American universities, and arranging "leader grant" visits to the United States for selected Nigerian officials, politicians, intellectuals, and others likely to occupy positions of leadership in the future. It all seemed reasonable enough when viewed from Washington. It was to be considerably more difficult on the ground.

2

Ju-Ju and Black Cowboys

The Nigerian detective in a dark wool suit and the uniformed constable who were seated in my stuffy, ground floor office in downtown Lagos seemed slightly embarrassed. It appeared they'd had little experience calling on foreign diplomats, and they seemed uncertain of their authority. I'd had to shut the dusty louvered windows so we could hear each other over the racket of the Lagos traffic and the shouts of street traders. The promised air conditioner had been late in arriving, and my office had the sticky ambiance of a Turkish bath. The detective wiped the perspiration from his ebony forehead with a damp handkerchief. Dark oblongs of sweat had appeared under the arms and along the back of the constable's khaki uniform.

"Mister Simpson, sahr," the detective began, "how many bodies have you found on your beach?"

"Three," I replied truthfully.

"And you notified the police each time?"

"I did."

My questioner then wanted to know whether the bodies had been "tampered with" in any way.

"Tampered with?" I asked.

"Parts missing, or skull opened?"

"No," I replied, "I didn't examine them closely." I didn't tell him that the most damage had been done by one of his own men. A constable had dropped a heavy rock onto the bloated belly of a rotting corpse to keep it from floating back out into the bay as the tide came in.

"We are most sorry, sahr," the detective said, signaling his colleague that it was time to leave. He handed me a cheaply embossed business card. "Please call me if it occurs again."

Once the visitors had departed, I summoned the senior local employee into my office to explain the purpose of the police visit. He was a gray-haired, bespectacled, mission-educated Ibo who took everything most seriously. It was only through him that I could forestall wild rumors among the staff. When I mentioned the query about bodies being "tampered with," he nodded and shook his head.

"Ju-ju, Mr. Simpson," he said gravely, "they seek evidence of ju-ju practice."

It had begun two months earlier, after we'd moved into a government-leased beach house near Wilmot Point at the mouth of Lagos harbor. It was a long, one-story dwelling set off the ground on short pilings. There were screened porches, a small pier, and a concrete seawall. Some fan palms faced the seawall and others surrounded a circular concrete patio. The wind from the sea was usually fresh and cooling, blowing away the heat and countering the smell of sewage from the harbor.

One day I returned home to a new, unfamiliar odor. My wife had been forced to close all the doors in an attempt to escape the stench. The body of an African male was being rocked gently by the slight surf washing against the seawall. He'd been in the water a long time. Other corpses followed in the weeks to come. One was discovered by our daughter and another was signaled by the barking of the small dog belonging to Demaris, Shawn's Yoruba nanny.

Why our beach? At first I thought it was some trick of the harbor's currents and back eddies. Early on a Sunday morning, as the neighboring Motorboat Club was preparing for a midday reception, I found a partial explanation. While I was standing in the sunshine sipping a cup of tea, I noticed an unusual movement offshore. I walked to the pier for a better view and exploded with instant anger. A Nigerian employee of the Motorboat Club was swimming slowly toward our beach, pushing a corpse before him through the calm water with every intention of leaving it against our seawall. It was an unusual sight: the beach boy's measured kick, the ripples spreading shoreward from the body's progress, the soles of the corpse's feet and the palms of the hands showing yellow in the sunlight.

"Out!" I shouted, gesturing him away, using every curse I could think of until the paddler turned slowly around, pushing his stiff-armed charge back toward the club's waters.

This explained the unusual number of dead found on our beach, but it did not explain their provenance. A British officer of the Nigeria Police—and a member of the Motorboat Club—provided a simple answer. The villages along the Ogun River, the Ojo Lagoon, and the Kradu Water were built on swampy land that often flooded during the downpours of the rainy season. The rapid deterioration of corpses in the tropical heat meant that the dead, of necessity, were committed to the waters. Some of them then floated to the mouth of the Lagos River and to our narrow strip of beach.

The beach house, rented from an Armenian businessman, was our third move since arriving in Lagos. Our first lodging had been the Ikoyi Rest House, an old colonial complex of one-story, concrete bungalows with sun-heated, corrugated tin roofs. It was not a welcoming sight. Nor did the large orange and black lizards lounging and defecating along the pathways add to the location's charm. Our arrival and the unloading of our baggage attracted the attention of the white-robed Hausa traders squatting in the shade of the palms. They came forward, insistently offering their faux-ebony sculptures and bird replicas fashioned from cow skin. It was the first time I'd ever been called "mastah" and it came as a shock.

A more definitive shock came with the news that no housing would be available in the immediate future. This meant at least several weeks in the rest house. The term "rest house" applied because British colonials, district officers, and businessmen working in the "bush" used these barrackslike facilities for R&R (rest and recreation). We would soon learn that some temporary residents considered the rest house luxurious compared to their normal quarters upcountry, where ice was rare and toilet facilities consisted of a portable "thunderbox."

In retrospect, rest house living provided a good introduction to the realities of West Africa. If Kipling believed the East was impervious to Western "hustle," it did not take long to realize that Africa also moved at its own particular pace.

Exhausted from the prop-lag of the long journey, we had resolved to sleep in during our first morning in Lagos. But a heavy knocking awakened us at 6:00.

"Tea, Mastah!" the roomboy bellowed.

For the next three days I attempted to change this routine. From the front desk clerk to the room boys, I tried to explain that we were not to be disturbed before 8:00 and that we drank coffee, not tea. But years of training and routine were not for changing.

"Tea, Mastah!" came the continued summons at 6:00 each morning, regardless of my earnest protestations. Clearly, the situation called for compromise and adjustment—on my part. In fact, early morning was the only cool part of the day, and the coffee was so vile and watery that strong tea was the only answer.

The consulate general crew in those days did not make up a particularly happy ship. The director of the USIS operation when I arrived in Nigeria was a complex, mercurial person, difficult to understand. He was at post alone, but he did not once invite us to his government-supplied house during our rest house purgatory. He refused to recognize the presence of my wife, leaving her off invitation lists and often failing to address her directly. At one point he cautioned her not to call the office during working hours. He and I were to work together during what remained of his Nigerian tour, but we would never be friends.

The consul general was a tall, thin, mustached career officer who looked more British than American. Nevertheless, at our first meeting, he informed me that shorts and knee socks were not to be worn in the office as they projected too colonial an image. He spent a great deal of time in the garden of his large residence tending the calla lilies. He had also adopted the colonial habit, at the end of a dinner party, of asking the male guests if they would like "to see Africa." He would then lead them through the patio doors to the garden, where they would line up to urinate under a full tropical moon.

Jim Parker, the consulate's administrative officer, was an African-American who had previously been assigned to Monrovia. That experience served him well in Lagos, where administrative problems were frequent and unavoidable. The "buck" not only stopped on his desk— it often returned there, again and again. Through it all Parker maintained a remarkable surface calm. He, his good-humored wife Odessa, and their courteous children were an oasis of domesticity amid the tensions of the small American official community.

As long as we remained in the rest house, the bar, with its ceiling fans, torpid flies, and odor of stale ale, was the center of evening activity. Sunburned British construction workers with Yorkshire or Geordie accents shook dice for rounds of Beck's beer or gin and tonic, jokingly calling for "Gin 'n Harpic!" (the latter a searing toilet cleanser). Alcohol had gotten to some of the bar's customers. Florid-faced "coasters" chugged down ale and lager at lunch and whisky-ginger, Scotch and soda, or brandy and port before and after their lukewarm dinner claret. Bush-jacketed district officers from their posts in Makurdi or Ilorin sipped gin and bitters while reading week-old editions of the London press. The occasional married couple took their predinner drinks at a table, a safe distance from the rowdy bar trade.

There was romantic intrigue there too. A shapely, desirable Welsh wife, whose engineer husband was often upcountry, appeared alone each night to sip Scotch before retiring. Her cleavage, revealed by a low-cut green gown, was the focus of every male eye. You didn't need a Somerset Maugham to reveal the outcome. Her eventual affair with a British district officer was soon an open secret. Shortly after—to the consternation of the bar's habitués—we learned that she, her lover, and her husband had agreed to live out their Nigerian tour of duty as a ménage à trois.

The rest house dining room was frozen in a previous time. The overhead fans occasionally threw out sputtering sparks. If a perspiring diner asked that a fan be put in motion over his table, the waiters had to seek approval from the frowning and officious Nigerian maitre d'hôtel. The amiable, inefficient waiters wore white cotton jackets spotted with food stains, loose red cummerbunds, and a type of soft red fez. The chef's specialties were ground nut (peanut) stew, with the jaundiced eyes of a sliced hard-boiled egg staring out of the lukewarm gravy, gray-sauced chicken curry (Saturdays only), and a peppery mulligatawny soup.

Our second lodging was a third-story, two-bedroom flat in a Nigerian government housing complex. Most of the flats were reserved for visiting politicians from Nigeria's regions during the sittings of the colonial Federal Parliament. It seemed a paradise after our rest house experience. There were newly laid parquet floors and views out onto the tall, graceful palms used for the production of palm wine.

Our solitude ended abruptly with the arrival of the politicians and their families and animals. The extended family of a turbaned northern parliamentarian moved in above us. They traveled as a self-sustaining unit, complete with goats and a few sheep as an on-the-hoof meat supply.

Although the sheep were normally tethered outside, a goat was kept in the apartment to supply milk for the children. We could tell its periods of residence by the pungent smell and the tapping of its diminutive hooves. From the wrenching, prying noise of wood cracking, we guessed that some remodeling work was being done in the upstairs flat. A bit later, we were alarmed by the smell of burning wood and puffs of gray smoke issuing from the windows above us.

Rushing up the narrow stairs with visions of accomplishing a dramatic rescue, I banged on the door of the northerner's apartment. False alarm. There was smoke and fire, but the low flame was confined to a corner of the living room. Sections of the parquet floor had been torn up to provide fuel, and some bloody cuts of mutton were prepared for grilling on a makeshift barbecue. I withdrew after sipping the mandatory glass of sweet tea surrounded by large-eyed children who obviously found my presence amusing.

The arrival of my new boss, Pat Belcher, his wife Louise, and their ebullient sons was like a breath of fresh air. Pat was a thoughtful, unflappable officer, and we got along well, sharing the workload and developing a practical program. The Belchers opened the seldom-used USIS residence to a wide range of contacts, adding many Nigerians to their circle of friends and bringing the sound of local "high life" music to residential, expatriate Ikoyi.

Before leaving the government flat, Mary Alice and I learned we were to be parents for the second time. By the time we'd reached the beach house it was time to find an obstetrician. We found one in the person of the gruff, tea-swilling, no-nonsense Briton who ran the Northumberland Nursing Home. As a former nurse with her own ideas about childbirth, my wife was not impressed. The sight of the doctor's blood-smeared surgical gown and his chain-smoking did not inspire confidence. At one point, under her critical questioning, the doctor threatened to throw us out of his nursing home.

Despite this, we formed an alliance of necessity. Lisa was born on February 9, 1958, while Mammy Wagons, large buses with goods piled on their roofs, emblazoned with such slogans as "God Loves Us" and "Justice and Truth" roared past on their way to the early morning markets. Everything went well, and the doctor offered us the choice of a celebratory cup of tea or a Guinness. We chose the latter. One swallow of "the black stuff" and Mary Alice entered a deep, restorative sleep.

Our fourth abode was in the residential area of Ikoyi and belonged to a shipping company. The apartment was shaded by trees and had an airy second-floor balcony. It was here that I began to appreciate the importance of ju-ju, or tribal witchcraft, in the life of everyday Nigerians.

Lawrence, our cook, was a thoughtful, polite man. He kept his kitchen clean and produced tasty, well-prepared meals. We congratulated ourselves on having hired him and felt more secure with him around the house. Suddenly, everything seemed to fall apart. His kitchen became dirty, he was late for work, his clothes were untidy, he became sullen and uncooperative. I made a special effort to discover the cause of this sudden deterioration, cornering Lawrence in the kitchen one morning and insisting we discuss what was bothering him.

It was not easy, but the story finally came out. Lawrence was involved in a family dispute. His brother, with the help of a neighborhood witch doctor, had put a ju-ju spell on him. Since then, Lawrence explained, "I have been followed."

"But who is following you?" I asked, thinking that a police warning in the right ear might solve the problem.

"A bee," Lawrence replied in a low voice, as if someone, or something, might overhear him. Now that he had begun to speak, the words poured out. Each morning, as he left for market on his bicycle, the bee was waiting. It followed him to the market and from stall to stand, disrupting business and causing the stout Mammy traders to curse Lawrence and refuse to do business with him.

"It is the same bee every day, Mastah," Lawrence insisted gravely, "I know it for sure."

I tried logic but it did no good. I even volunteered my help in killing the troublesome insect. That suggestion seemed to cause more fear than the bee itself. With each passing day Lawrence became more of a psychological mess. He was definitely losing weight, spending hours sitting outside, staring into space. Finally, acting on a hunch, I decided to inspect Lawrence's room in the servants' quarters in the hope of finding some ju-ju symbol planted there by those who wished him harm.

I found a beehive high in the upper corner of his closet. It was dry, delicately layered, gray, and still active. Sluggish bees moved in and out of the entry and disappeared through a crack in the closet that provided egress to the outdoors. A hesitant Lawrence viewed the hive reluctantly before I had it removed. The next morning he was not followed to market, his cooking returned to normal, and he soon regained his lost weight. But he clung to his own story. "It was the same bee, for sure, each day," he insisted.

A short time later our nanny, Demaris, began to exhibit some of the symptoms Lawrence had developed. Her clothing—previously spotless and neatly pressed—became soiled and wrinkled. She stopped wearing shoes or sandals and ignored the usual bathing time for Shawn. She was late for work or failed to appear at all. This time it was Mary Alice who probed *en tête-à-tête* for the cause.

Under cross-examination Demaris said she had seen "a big snake" in the garden. The snake had spoken with Demaris, or looked at her a special way, or left a sign in the sand. We suggested Demaris take some time off to rest and try to rid herself of her fixation. When she returned, it was obvious this particular snake had very special powers. Demaris was definitely pregnant. She gave her notice, announced she was returning to her village, and left a small going-away gift for Shawn.

Although many Americans were to serve in Nigeria and other African nations without direct contact with ju-ju, the wife of one American consul general in Lagos did have a disconcerting experience. Feeling uncharacteristically nauseous, she called in a local British practitioner. He treated her over a period of days, using the standard remedies, and was surprised to find no improvement. Luckily, this physician was an old Africa hand. One day, during the cook's absence, he took the time to inspect the kitchen. Hidden in a tin he found a ju-ju item, a tightly rolled ball of chicken dung and feathers. The cook was roused from his slumber and made a full confession. The ju-ju was being put in Madam's coffee each morning to "make Madam love me." The victim recovered, the cook sought employment elsewhere, and the incident became a bit of local folklore.

But ju-ju was no joke. Belief in the power of ju-ju and in its practitioners can have definite physical and psychological results, both good and evil. I would eventually learn of its more sinister side.

Buea was damp and shrouded in the mists that swirled around the impressive 13,350-foot heights of Mount Cameroon. This mountain town in the British Cameroons still bore the imperial imprint of its pre–World War I German rulers. The sculpted stone head of a sweep-mustached Otto von Bismarck graced a water fountain in the square, and the alpine chalets clumped together on the slopes seemed strangely out of place at the edge of the African forest.

I was quartered in the newly built Mountain Hotel to interview candidates for study grants to the United States. Normally this would have been handled by a cultural affairs officer, but the application deadline was approaching and I'd been asked to step in. I had the files of three candidates scheduled for interviews in Buea and four more covering those in Yaounde, the administrative capital.

The first evening in Buea I walked some distance from the hotel toward the base of Mount Cameroon. The road came to an abrupt end at a thick stand of yellow-leafed plants. Ahead lay a narrow jungle trail spiraling up the mountain. I climbed 50 yards up the track and paused in the fading dusk, listening to the sound of dripping moisture and the clicks and shrieks of what I took to be distant monkeys. A newcomer to Africa, brought up on Hollywood myths of the "dark continent," I decided any further exploration could await full daylight.

I had just turned to retrace my steps when a strident trumpeting carried down from the mountain. It was the first and only time I have heard a wild elephant in its native habitat. The call was repeated three times, each time a bit less loud, a bit less insistent. There was a melancholy quality to the trumpeting, as if a lone bull elephant were signaling the demise of a scattered herd, the end of an era.

One of the student candidates didn't appear for his interview. The second arrived with a briefcase filled with written recommendations from "well-known people." His father was a civil servant whose son had learned the fine art of name-dropping. Unfortunately for him, my knowledge of Cameroonian politicians and VIPs was limited and his litany of self-importance failed to impress.

The third candidate was a youth named Moses. He had walked barefoot for three days and nights to reach Buea, his cheap tennis shoes slung over his shoulders. There were the raised keloids of tribal scars on his cheeks and he had a broad, infectious grin. But he was serious when he handed me the recommendation of his schoolmaster. It was obvious that Moses would need intense coaching in conversational English, but his determination was impressive. He had somehow learned some basic facts of American history. These he solemnly recited, his grin replaced by a frown of concentration. Sitting in a hotel room at the foot of Mount Cameroon, with the mist swirling outside, I listened to excerpts from Lincoln's Gettysburg address delivered in something close to pidgin English. When I tried to cushion Moses from the shock of a possible turndown, Moses would have none of it.

"Oh no, Sahr," he assured me, "I *must* go to study in your land." When I returned to Lagos and completed my report, Moses was near the top of my list.

Months later, our entire office had been turned into an auxiliary inoculation center during a local smallpox epidemic. In the chaos of screaming children and swooning mothers I heard a timid knock at my door. A beaming, diffident Moses, resplendent in a starched white shirt, had come to call. He was on his way to the United States for a year's study, and he had brought a gift. He had painstakingly carved a fire-hardened piece of bamboo with the squares and line symbols of his tribe to produce a unique walking stick. For a fleeting second I considered returning the gift with thanks. But that would have been impossible without offending or hurting him. It was too personal an offering, too innocent a gesture. As I write, the bamboo stick is in my study, sharing space in a large Chinese vase with a heavy blackthorn stick from Northern Ireland and a cane that once belonged to a French general.

Another trip during the same period found me driving the family to Ibadan, the heavily populated capital of the Western Region, seat of the Yoruba tribe, and site of the University College of Nigeria. I was sent there to fill in briefly for a USIS officer who had been called to the United States on family business. Apart from some select areas, the main city was a depressing vista of tin-roofed huts, open drains, scavenging dogs, and fly-plagued markets. Large woven paniers packed tightly with monkey heads in a circular pattern were a choice market item.

The African-American officer I was temporarily replacing had covered the closed windows of his rented concrete house with treated black paper. This had effectively turned the interior into a dark, hot furnace peppered with the remains of dead flies. With the paper removed, the windows opened, and the flies swept up, we came under the close scrutiny of several golden-eyed goats. They seldom strayed far from the open windows and seemed to find our simplest activities fascinating. At night a nearby church shook the neighborhood with exuberant gospel singing until a very late hour. Fortunately, our stay in Ibadan was short.

The Nigerian rainy season seemed much heavier than the seasonal downpours we'd experienced in Vietnam. The darkness came in the middle of the day, rolling in from the Gulf of Guinea as a violent wind tossed the palms back and forth on their long trunks. When the sky opened, sheets of rain fell like successive curtains on a darkened stage. It hissed onto the streets and drummed on the steaming roofs.

The streets and roads flooded, and the inhabitants of Lagos picked their way cautiously through knee-deep water on their way to work, the men wielding black brolleys and the women, with beach parasols, balancing briefcases, folders, books, and lunch packets on their heads.

My route into town took me through axle-deep flooding that concealed the road's edge, making it difficult to navigate. My official Jeep station wagon performed well, and I often picked up stranded commuters along the way. Although soaked to the skin, they were invariably in good humor. Taciturn vegetable vendors climbed onto their thatch-roofed stands to avoid the flooding, sometimes sharing their shelter with prostitutes who worked the road to Ikoyi.

The end of the rain always came abruptly, as if some heavenly hand had closed a spigot. The flood waters sluiced noisily into the culverts or soaked quickly into the porous ground. The dark clouds fled inland, and bright sunlight hit the draining macadam, raising another haze of steam. This was the moment of impressive color contrasts: the cobalt blue sky, white clouds replacing gray, the bright green of rain-washed foliage, and the appearance of skittering black dots ahead. These large land crabs, flushed from their holes by the rains, moved sideways across the road like crustaceous lemmings, one large claw held aloft. Unavoidable, they popped under the tires of the station wagon like punctured balloons.

Working with the Nigerian media was a very special experience. Some of the Lagos dailies printed wild, imaginative stories about sex and crime that would have made a London tabloid editor blush. The fact that these florid exposés were often written in precise, archaic English only increased their bizarre quality. Although the British Information Service (BIS) had an inside track to the Nigerian press and radio, part of my job was to see that the local media received USIS news bulletins and feature articles. Ensuring the use of this material was another matter.

Articles or commentary on U.S. African policy or Nigerians visiting the United States was not too hard to place. But, with the Cold War heating up, Washington was filling our daily wireless bulletin—supplied to the Nigerian media free of charge—with material on the dangers of Soviet hegemony and the misdeeds of the KGB. This was hardly the type of copy Nigerian editors would rush to shoehorn into their limited space.

The launch of the world's first artificial satellite by the Soviets in 1957 impressed and seized the imagination of many Nigerians. Sputnik was an international propaganda victory that we found difficult to match. Some of our Nigerian and British media contacts and friends, shocked at the apparent lapse in America's scientific prowess, were vocal in expressing their concern.

But counterpunching the Soviets in the Cold War arena was not an urgent daily task in Nigeria. We were in for the long haul and trying to establish trust and understanding in one of Africa's largest nations. The average Nigerian knew very little about the United States in 1957, and our professional job was to provide the information they sought as their nation moved toward full independence. This didn't mean pushing sugar-coated versions of a Norman Rockwell never-never land. It did mean frank discussions of America's race problem. Nigerians were mightily confused in 1957 by the call-out of the Arkansas National Guard by Governor Orville Faubus to prevent public school integration in Little Rock. Their confusion doubled when President Eisenhower ordered federal troops to Arkansas to ensure compliance with the court order for desegregation.

I spent long, sweaty hours with Nigerian editors and "leader writers" trying to explain administration policy on desegregation or delving into the historic background of slavery and the causes of racial tensions in the United States. It was often a thankless job. Relevant history can't be taught and absorbed in an hour's time, and cultural differences leave voids of understanding. It's hard to explain the significance of endemic hate in race relations to someone who was raised in a village where the colonial district officer was seldom seen or was greeted like a god when he did appear. Even someone who struggled up through the British school system on merit to the point of joining the select group of Nigeria's media representatives found it hard to understand. The prime local residual hate appeared to be tribal and that was often veiled or impersonal. It would appear with a vengeance after independence, during the war in Biafra.

If the battered, ancient linotypes in many Lagos newspapers survived on generous squirts of oil, the newsmen kept limber and good humored with generous daily rations of iced beer. It was during such antidehydration sessions, around a table studded with quart bottles of lager, that I made my real contact with the Nigerian media. Following one of these bibulous meetings, I was nominated for membership in the Island Club.

Colonial Nigeria reflected the British fondness for clubs and club membership. In our desperation to occasionally escape the rest house bar at the beginning of our stay, we had joined the Ikoyi Club. This bit of transplanted Britain had tennis courts, cricket grounds, manicured lawns, shaded tea tables, a swimming pool with an unacceptably high urine content, and adequate bar facilities. A few prominent Nigerians were members, but the Ikoyi Club was primarily a White preserve and last stand of those embittered Brits who gritted their teeth at the mention of independence. The same people tended to blame Americans for the twilight of their empire and it was difficult to feel comfortable among them.

The Island Club was primarily African. Caucasians aspiring to membership risked being "white-balled" by the Nigerian members: doctors, lawyers, businessmen, newsmen, politicians, and government officials. My introductory Saturday lunch at the Island Club provided an opportunity for the voting members to eyeball me as a membership candidate and make their decision. Drinks began at noon, lunch was served at 1:00 P.M. The main dish was an eye-watering, red-sauced curry on a huge pyramid of rice spiked with scattered condiments. Beer was king, the pint mugs were kept filled, and hearty laughter punctuated a succession of tall tales. We left the table at 4:00 P.M. A few days later a brief note arrived at the office informing me that I'd been accepted for membership. I had been spared the ignominy of a "white ball."

All of our efforts weren't aimed at the media audience. Mobile film units were used to reach outlying communities and far-off villages. A film titled *Cowboy*, depicting the real life of contemporary cowpokes in Montana, was particularly popular among the cowherding Fulani tribe. Their favorite moment in the film was a cattle roundup during a heavy snowstorm. How such screenings advanced U.S. foreign policy goals is debatable, but there was little doubt that the arrival of the USIS film unit was a major local event out in the bush.

A more sophisticated Youth Club audience in Lagos viewed the same film and listened to my brief talk on the American West. Luckily, I was prepared for what followed. A bright-eyed teenager was quickly with the first question.

"Why were there no Black cowboys?"

I assured him there had been Black cowboys, still might be a few, and passed around a large book containing photos of famous Black American cowboys and Indian scouts. I then mentioned the "Buffalo Soldier," the Black troopers who filled the ranks of some U.S. cavalry units in the old West.

"You mean like John Wayne?" someone asked, obviously puzzled.

"Well . . ." I hesitated.

"No, you fool," a student snapped at the questioner. "No Black fellah would ever be an officer!"

I explained that the first Black American general had served in World War II and that, since 1953, desegregation in the U.S. military had seen many Black Americans attain senior rank. My statement was greeted with a polite but skeptical silence.

"I tell you," one youth finally commented, "there are Black sergeants!"

"How you know this?" one of his friends demanded.

"I see it in the cinema!" he replied, nodding his head affirmatively to end all argument.

Some of our films did carry more political freight than *Cowboy*, but fighting the propaganda Cold War in African villages through film was a doubtful tactic at best. Reports on showings prepared by our film section employees dutifully listed a head count of audiences and reactions to the films shown. The audiences were invariably "large," the reactions "enthusiastic." A film on American naval power drew "oh's" and "ah's" from an inland audience. However, this was not because they were impressed with U.S. naval might and its strategic significance, but because they had never seen the sea and enjoyed the visual drama of plunging decks, flying spray, and aircraft launches from a flight deck.

Once, checking on a film that was being monopolized by an Oba, or tribal chief, I discovered that he'd insisted on having the film shown over and over again. The film technician assured me there was always "much laughter" from the Oba's guests. Further investigation revealed that a film of U.S. foreign policy containing footage of official visits was considered high comedy in the Oba's compound. This was not because of its subject matter but because, when the film was run backward and at high speed, the arriving and departing statesmen had the air of agitated circus clowns in a silent comedy epic.

One of the drinks parties we gave at the beach house introduced the American dry martini—stirred, not shaken—to British and Nigerian officials, newsmen, and Lagos-based diplomats. Considering the steady consumption of alcohol I'd observed since arriving in Nigeria, I didn't hesitate to recommend the iced martinis to our guests. Alas, I had overestimated their capacity or they had underestimated the power of a mix containing a few drops of vermouth to each glass of gin. The noisy party became noisier, and some male guests swayed in place while their wives' conversation became bawdy. Hidden antagonisms and desires surfaced as the sun went down, a religious sect on a far beach made music with drums and bottles, and I mixed more martinis.

The next day all was quiet on the Lagos front. Official business had slowed in more than one office. The director of the British Information Service sent a hand-carried note headed "Black Friday!" accusing us of unleashing a new American "secret weapon." Some members of the Nigerian Broadcasting Service failed to appear for work. The potency of the martinis was best demonstrated by the young British officer of the Nigeria Police who spent the night sleeping behind a bush in our garden, fully uniformed, his swagger stick at his side. When he appeared on our screened porch next morning, rumpled, bleary eyed, and in search of strong tea, Shawn pointed and alerted us with one word, "Man!"

3

Fire Ant Fandango

If the late 1950s was the period of the "New Africa," it was also a time when the Foreign Service community in Washington experienced the emergence of the "Africa can do no wrong" syndrome. A small but influential group of official do-gooders working on African policy were trying to make up for years of diplomatic neglect. In their rush to understand Africa and the Africans, they were doing both a disservice by rejecting the negative realities of the continent. Their optimistic hopes for Africa often blinded them to the dangers of militant tribalism; the residual, sometimes clandestine influence of former colonial nations and their skill at power politics; and the sad fact that few of the new African nations had the infrastructure or trained personnel for efficient self-government. The clock of world history could not be turned back, but a more frank and critical analysis might have eased the transition period and helped avoid the tragedies ahead.

There were a number of ritual killings in Nigeria during our second year in Lagos. A mass grave had been discovered near the town of Abakaliki in the Eastern Region. The bodies had been "tampered with," and the first reports spoke of ju-ju as the cause. One of my contacts in the Nigeria Police explained that the case was a bit more complicated. The murders were in reality linked to a mafialike protection racket run by a village chief who was using supposed ju-ju practices as a cover. The details of this case were finally made public and headlined in the Lagos dailies.

Another case was definitely linked to ju-ju. A man had taken the head of a young boy, swinging his razor-sharp "matchet" in full view of a market crowd. The killer had then dropped the head into a jute sack and gone on his way. Arrested, he'd admitted he was selling the heads of male youths for a good price. The brains were being used to produce a salve that was said to restore the potency of aging tribal elders.

Following this incident, another event hit closer to home. A newly arrived USIS officer was preparing to drive to his post at Enugu, the capital of the Eastern Region. I pointed out that his route would traverse zones where ju-ju killings had occurred and suggested caution. I recommended that he not stop en route, no matter what he might encounter. I could tell from the newcomer's expression that he wasn't taking my warning seriously.

Very early the next morning, over a clicking, buzzing line, the traveler breathlessly described his experiences. Things had begun to go wrong when his driver pointed out an empty sedan, or "ghost car," parked by the side of the jungle-bordered road. He'd begun to take the "ghost car" designation seriously when it appeared again many miles on, parked and still unoccupied.

Later still, well after midnight, they'd seen something on the road ahead and pulled to a stop. Glistening in the glare of their headlights lay the mutilated remains of a man—a head, torso, limbs, and intestines extended across the tarmac.

"What did you do?" I asked.

"We got the hell out of there!"

The shaken officer had reported his gruesome find to the police in the nearest large town. An insouciant, note-taking constable had classified the incident as a ju-ju warning, a no trespassing sign, and agreed that our man had done well to leave the scene.

As more and more African countries became independent, USIA decided to launch a project that would task each post in Africa with contributing film footage to be edited in Washington and incorporated into an African newsreel. The footage would cover everything from U.S. assistance to African "nation building" to African-American educational cooperation, from economic development to medical research, from police training to fisheries development. I thus found myself in the role of a newsreel writer-director teamed with Olojo Kosoko, a young, good-humored Yoruba cameraman.

It was easy enough to come up with short subjects in and around Lagos. But Pat Belcher and I were looking for material that would allow us to develop a theme for short features with national appeal. With Nigerian independence moving ever closer, tribalism and its effect on national unity were obviously major concerns. It was not difficult to identify the army and the police as the two federal institutions that (1) had the physical ability to maintain order and hold the new nation together and (2) had melded the main tribal groups and religions of Nigeria into a viable whole—or so we thought. Naively, we presumed that barracks cohabitation must have produced mutual friendship and respect.

My call on a somewhat skeptical British brigadier general obtained a clearance for filming a report on the Queen's Own Nigeria Regiment. This British-officered infantry unit had distinguished itself in Burma during World War II. It was now to form the nucleus of an expanded national army following independence. The general provided the necessary orders for transport and housing. Kosoko was hired to join me for the 500-mile overland trek to Kaduna and Kano in the Northern Region. Before leaving, I dug deep into my stored effects to retrieve the parachutist's bush hat I'd worn on operations with the Franco-Vietnamese forces in Indochina.

We traveled in an army Land Rover driven by a silent sergeant who scrupulously observed Muslim religious ritual, pausing by the side of the road to wash with water from his canteen before praying. We bounced over long stretches of red laterite roadway, the Land Rover's engine emitting an ominous, high-pitched whine. The further we went, the more I suspected the smiling brigadier of offering us the Land Rover as a private joke. I pictured him chuckling over his gin and bitters as he told his fellow officers how he'd managed to give one particular Yank his first, rough-riding "feel for Africa."

Speeding, swaying, overloaded Mammy Wagons roared past, leaving us in a rosy haze of settling dust. Thatch-roofed villages came into view where long-horned, hump-backed cattle sought shade under a single thorn tree. We slowed for a procession of children in Ogbomosho, their blue and white school uniforms neat and starched, and drove on to Ilorin.

We found lodging in a local hotel that made the Ikoyi Rest House look like the Paris Ritz. Covered with red, sweat-caked dust, I insisted on a bath before dinner. I found the lockless bathroom on the second floor and banged on the tub with my fist to send the lolling cockroaches down the drain. There were four distinct rings around the tub's grimy interior, and the fouled, seatless toilet by the open window was clogged. Halfway through my bath, while I was kneeling in eight inches of rusty water, a skinny, middle-aged Briton pushed open the door. He was missing teeth and his complexion was an unhealthy, lemony shade in the dim light from the naked, overhead bulb.

"Allo, mate!" he said, striding past the tub to drop his pants and perch precariously on the soiled enamel of the toilet. "Bit of the trots," he informed me, lighting a cigarette and getting down to business. I dried myself and departed quickly, leaving him the sole occupant of the bathroom from hell.

The next morning some Yoruba musicians entertained us with their "talking drums" aboard the overloaded ferry that took us across the wide, slow-flowing Niger.

The further north we traveled, the hotter it became during the day and the colder at night. The jungle green of the south gave way to flat, desolate stretches of semidesert dotted with scrub bush and the occasional tree. North of Minna, pink-bottomed baboons erupted from cover to race ahead of us, screeching abuse, while their beady-eyed doyen observed the scene from a roadside perch, picking at his yellowed canines with a small twig.

We arrived at the headquarters of the Queen's Own Nigeria Regiment outside Kaduna shortly after daybreak. Wind zephyrs raised the dust of the parade ground in thin spirals, a hot, yellow sun emerged from the gray haze, and a cawing crow perched on one of the whitewashed stones that lined the pathways. The British flag snapped on its halyard high above the headquarters building and a squad of soldiers was drilling near the compound's gate. We were far from India's Northwest Frontier of the 1800s, but I half expected to see Cary Grant and Victor McLaglen appear at the mess hall door.

We had arrived at the same time as a truckload of new recruits. The young British captain assigned as our guide explained that some of these men were from the warrior tribes of Chad and the northern Cameroons. Neither Christian nor Muslim, they were officially classified as "Pagans." Pushed into something resembling a military formation by a tall Fulani corporal, the recruits fell silent. Muscular men with high cheekbones and skin like powdered chocolate, dressed in khaki shorts and white T-shirts, they shifted their bare feet in the dust and squinted at the sun.

A stout British major hurried toward us, accompanied by a translator. He eyed us suspiciously, took up his position, and cleared his throat before welcoming the newcomers, pausing periodically to allow for the shouted translation. Roused from my early morning torpor, I signaled Kosoko to start filming. When the time came for the ceremony, each man swore allegiance to the queen in his own language. He then extended his tongue—as if to receive a communion host—and licked an unsheathed bayonet.

The commanding officer and his staff at Kaduna cooperated fully once they saw we were there to do a serious job. I explained our filming needs to the colonel over a frosted pewter mug of pale ale in the fan-cooled, mud-walled officers club. No, we were not seeking footage of ceremonial parades. Yes, we did need shots of simulated combat action.

The next few days found us up at dawn to beat the heat and loading our filming equipment into the Land Rover. We were watched closely each morning by several large, ugly desert vultures perched along the mess hall roof, waiting to swoop down on any scraps thrown out by the cooks. I had an uneasy feeling they'd be in quick, close proximity if one were rash enough to stretch out on the parade ground for a siesta.

Two infantry companies, an armored car, and a mortar section were involved in the "combat" scenario I worked out with the cooperative captain. The operation involved the stealthy approach by scouts on an enemy position (a storage bunker), followed by a general attack signaled by a Bren gun opening fire.

Unfortunately, I'd failed to consider the fact that Kosoko had never experienced heavy, close-proximity small arms fire. I should have noticed a certain nervousness on his part as I placed him next to the Bren gun. But I was too busy acting the poor man's Darryl Zanuck, instructing the driver of the armored car when he should move into camera range. I was also unaware that British blank cartridges were much noisier than the U.S. version.

Watches were synchronized, helmets donned, and the wiry northerners fixed bayonets and settled down to wait as the scouts crept forward. Kosoko moved a bit closer to the Bren after I told him to catch the ejecting empty cartridges on film. When the scouts signaled they'd reached the objective, I tapped the gunner on the shoulder. "Now!" I told him.

The Bren's first ear-numbing burst sent Kosoko a good foot into the air. The camera flew out of his hands and landed with a thump in the dust. The armored car moved forward, grating its gears, and the infantry clustered behind it, using the vehicle for cover, either instinctively or through training. I felt like a circus ringmaster who'd lost control.

"Hold it!" I shouted. "Cease fire! Come back!" At that point the heavy machine gun of the armored car opened fire, drowning out my shouts. I banged on the metal turret but the gunner was undeterred. The captain finally brought order to chaos. For the second take I lay beside Kosoko, helping him brace the camera and steadying his grip.

It took us a whole day to complete filming the exercise. Kosoko adapted quickly to his new role as an apprentice combat cameraman. He obtained some good footage, including the northern infantrymen charging toward him, shouting their battle cry...not a particularly pleasant experience for a Yoruba.

We then covered the more prosaic features of garrison life: the bugler at dawn, the mess routine, medical procedures, vehicle training, English classes, and sports. During this day-to-day exposure to Nigerian military life, my preconceptions were changing. The northern Muslims—Hausas and Fulani—and a considerable number of Pagans made up the majority of the combat soldiers in the enlisted ranks. The mission-educated Yorubas and Ibos from the south, most of them Christians, were the mainstays of the Nigerian officer corps and occupied most of the clerical and specialized noncom positions. These basic divisions ran through the regiment like fault lines. A retired British officer who had served with the regiment in Burma expressed his opinion with a tongue-in-cheek comment.

"The Yorubas and Ibos were a great pain in the arse," he recalled. When I asked why, he grinned and replied, "Because they learned to read and write!" Regardless of die-hard colonial attitudes, you didn't have to be a military analyst to sense that the regiment's toleration of tribal and religious differences could well disintegrate with the departure of the British officer cadre.

Nevertheless, the short feature was in the can and on its way to USIA, Nigerians and their African neighbors would soon view the film on the federal intertribal army, the brigadier was happy, and Kosoko was brimming with new-found confidence.

With our military filming done, we headed the Land Rover further north to Kano, where the local population was celebrating the emir's birthday. Still under the army's sponsorship, we were housed in the thick-walled, adobelike officer's quarters. The mess was cool and hospitable, the ubiquitous, greasy ground nut stew unavoidable.

Kano in the late 1950s had the look of a classic desert outpost. Dilapidated mud walls of russet hue circled the old city, the cry of the muezzin echoed through the unpaved alleys at prayer time, and camels growled in the marketplace. Belled goats dozed in the shade and dyers with indigo-stained arms worked over ancient, sunken stone vats half shaded by latticed drying racks. Sixty miles to the north lay the border with the soon-to-be-independent French colony of Niger, and 50 miles beyond that the desert post and town of Zinder. This was still a land of camel caravans, tribal intrigue, smuggling, and rule by the feudal emirs under the watchful eyes of British district officers.

Mounted emirs and tribal leaders were arriving in the city from Sokoto, Katsina, Zaria, and Gaya, surrounded by their retinues of colorful armed horsemen. The emirs, blue or white turbans low on their foreheads, were sheltered under large, tasseled parasols held by aides on nervous, prancing mounts. Swaths of light cloth protected their faces from dust and sun, and many of them wore impenetrably dark sunglasses. Repetitive blasts from a heavy silver horn announced the VIPs' arrival and cleared the street ahead.

Cross-hilted broadswords in cowhide sheaths were slung over the mounted warriors' shoulders. Spade-bladed spears gleamed in the sun, and some conical metal helmets with protective noseguards appeared to be modeled on those worn by Saladin's conquering hordes in the 1100s.

Our driver, normally uncommunicative and silent, called to one of the horsemen and motioned for him to approach. The Fulani was wearing an ancient, much-repaired coat of chain mail. While his horse shifted and tossed its head, we tried to question him on the origin of the chain mail. He told our driver only that it was "very old" before urging his mount forward at a canter.

Rumor had it that some of the chain mail on display dated from the time of the Crusades. Considering the ebb and flow of weapons and military artifacts in Africa over the centuries, this was entirely possible. My guess was that the protective mail was more likely fabricated at a later date, perhaps by a Sudanese armorer employed by the *Mad Mahdi* in 1898 or some contemporary metalist working in the back streets of Kano or another city in northern Nigeria.

The highlight of the birthday celebrations was the show of horsemanship, or *Jahi*, performed outdoors in honor of the emir. We'd obtained permission to film the event. Kosoko had set up his tripod and camera at a respectful distance from the emir's throne. Other emirs and tribal leaders of lesser rank were seated under a flapping canopy, their armed escorts gathered in a dusty cloud of milling horsemen some 300 feet distant.

I wasn't sure what to expect, but I'd asked Kosoko to shoot it all and we'd worry about editing later. The desert sun was now very hot. Like a neophyte to the tropics, I'd left my bush hat in the Land Rover and had to make do with a handkerchief as a headcover. My damp shirt was clinging to my back and my bare arms were prickly with the serious warning of future sunburn. The emirs and their entourage, although turbaned and swathed in varicolored loose cloth, seemed impervious to the heat. They sat in silence, some wearing mirrored sunglasses, swinging their horsehair fly whisks, waiting for the performance to begin.

The emir of Kano finally arrived. He was sitting on a fine white horse of Arabian lineage bedecked with colorful, embroidered cloth and silver ornamentation. The emir's aides helped him dismount, rearrange his clothing, and take his seat. He too was wearing darkly tinted glasses.

A perspiring, redheaded British official tapped me on the shoulder. "I'd stand a bit back if I were you," he said, pointing toward the distant horsemen. "They come along quite fast, you know. Bit dangerous where you are."

I took his advice. No sooner had I moved behind the tripod when the first cavalcade of horsemen galloped toward us. Once again Kosoko was in an unenviable position, but I convinced myself that it was all part of his new trade.

The thunderous charge came closer, the horses straining forward, ears back, manes flying. Their riders, dark blurs in flowing white robes, lifted their flashing swords, waved their spears, and twirled their rifles. For a few breathless seconds, I had a fleeting impression of what it must have been like to stand in a British square at Omdurman waiting for the shock of a mounted assault. Only yards away the horsemen loosed a ragged fusillade of rifle shots into the air and reined in their mounts. The horses' hooves dug into the earth as they stopped only feet from the seemingly tranquil emir. A huge cloud of amber dust engulfed us all.

Our return trip was leisurely, and we took time to slake our constant thirst with visits to roadside beer halls well stocked with Beck's, Heineken, Bass, and the local brews. At one stop a somber Nigerian constable took a professional interest in the unusual multinational makeup of our team. When the driver explained our mission, the now-grinning constable insisted on posing with us in front of the Land Rover for a photo.

A later stop to refill our canteens from a village well revealed another aspect of bush Africa. A local prostitute was resting in a seductive position on a nearby stone wall. Her hair was done in orderly corn rows, bright red lipstick contrasted with her ebony skin, and her eyelashes were naturally long and curled. She was clothed in a dark wrap-around shift of thin cotton that accentuated her young breasts and molded itself to the curve of her high buttocks.

Kosoko had tipped me to her profession on our arrival, but no one could have mistaken her trade. I had never seen such a naturally sensuous creature. Every move, each attitude seemed part of a sexual ballet, a dance of professional temptation. When she came over to cadge a cigarette from our driver, her hip-swinging progress would have enlivened any sex emporium from Paris to Las Vegas. Informed that we were not in the buyer's market, she shrugged and left without a word. But the message of her parting smile was that we—as reticent males—were the real losers.

Eager to return to Lagos and not risk another dodgy hotel, we decided to take a long, restorative siesta in the late afternoon and drive on through the cool night. Kosoko and I stretched out on mats near the Land Rover, while the driver stayed with the vehicle, his long legs protruding through the open window.

Traveling at night was a different experience. The open fires of isolated villages without electricity appeared ahead of us like the camps of an unknown army. When we stopped by a crude roadside grill for roasted goat, the African night was full of noise: dogs barking, drumming, laughter, and the BBC World Service tuned to high volume. We arrived back in Lagos by midmorning, a crew of dust-covered pirates, after a round trip of well over 1,000 miles. Later, watching the laterite-tinted water rush down the shower drain, I resolved that any future trips to the north would be made by air.

The coming end of empire in Nigeria saw a flare-up of colonial fervor rather than a diminution. It seemed almost a gesture of defiance in the face of irrevocable change. The Queen's Birthday and traditional garden party at Government House, the seat of the British governor general, was a well-attended event and a symbolic social statement. It emphasized that, although independence was coming, it had not yet arrived. The British women wore white gloves and wide-brimmed hats in pastel colors, while their red-faced spouses perspired in jackets and club ties. The Nigerian women wore either British fashion or colorful tribal dress, while some of their civil service spouses suffered even more than their British counterparts, perspiring heavily in dark suits cut from light wool. The drinks flowed, the sun did its work, the laughter and chatter increased by many decibels, and some of the invitees became rubber-legged. The British and Nigerian characters from Joyce Cary's *Mister Johnson* were alive and well at Government House on the Queen's Birthday.

The Nigeria Police was another institution that insisted on retaining its tradition of spit and polish to the end. Although more Nigerians were entering the officer ranks in the late 1950s, the majority of senior officers remained British. The members of the staff of the Nigeria Police Academy near Lagos, with their iron-creased shorts, shined boots, and swagger sticks, were working hard to turn new recruits into police officers in time for the turnover of power in 1960. Each graduating class had its garden party on the spacious lawn in front of the academy buildings. One such fete had a very special effect on the guests. It was an unforgettable evening.

The flame-colored African sun was sinking behind a latticework of horizontal gray clouds. The prisoners, who had been trimming the academy's lawn with sharpened matchets, were returning to their cells. Some smartly uniformed young officers, both British and Nigerian, mustered near the circular driveway to greet the newly arrived guests. Several tables were scattered over the lawn, crowded with punch bowls, bottles, and platters of hors d'oeuvres. Nigerian stewards in white serving jackets were fanning away the flies and watching the ice melt.

The black sedans of government officials, diplomats, chiefs, obas, and business leaders began to pull into the drive. In the late 1950s no one yet seemed to have tumbled to the heat absorption qualities of the color black. Black was still the color of prestige.

This was a less formal crowd than those at Government House. There were fewer women in hats and gloves. Many of the British police officers' wives were smartly dressed and coiffed. Nigerian families arrived in rented sedans with drivers, the women's tribal costumes a bright splash of variegated color against the grass. Most of the men not in tribal dress were still in heavy churchgoing black, although a few sported seersucker or linen. Children of all ages, dressed in their Sunday best, scattered from the cars like buckshot, drawn by the magnet of the refreshment tables. But nothing was to be served until the guests were welcomed. The superintendent of the academy then made a short speech, the police band played "God Save the Queen," and the assembled guests got down to serious drinking.

Then something strange happened. The attractive wife of a British police officer lifted her unsteady spike heels from the turf and said, "Oh!" Speaking in a louder voice she said "Ouch!" and spilled some punch while she reached for her ankle. Yards away a stout Yoruba woman in flowing blue robes and a carefully tied yellow butterfly headdress did a quick sidestep and stamped her foot on the ground. Things deteriorated rapidly. Women were hopping, shuffling, and retreating toward the drive. Decorum had been abandoned, there were squeals, and the academy staff mustered the stewards and some constables, admonishing them to "do something."

I approached the heart of the turbulence, where a perspiring steward was ineffectually striking at the lawn with his serving towel. The culprits were there, disturbed and frenzied by the sudden assault of crushing heels and soles. The African fire ants were seething among the dry blades of grass like small red peppers, biting anything and anyone they encountered.

There was no denying the comic element to the scene: the gyrating, dancing guests, the yelps of pain, the ineffective countermeasures. Jerry Lewis or Abbott and Costello would have fit perfectly into the scenario. Women weren't the only persons under attack. It took the fire ants longer to infiltrate the men's trousers and socks. Once there, however, the spiteful insects were harder to remove. Whimpering, bitten children were being taken back to the cars.

Retreat was the only sensible alternative. The ant stings were no laughing matter. They raised burning, quarter-size welts. The walking wounded were being treated with salve and ice from the bar buckets. A valiant attempt was made to relaunch the reception. A few diehards stood by the bars, glass in hand, eyeing the grass with suspicion. But it was really all over. Nature had won again.

The two dark-suited, sober-faced Nigerian lawyers shook my hand and sat opposite my desk, their bowlers on their knees, their furled umbrellas at their sides. They had come to my office on behalf of their client, our former house steward. He had been implicated in the theft of 115 pounds from our apartment in Ikoyi, and, although the police suggested I keep him on so they could better watch his movements, his surly manner and poor work performance had forced me to let him go. Now, within weeks of our planned departure from Nigeria, he was threatening to take us to court for "unfair dismissal." His somber lawyers suggested that perhaps I would prefer to settle the matter out of court. When I refused, they informed me that the matter would go before a judge and left with even longer faces.

This was exactly the type of complication we did not need, and I hastened to seek legal advice. My lawyer was a thin, smiling man-about-town nicknamed "Sonny." He assured me there would be "no problem," asked me to write out a full statement, and promised to keep in touch with the court.

The days sped by, arrangements were under way for our home leave in the United States, and I was anxiously awaiting word on my next assignment. Mary Alice was preparing our two young daughters for the trip and readying our household effects for shipping. But the upcoming court case was a cloud on the horizon. I had to face the fact that my departure from Nigeria could be delayed. I also knew that a clever but unscrupulous lawyer could turn the case into a White versus Black, have versus have-not scenario. "Not to worry," Sonny told me cheerfully.

Finally, an early phone call advised me to be in what amounted to a small claims court at 10:00 A.M. In reality, it was a former theater, not a courthouse. It was also a bedlam of disputatious Mammy Traders, noisy family members, shouting bewigged lawyers, and a scattering of bored court officers and constables.

I waited and waited. Sonny arrived, gave me a big wave and sat with the lawyers. The old overhead fans were too high to provide adequate ventilation and everyone was perspiring.

The judge's appearance on the theater's stage caused a stir. He was a short Nigerian wearing rimless bifocals and the long, tightly curled wig of judges in the British court system. The wig was yellowed with age and slightly askew. All of us stood, and an official declared the court in session. The judge sat at a wide-legged table under a sun-bleached color photo of Queen Elizabeth II. His first act was to kick off his shoes. Then he concentrated on his cases, hardly raising his head to look at the lawyers or their clients. His gavel fell in judgment with the rapidity of a pile driver. He cleared his court calendar with a speed that would have been the envy of his professional colleagues in the Bronx.

He wasn't able to railroad every case to a hasty conclusion. The Mammy Traders—no strangers to the court—had their own way of playing the game. Enormous, heavy women with voices that would send a lion whimpering into the bush, only the Mammy Traders dared to differ with the judge. It was pure theater. They cried, they disputed the judge's findings, they questioned a prosecuting attorney's manhood, they gave testimony peeling and eating a banana, and they did not hesitate to vilify their husbands ("Dat mon, he be no good at all") and pose as the sole hope for their family's survival. When all else failed, they fainted. Anyone daydreaming in court would be brought back to reality quickly when a Mammy Trader fell to the floor. The judge's order to clear an "unconscious" Mammy Trader from his court was a pure verbal formality. Not until the Mammy Trader was willing to assist the court's officers by becoming at least partially mobile could the judge's order be carried out.

For three days I sat in the muggy court, listening to the drama and minor tragedies of Lagos. It was the equivalent of a crash course in pidgin English, and I marveled at the judge's ability to switch from the Queen's English while addressing a barrister to pidgin when he explained his sentencing of a petty thief to the man's family.

I was prepared for another wasted day when Sonny approached me prior to the judge's arrival.

"It's today," he announced. "It should be over by noon."

An hour later the clerk called our case. I breathed a sigh of relief, sitting on the edge of my chair. Sonny and our former steward's lawyer were called to the judge's table for consultation. There appeared to be a problem. The judge called the court clerk, the clerk summoned a messenger, and the messenger ran from the court, mounted his bicycle, and rode off into the rain.

"He's gone to the records office to get your file," Sonny informed me. "It will take time. Go have a beer."

Too nervous to leave the court, I sat through three more rapid-fire cases before the click of the clerk's faulty bicycle wheel heralded his return. Soaked to the skin, he left a trail of wet footsteps up to the table, where he whispered in the judge's ear. For a few short seconds the judge looked directly at me before his gaze slid away. I strained to hear his words . . . "official file missing . . . declare this case a mistrial . . . next. . . ."

I could not believe my ears and looked to Sonny for an answer. In response, he gave a conspiratorial wink and gestured toward the court's exit. I never did find out what happened to the case file. Sonny remarked that they were "always losing things over there" in the records office and refused to accept a fee. If the steward had not been attempting a blatant shakedown, I might have had some qualms about the file's unexplained disappearance. As it was, I decided to abide by the judge's ruling and the customs of a Nigerian court.

My orders arrived in the form of a telegraph from Washington. I was to be the regional public affairs officer, with the rank of consul, at the consulate general in Marseille. I had finally broken into the "European Club," and it was a choice assignment. My operational territory would stretch from Narbonne and Montpellier to Nice, Monaco, and the Italian border. It would include a number of French départements, among them the Bouches-du-Rhône, the Gard, the Var, the Vaucluse, the Alpes-Maritimes, and Corsica.

I was anxious to see Marseille for the second time. During my short exposure to that rough, gutsy, but beautiful old city in 1945 I had come to appreciate what M. F. K. Fisher would later praise as "a considerable town."

4

Pastis, Pagnol, and
a President

The water of Marseille's Vieux Port sparkled under a hot sun in May 1959. The fishwives on the Quai des Belges were sluicing seawater over their trays of sardines, squid, rouget, rockfish, and sea urchins to keep them fresh. The small ferryboats were chugging across the harbor to the hôtel de ville (city hall), built by Louis XIV. The odor of grilled fish and *soupe de poisson* wafted from the waterfront restaurants. The Bar de la Marine, so dear to Marcel Pagnol, was still serving iced pastis and green olives to a clientele of hoarse-voiced fishermen in visored black caps.

I stood near the moored launches that took tourists out to the Chateau d'If and remembered my introduction to Marseille 14 years earlier as a 20-year-old GI. Things had been different in August 1945. The Germans had blown up a section of the old city behind the Quai du Port—a favorite refuge for both the Résistance and the underworld. They had filled the inner harbor with wreckage from the once tall *pont transbordeur* and sunk a number of small craft in an attempt to disrupt the port as long as possible. Cranes were still hauling twisted metal and debris from the water.

As veterans of the European campaigns preparing to sail for the invasion of Japan, we'd become inured to destruction. Our prime interest during leave from our sun-baked camp near Arles had been the full-bodied, dark-haired prostitutes of the Vieux Port, whose primary diet seemed to consist of tomato and onion sandwiches. How to avoid the

MP patrols determined to keep us out of this off-limits zone had been our secondary concern.

I'd returned once again in 1949 when studying in Paris. But my main goal then had been to follow the Van Gogh trail in Arles and I'd spent a very short time in Marseille.

Now, as an officer assigned to the U.S. consulate general, a married man, and the father of two daughters, I considered myself particularly lucky to be back in Marseille. I had often heard the clichéd caution about never returning. But somehow, with the sun on my face, listening to the raucous shouts of the fish vendors and watching the busy activity of the port, I felt a special affinity for the ancient, colorful city.

We were housed temporarily in the Hôtel Porte de l'Orient while my predecessor, Jack Hedges, and his family prepared to leave the USIS director's residence on the rue Saint Jacques. Paul Child, the previous public affairs officer, and his ebullient wife Julia had also served in Marseille. Her long exposure to Provençal cuisine surely contributed to her establishment as one of America's great chefs and a national television personality.

Hedges too was a special person. One of the original radio "quiz kids" and a Harvard graduate, he was a large, intelligent man with a refreshing sense of humor and a W. C. Fields delivery. A navy veteran, he had previously served with the Mutual Security Administration in Paris and Saigon before joining USIA. During his two-year tour in Marseille, he had fit into the local scene with ease, equally at home discussing economics with members of the chamber of commerce over a multicourse luncheon or sipping pastis with local artists in one of their favorite cafés. Skillful at the keyboard, he could liven any party with jazz and honky-tonk piano, while a trademark Gauloise cigarette hung from a corner of his mouth. Hedges was now on his way to the Paris embassy as the assistant press and publications officer.

Shortly after my arrival, Jack insisted that I accompany him on an official trip that would serve as his farewell to the region and introduce me to his working contacts along the coast. From Marseille to Toulon and from Saint Tropez to Cannes and Nice we called on local politicians, mayors, and regional deputies; writers, editors, and television personalities; naval officers; and police officials.

Once back in Marseille Jack and his wife, Peggy, picked us up in the office sedan for a tour of the city by night. High above the notorious Panier quarter we watched the nocturnal invasion of large, gray rats scurrying and tumbling down the steep stone steps toward the restaurant district in search of food. Later, Jack introduced us to his favorite nightclub not far from the Marseille docks. We met Madame, the owner, who had fluffy, dyed hair the color of straw, a pneumatic figure that had seen better days, and alert brown eyes that recorded every event in her establishment. She also had the disconcerting habit of breaking into German marching songs after a few cognacs and beating out the cadence on the bar with a clenched fist. We were introduced to the pianist, a small, bald man who pounded the piano each night from his darkened corner, and to the professional women who worked the bar, a ribald gathering of Mediterranean Sadie Thompsons, their healthy curves a living tribute to a Provençal diet of fish, pasta, and olive oil.

A few days after our nighttime sortie, Hedges began planning a diplomatic reception at the USIS residence that would introduce me to *le tout Marseille:* the consular corps of 13 nations, the local French government civilian and military officials, the university rectors, the members of Franco-American groups, business leaders, and the media.

Jack had informed me we were to have live music, so I was not too surprised when the nightclub pianist arrived just before the first guests and ran through a quick familiarization course on the house piano. The guests were a patchwork of opposites. Our stuffier consular corps colleagues drew in their breaths when Jack introduced them to the officers of a Socialist—but anticommunist—labor union. The doyen of a venerable French university looked particularly pained when he was left alone to chat with a bearded American Fulbright scholar who spoke execrable French. One of Jack's most questionable contacts, a swarthy Corsican rumored to have underworld connections, turned pale when introduced to one of the newly assigned narcotics agents working out of our consulate.

The party peaked at about 9:00 P.M. From that moment on we were on a downward curve. I was talking to the president of a local Franco-American friendship society, a stout, forceful businessman with very definite ideas about France, the United States, and the world. He had backed me into a corner of the reception room between a Louis XIV table and a large standing lamp.

The more bourbon the president consumed, the harder it was to follow his commentary. It was filled with strange pauses, disjointed phrases, and vague admonitions to "listen carefully." His spectacles had slid down his nose, and a blank smile was spreading over his face at frequent intervals. I was about to suggest that we join the other guests at the buffet when he began to sway like an elm in a high wind. Back he went, then forward, with a slightly puzzled look. I watched for several seconds, transfixed. When I reached out to steady him it was too late. His backward sway was beyond recovery. He went down in slow motion, his free hand clutching the lamp shade for support. The lamp went with him. Even the music couldn't cover the din of his descent. Fortunately, no one was injured, but the president's wife was mortified. That particular incident spoiled *monsieur le president*'s taste for bourbon.

Hedge's briefings on the new job were irregular but thorough. He broached specific requirements and projects as they came to mind. As in all handovers, he had his ideas and I had mine. Within a week's time I learned that I was to act as a public affairs adviser to the U.S. 6th Fleet when it was within our jurisdiction along the southern coast of France. Each May I could count on being appointed to the official U.S. delegation to the International Film Festival at Cannes, and by September I could expect an invitation to the International Wine Fair at Montpellier.

Other, grayer areas required continued U.S. support for certain non-communist labor unions and a small but determined local group supporting European unity. The Cold War was at its chilly height in 1959, "massive retaliation" was the motto, and Europe was a stage for East-West espionage of all kinds. France was a nation still torn by political rivalries and bitterness from the war, the *epuration* (purification, or evening of scores), and its immediate aftermath. The "Yankee Go Home" graffiti of the late 1940s had faded from the walls, but the French Communists were still a potent, well-organized force. Few Americans realized the real danger this Moscow-oriented and -supported party posed to the French republic.

The republic was also threatened to a lesser extent from the hard-liners of the right, those who had managed to erase their past association with the Vichy government or their flirtation with the occupiers. These militants were prospering in the Cold War environment, seeking social contact with American diplomats and offering their doubtful services sotto voce as experienced, dedicated anticommunists.

The Communists were particularly strong in Marseille, where they controlled the docks and many key industries through the powerful national labor union they dominated, the Confédération Générale du Travail (CGT). They were also active on the cultural front, with intellectual militants turning the most innocent function into a political manifestation or a Marxist history lesson.

Like all good "cold warriors" I was tasked to keep an eye on our Iron Curtain rivals in Marseille and their French surrogates. I also had to keep certain virulent anticommunists—who would have liked nothing better than the launching of World War III—at arm's length.

Shortly after Hedges departed, I was faced with a lukewarm Cold War situation. He had told me of the earlier special effort the Soviets had made at the annual Commercial Fair of Marseille. They'd built their own elaborate pavilion and filled it with machine tools, farming equipment, caviar, and vodka. They had sent a large trade delegation of well-fed glad-handers to talk business with the merchants of southern France and had twinned the cities of Odessa and Marseille. Due to sound practical reasons, reinforced by budget problems, the United States had been content with a small exhibit on the theme of "Visit the USA," a valiant effort to bring tourist money to the United States.

Now, the Marseille dailies were bannering the latest Soviet project: a booth at the Montpellier Wine Fair featuring Georgian wines and other vinous products of the USSR. As America's newly arrived regional propagandist and a wine-drinking Californian, this was a challenge I could not ignore. If the French were about to taste Georgian wine, they should also be allowed to savor the product of American vineyards.

A quick letter to the California Wine Institute brought maps, photos, and material needed for a speech. Some hurried research revealed the existence of the perfect "peg." There was a bronze statue in a Montpellier park dedicated to the California winegrowers who, many years before, had donated their vine cuttings to their French colleagues after a plague of phylloxera had destroyed the local vineyards.

The mayor of Montpellier was overjoyed to learn that the United States would be represented, and the president of the fair expressed the belief that no field of Soviet-American rivalry could be found that would better serve humanity. There would be an "America Day" at the fair and I was guaranteed an audience of curious, if skeptical, winegrowers and tasters.

I then faced a major problem. Where was I to find some California wine? It was too late to order it from the United States or even from the embassy commissary in Paris. The deep bellow of a freighter pulling away from the Marseille docks provided the answer. I charged into the consular section and checked the arrival and departure schedule of

American ships. Luck was with me. An American flag cargo-passenger ship was in port. A half hour later I was explaining my problem to a puzzled chief steward. I told him of the challenge of Soviet participation at the fair, the phylloxera story, and "America Day." He gave every indication of thinking he was dealing with a demented secret agent. My eagerness to put my hands on some California wine was matched by his obvious desire to get me off his ship as soon as possible.

He took me down to his *cave* (cellar), well below the waterline. A small electric fan had been installed to fight the heat, but someone had switched it off. The bottle I felt was warm to the touch. "Take your pick," the steward said, folding his arms.

I selected ten bottles, red and white from different vineyards. My feeling of accomplishment was dulled by the fear that some of the warm bottles might be more appropriate for a vinegar-judging contest.

The drive to Montpellier was pleasant, the day was warm, and the rich perfume of harvested grapes was in the air. My carefully selected bottles were beside me, stowed in a large carton and carefully wrapped to avoid jarring.

The president, vintners, merchants, and tasters were waiting for me—a robust, ruddy-cheeked crew. They listened to my speech and a murmur of interest ran through the hall when the bottles and glasses were placed on a table. They came forward in a body, shook my hand, and waited for their glasses to be filled. They swished the wine and applied their noses; swished it again and shut their eyes. I watched with a nervous smile. Then they tasted, filling their cheeks like chipmunks, pursing their lips. The president smiled and put his hand reassuringly on my shoulder.

The tasting continued, from bottle to bottle. The tasters exchanged murmured comments as they waited for new glasses. Normally they would have been spitting out the wine and preparing their palates for a different taste, but this was an informal tasting, a relaxation.

"You see," said the president, "they are swallowing it." I blessed the hardiness of the wine and its ability to withstand mistreatment.

Finally, one of the elder tasters turned toward me.

"Most interesting," he said. "One of the reds is equal to a minor Beaujolais. But the white..." I held my breath. "They are very good. The *terroir* is strange to our palates, but they do have merit." That evening the "America Day" festivities were capped by a dinner of *cuisses de grenouilles* and *tournedos Rossini* accompanied by the appropriate wines, salad, and cheeses. The Soviet delegate to the fair found it impossible to attend and sent his regrets.

The next morning I drove back to Marseille with a slight headache and the impression that I had shattered the French cliché of the average American as a milk-sipping milquetoast. I had also found a common ground of understanding and interest among an influential and vocal group of French citizens.

A few weeks later, after the Montpellier expedition had faded into a pleasant memory, a thick letter arrived on my desk. It was from the New York wine industry. In a polite but firm tone it expressed surprise and shock that a government official should be pushing American products on a regional basis—particularly when the region in question corresponded to the official's home state. Enclosed with the letter were copies of similar missives sent to the director of USIA and the Paris embassy.

My response leaned heavily on the links between the California vintners and their Montpellier counterparts, the large participation of the Soviets, and the success of our minor project. The complainant eventually sent me a standing invitation to visit the New York vineyards, the agency relaxed, and the embassy was amused.

Serving as the regional public affairs officer, press spokesman for the consulate general, and overseer for the operation of the Centre Culturel Américain, a modest in-house library, exhibition space, and advice center for French students and academics, ensured a wide variety of local contacts. Whether media representatives, artists, civic officials, the military, members of one of the oldest chambers of commerce in Europe, or even fellow diplomats, all of these individuals provided keys to knowing and understanding Marseille and Provence.

Doug Smith was the second USIS officer at the post and an old friend from service in Indochina. Doug was young, energetic, and a hard worker. The son of missionary parents, he was a bit naive, but Marseille's rough edges would soon dispose of the naïveté.

Much of the direct input of local knowledge following my arrival came from our small French staff headed by Ramon Garcia, a former American citizen who had served in the U.S. Army during the Korean War and who had returned to France after that conflict. Garcia was relaxed and pragmatic, with a deep appreciation of Provençal living. He had an easygoing approach welcomed by the Marseillais. Our small branch office at the Nice consulate was run by Gilles Daziano, a talented man with a good sense of humor. He needed it. Answering to me in Marseille and pleasing the American consul in Nice was no easy task. Add the pressures of the 6th Fleet admiral based in nearby Villefranche and the large colony of resident Americans in the Nice region, including culture vultures and gung ho veterans, and there was little wonder that Daziano often began our telephone conversations with a sigh.

I came to know the city of Marseille through exploratory walks, stand-up lunches at the *zinc* of innumerable cafés and sipping pastis in waterfront bars. Listening to what went on around me was a good learning aid. Perhaps it wasn't the orientation of a classic diplomat but it suited my purposes. I could walk to a late afternoon call on a city official in the hôtel de ville to discuss the mayor's presence at an official American function and then take the small, open ferry across the Vieux Port for an apéritif at le Peano, a rendezvous for Marseille's artists and writers. On another occasion I might stop for a *pression* in a small bar on the rue Davso, where the city's "bad boys" rubbed shoulders with off-duty plainclothes men of the Marseille police. Walking up the rue Paradis, I could hear the heehaw of police vans—the serenade of the city—and the sound of flamenco music coming from a second-floor window, and sniff the odor of strong coffee and grilling *merguez* sausages. Turning right onto the rue Saint Jacques and coming within sight of our government-leased townhouse, I inevitably encountered two or three prostitutes. High-heeled regulars with their assigned sidewalk stations, they greeted me each evening with a deferential but friendly "Bonsoir, monsieur le consul." Once when a new girl on the block approached me, offering action, the regulars quickly shushed the newcomer. The senior regular later apologized for her young colleague's gaffe.

On December 2, 1959, a heavy rainstorm struck the pleasant coastal town of Fréjus approximately 75 miles east of Marseille. The force of the storm ruptured a dam at Malpasse, and the resultant flashflood proved both lethal and devastating. The storm created havoc in other coastal communities, disrupting power and telephone services, but none were so hard hit as Fréjus. Normal emergency services were swamped with demands, and both the British and U.S. consulates in Marseille decided to lend a hand. Gerry Clode, a British vice consul who had served with de Gaulle's Free French Forces during World War II, and I loaded our small utility trucks with hundreds of freshly baked baguettes and cases of bottled water. These supplies were badly needed for the survivors and rescue workers.

I reached Fréjus early in the morning over a circuitous route taken to avoid flood-damaged roads. It was like entering a war-battered town in Alsace rather than a Mediterranean resort. Mud like liquid chocolate still clogged most of the streets, vehicles had been tossed one onto the other by the flood waters, and bodies were being hauled from the muck. A makeshift morgue had been set up in the local church. Residents with handkerchiefs held over their noses were passing silently before the stiff and muddy dead—men, women, and children—searching for missing family members.

Our cargo unloaded, Clode and I agreed that there was not much else we could do. The French authorities had the situation in hand. I did get a message through to the consulate on the urgent need for more blankets. A U.S 6th Fleet destroyer delivered blankets and other relief supplies within 24 hours.

With more dark clouds piling up, the wind rising, and continued rain predicted, I decided to head back to Marseille. A representative from the mayor's office thanked us for our assistance, but we made it clear we wanted no publicity for our small contribution. In retrospect I've often wondered if we were automatically scrambling for Cold War points. I think not. Like the gratis smallpox inoculations in Nigeria, it was the kind of thing that was done.

Shortly after the Fréjus disaster, the first in a series of classified telegrams from the State Department and the White House began to arrive at the consulate general in Marseille. We were informed that President Eisenhower would be making an official visit to France later in December. He would be landing from the 6th Fleet flagship, USS *Des Moines*, at the French naval port of Toulon. From the moment the president set foot on French soil in Toulon until his official train headed north out of our territory on its way to Paris, the success of his visit would be in our hands.

I had never experienced a presidential visit before, but my more experienced colleagues warned that I'd better put any plans for a normal life on hold until the visit had ended. How right they were. We were forewarned of the imminent visit of a White House advance team, and the decoding capabilities of the consulate were sorely tried until additional personnel were sent down from Paris. The embassy was already scheduling meetings in Toulon, where we were to plan details of the visit with the staffs of President Charles de Gaulle and Prime Minister Michel Debre; the foreign ministry; the ministry of the interior (security); the prefect of the department of the Var; the French navy, army, and air force; the mayor's office of the city of Toulon; and a plethora of regional police officials.

It was not long before the presidential visit became public knowledge. This relieved some of the pressure on the code clerks, but it unleashed a telephone offensive on our limited communication system. The words "White House on the line," at first a novelty, soon became a heavy burden. In a very short time we learned that everyone working within the White House, from the lowliest advance party gofer to the ranking planner, prefaced their request with "the White House wants..." or "the president requires...."

I must admit, of all the White House crews I was to work with, the members of Eisenhower's were the calmest and most methodical, approaching their task with military precision and a great reliance on staff work. Kennedy's "Irish Mafia" was to prove more flexible and flamboyant, a close-knit team enjoying private jokes and eager to wrap up the day's work in order to explore the local watering holes and restaurants. Johnson's Texans were polite but leery of foreign methods and ever alert to the changing moods and mercurial temper of their trail boss. Nixon's buttoned-down crew was serious and withdrawn, its members quick to throw their weight around but equally quick to hand out praise when things went well. Carter's country folk were generally easygoing, perpetuating the good 'ol boy image and retaining a certain suspicion of "Eastern establishment" Foreign Service officers.

With the Eisenhower arrival in Toulon set for December 18, 1959, and a number of planning meetings completed, I now had a pretty good idea of my responsibilities. Lowell Bennett, our press attaché in Paris, and Jack Hedges, his assistant, would be traveling to Toulon aboard the presidential train to receive and cosset the White House press corps traveling with the president.

Bill Cody (a distant relative of the original Buffalo Bill), the embassy's counselor for public affairs and our overall boss, would also be on the train, but he seldom involved himself in media matters, preferring the cultural side of our operations. He was a stout gourmand who had spent long years on the Left Bank in prewar Paris. How he made the switch from his bohemian past to that of a conservative stickler for diplomatic protocol remains a mystery.

My job and that of my staff would be to see that the accredited American, French, and international TV networks and photographers had adequate filming access for the president's dockside arrival. We also had to ensure visual access for the written press and radio reporters, sound feeds, and ready texts of the president's arrival statement in French and English. In addition, we were charged with making sure the White House press moved quickly from the USS *Des Moines* to the presidential train following Ike's brief speech. Presidential trains depart on time. Any dallying press representatives would have had to make their own way to Paris.

Our major priority was to see that all TV footage of the arrival was collected and delivered to the train prior to its departure. This was well before satellite transmission, and exposed film, secured in its cans, had to be airshipped to the networks for development and editing. It had been agreed among the major American networks that their footage would travel on the train to Paris, where motorcycle dispatch riders would rush it to Orly Airport for a flight to the United States.

I was to be in Toulon a week before the presidential arrival to attend more meetings and iron out any media-related difficulties. Just prior to my departure, a priority telegram from the White House suggested that the consulate general in Marseille might want to assist in drafting the president's arrival remarks. A White House "suggestion" being the equivalent of a shouted command, we readily agreed to contribute. A copy of the first White House draft duly arrived on my desk. I recall that the text was the standard, boilerplate pablum that professional speechwriters turn out with ease.

My previous experience drafting a VIP speech had not been felicitous. In 1955, when the religious-military sects of Vietnam were preparing to revolt against the Diem regime, I had been asked to work on a crucial speech for President Diem. In a pugnacious paragraph I had spoken of the fragility of democracy and the government's responsibility to protect it by the force of arms. These words, when delivered, were said to have contributed to the sects' decision to fight.

I was facing no such danger with this bland arrival statement, but how often, I questioned, must we dredge up Lafayette and shades of our old alliance with France? Suddenly, I thought of the tragedy of Fréjus. It was still fresh in France's memory, particularly in Provence. The town was only some 50 miles distant along the same coast. It seemed a natural, and I added a brief expression of sorrow and sympathy from the president to Fréjus and its inhabitants. It fit Ike's image as a down-to-earth, caring father figure. With this contribution duly telegraphed to Washington, I said my family goodbyes and headed for Toulon in the USIS station wagon driven by Eugene Druzniak, our gravel-voiced chauffeur, caretaker, and general factotum.

The Tour Blanche Hotel, high above Toulon, had been chosen by a scouting detachment from the White House to house various elements of the Eisenhower advance party. My arrival coincided with that of a strong Secret Service detachment with all their baggage and carefully packed working tools of a more lethal nature. They had been met at the airport by some of their French counterparts, who were doing their best to accommodate the visitors. But there was definitely a language problem.

A French security official, hearing me speak French to Eugene, approached to seek my help.

"Monsieur," he said. "Can you ask your friends to remove their luggage from the lobby?"

This seemed a strange request. Luggage was still being brought in from the cars and the lobby was in a state of flux. Why, I asked, was it so important to move the bags?

"Look," he said, indicating a large and expensive leather holdall. "It is most embarrassing."

Still puzzled, I examined the bag that troubled him. Then I understood. It was embossed with gold letters that spelled out the owner's name. Under the name, in larger lettering, was the clear designation "U.S. Secret Service." This was a public admittance inimical to French bureaucratic logic and particularly troubling to Gallic security specialists to whom the word "secret" had an almost religious significance. Rather than spend a half hour explaining the open status of the White House Secret Service in American society I suggested to the top Secret Service honcho that it would be best to clear the lobby before the arrival of a (nonexistent) tourist bus.

Over the next few days the hotel filled with communications experts, White House staffers, embassy personnel, and security officers. I went ahead with our press arrangements, making sure that selected newsmen from Marseille and Toulon were included in the planning. After all, I would be in the region long after the Eisenhower circus had departed. I also got to know the Secret Service agents informally, and they filled me in on their weapons and tactics. This honeymoon, however, was brief.

Three days before the president's arrival, I received an urgent summons to appear before the French admiral commanding the naval base of Toulon. I found this strange, particularly since there were officers from the U.S. naval attaché's office now providing liaison in Toulon. I had spent a pleasant half hour with the admiral when Hedges had introduced us during our coastal tour. Perhaps the admiral wanted to discuss press arrangements?

A frowning aide led me into the admiral's spacious office with its Dufy-like view of the harbor. The admiral was pacing behind his long desk, red-faced and clearly agitated. I soon learned that the Secret Service had managed to offend the French in a far more serious matter than their luggage marking.

In a dry run of the president's route through the naval base on the way to the train station, the Secret Service had discovered a blind spot. This blind spot meant that Secret Service agents in the follow-up car would lose sight of the president's armored limousine for several seconds as it negotiated a tight turn. To eliminate this blind spot, the Secret Service had decided that three feet of masonry would have to be shaved off a building along the route.

"No," the admiral told me. "It is impossible!" He explained that the building was a historic monument. It had been there for centuries! It was already ancient when Napoleon was a young artillery officer lobbing cannonballs at the occupying British garrison in Toulon! Without actually saying it, the admiral made it clear that perhaps the president would be more at ease landing at another spot along the coast. I did my diplomatic best to calm him and soon found myself in the role of middleman between the French navy and the Secret Service.

It took 24 hours of negotiations: telephone calls to Paris, telegrams to Washington, and tight-lipped bilateral meetings. The threatened clash of national wills was averted only after a heavy French lunch washed down with many bottles of Provençal rosé. The blind spot would be covered by armed Secret Service and French security personnel stationed atop the tiled roof of the intact monument.

We reviewed all the media arrangements at a meeting held the day before the president's arrival. Representatives of the French Gendarmerie Nationale, the Compagnies Républicaine de Sécurité (CRS), the Police Nationale, and the police of Toulon sat in on the meeting. This was important because their personnel would be restricting movement within the city, demanding official passes, and checking on accredited journalists. Security cooperation was particularly crucial for us, because Ramon Garcia and Eugene Druzniak had been assigned to deliver the exposed TV and newsreel footage to the train. Although they would both have official passes, we explained their route and the need for speed to our security colleagues, who promised to alert their men.

December 18 dawned cool and hazy. A thin surface fog hung over the calm water of the harbor until well after noon. The sharp prow of the USS *Des Moines* finally split the fog, and the cruiser moved slowly toward its berth. Ashore, the official greeting party, including Secretary of State Christian A. Herter, American Ambassador Amory Houghton, French Minister of State Louis Jacquinot, and French ambassador to Washington Herve Alphand prepared to greet the president.

When Ike appeared, there was a flurry of applause from the onlookers, French naval personnel, and civilian workers. It was the first time I'd ever seen Eisenhower. Here, finally, was my erstwhile World War II commander in chief in the flesh. He seemed smaller than I'd imagined, but his smile had a definite warmth and he seemed genuinely at ease. He was accompanied by his son, Major John Eisenhower, the latter's wife, and the multilingual Colonel Vernon Walters (later a general and deputy director of the CIA).

Then it was time for the speeches. The mikes that had been fussed over by White House technicians emitted the inevitable prebroadcast screech before Monsieur Jacquinot welcomed the president once more to France and Ike responded. I scanned our edited text, waiting for the mention of the Fréjus tragedy. It didn't happen. Some White House wordsmith had obviously judged the insert too lugubrious for the start of an official visit.

By 1:30 P.M., the president had arrived at the *salon d'honneur* of the railway station, where a group of politicians, including deputies and senators from the region, were waiting to shake his hand. Meanwhile, Garcia and Druzniak had gathered the last newsreel and TV footage of the arrival and were ready to drive to the station. Convinced they could reach the train easily through the cleared streets prior to the 2:00 P.M. departure, I hopped on a bus loaded with White House media representatives and we headed for the train.

Our planning was basically sound, but we hadn't taken into account the French tendency to change procedure at the last minute. As Garcia and Druzniak raced from the naval base to the station, they found their access barred by French security officers who (a) had just arrived in Toulon that morning, (b) had never attended any of the joint Franco-American planning sessions, and (c) had received no orders to let my staffers through to the train. After some desperate and quick talking on Garcia's part, they were allowed to leave their vehicle, lift the heavy boxes of film, and sprint for the train.

Inside the train, the members of the White House press corps were relaxing, preparing for the four-course luncheon with appropriate wines laid on by the French National Railroad. I was far from relaxed, hanging out the open doorway, scanning the platform. Lowell Bennett, a true pro, understood what was going on.

"Where are they?" he asked.

"They'll make it," I replied unconvincingly, watching the second hand of my watch.

Garcia rounded the distant corner of the station just as a conductor's whistle sounded. He was running like an Olympic athlete with Druzniak pounding along behind him. The couplings groaned as the train began to move. They increased their stride, perspiration coursing down their cheeks, the weight of the boxes beginning to tell. The train gathered momentum.

"Run!" I shouted, hoping for a miracle. A final effort put the box Garcia was carrying within inches of my outstretched hand. In French films, running men always make the train. They didn't on December 18, 1959. The exposed footage stayed in Toulon.

I understand the luncheon that day was excellent. I don't recall. I had lost my appetite. Network representatives, informed that their footage was still in Toulon, expressed their disappointment in concise, colorful language. One TV commentator became so abusive that Bennett, who had served with the Free French and—as a war correspondent with the Royal Air Force—been shot down over Berlin, threatened to knock him flat on his ass. This uncompromising riposte had an immediate calming affect on the other newsmen. Jim Hagerty, the presidential press secretary, asked if it was true the film had missed the train. When I confirmed the bad news, he burned me with a sulfurous glare and went back to editing Eisenhower's speech for delivery in Paris. Through all of this ruckus Bill Cody sat like a benign Buddha, imperturbably tucking into the first course of his lunch and sipping a full glass of the French railroad's best Bordeaux.

Echoes and rumors of hot wars reached me as I settled into my post in Marseille. The Diem regime in South Vietnam that we had worked so hard to put in place as a "bulwark against Communism" in Southeast Asia was becoming shakier with each passing month. The pin-prick

Viet Cong actions in the South were inexorably moving toward large-scale guerrilla warfare. The war in Algeria that had absorbed so many of the French units from Indochina was intensifying. My links with these conflicts were maintained by letters from friends still in Vietnam and encounters with French officers I had met in Indochina who were passing through Marseille on their way to or from Algeria. It was the luck of the Foreign Service toss that assignments in both countries were to be in my professional future.

5

Festival at Cannes

"**B**eware of Gaston Defferre," I was warned by a member of the embassy's political section, "he eats American officials for breakfast." Defferre was the tough Socialist mayor of Marseille and a deputy in the National Assembly. He had led a regional Résistance network during the war and distinguished himself after the German surrender by physically ejecting a group of Communists who had taken over the city hall. A no-nonsense Protestant who spoke in clipped phrases, Defferre was a colorful character. He had fought two duels with political rivals (pistol and sword—no serious wounds), was an able yachtsman, and owned *le Provençal*, the largest circulation daily in the Marseille region, and the afternoon *le Soir*.

The majority of Marseillais enjoyed their mayor's directness. They admitted to visitors that it took "a bastard to run a city like this" and often referred to him with the colorful label of "Gastounet." My informant in Paris had also made it clear that Defferre had little time for the consular corps members based in his city and had publically stated that he was not to be "pushed around" by either the Communists or the Americans. The fact that my request to call on him had not yet been answered tended to support this latter point.

A telephone call from our cultural attaché in Paris changed my request from a simple act of protocol to a matter of urgent business. Gaston Defferre had been nominated for a State Department leader grant (now known as the International Visitor Program), and I was to confirm his willingness to accept the offer, set a travel date, and work out a tentative program.

The International Visitor Program was, and is, one of the most imaginative and practical overseas cultural efforts of the U.S. government. Under its terms, candidates in many fields—politics, education, the arts, sciences, and defense—are selected by a special embassy committee for their present and future leadership potential. They are then offered working visits to the United States modeled to fit their interests and professions. This ongoing program has ensured that a large number of influential international personalities of various political hues obtain both a knowledge of the United States and direct, long-time personal contact with Americans in the same field.

A quick perusal of the Defferre file revealed that he had previously been nominated for a grant but that his political commitments had made it impossible to leave France. I put a call through to his chef de cabinet, stressing the matter's urgency, and obtained an appointment for the next day.

Defferre received me in his office with a firm handshake and indicated that I should sit down facing him over his ornate desk. A shock of white hair surrounded his suntanned bald pate, and his blue eyes fixed me with a "your time is limited" glare. I explained the situation. He seemed unimpressed. I emphasized how important it was to reach a speedy decision in order to start planning his travel program. He pursed his lips and said he wasn't sure he could leave in the near future. He finally agreed to make a decision within 48 hours, and I left documents with him detailing the procedures.

The 48 hours had become 72 before I again telephoned the hôtel de ville. The mayor was very busy and would call me back. He did not. I decided to camp on his office doorstep in the airy waiting room overlooking the Vieux Port. I had adequate time to study the fine plaster work of the ancient ceilings, the design of the wallpaper, and the framed Croix de Guerre awarded to Marseille for its role in the liberation. I also observed the constant flow of politicians, businessmen, and officials in and out of Defferre's office.

Finally, it was my turn. The same handshake, the same glare. I tried to lighten the procedure by explaining that I too had been a newspaperman before entering government. There was very little reaction. The mayor had, nevertheless, obviously read through the documentation and done some research of his own. He told me he "might" go to the United States if he could join Senator John F. Kennedy's presidential campaign trail. He presented this request as if it were a challenge. As if I, whom he probably considered an official of the Eisenhower administration, would flinch at such a proposal. This attitude alone seemed to justify an orientation visit to the United States. I promised to contact Washington as soon as possible and to inform him of the reply.

I had an answer by the end of the next working day. The State Department agreed that Defferre's proposal would be both interesting and profitable. I was urged to speed his commitment so the planners could go to work. I hurried back to the hôtel de ville. The mayor seemed a bit more relaxed. He even cracked a brief smile when I told him his proposal had been accepted.

"Now," I said, opening a small pocket calendar, "when would you be able to travel?"

"There is one problem," Defferre said, frowning.

"What problem?" I asked.

"The per diem (daily expense allowance) being offered is too low," he told me. "It would not even pay for the flowers I might wish to offer a hostess if I am invited to dinner."

He had a point. The official per diem was low. But Uncle Sam was prepared to pay airfares and lodging; to arrange ground transport, introductions, meetings, and interviews; and to generally see that the visit was pleasant and profitable.

I must have sat silently for several seconds with my mouth open. It was unbelievable! Here was the mayor of Marseille, a deputy in the National Assembly, a newspaper tycoon, and a yacht owner, quibbling over the rate of U.S. government per diem.

Recovering a bit, I explained that per diem was factored on a set sum for everyone, including government officials and leader grantees. Defferre seemed immovable. The promised calls that had never come through, the long waits outside his office, the cool, impersonal receptions, and now the per diem question, all combined to spark my anger. I am sure my face reddened. Suddenly—and unprofessionally—I didn't give a damn whether he left for the States or not.

"Monsieur le Député-Maire," I told him, "there are many other candidates on this list. If I don't hear from you by tomorrow evening, someone else will take your place."

I received a call at lunchtime the next day from Defferre's chef de cabinet. Yes, the mayor would be accepting the kind invitation of the U.S. government and he would prefer to leave at the most propitious time to join the Kennedy campaign.

Many weeks later, after Defferre's return to Marseille, I received an invitation to luncheon at his home on a hill high above the city. I arrived on time and rang the door chime. The mayor himself opened the door wearing a broad grin and a straw boater with a blue band and gold lettering proclaiming "Kennedy for President." Throughout the meal he enthusiastically described his experiences on the campaign trail and predicted that John Kennedy would be the next president of the United States. From that time forward our professional relationship, though never close, was cooperative and friendly. This was to serve me well when I returned to Marseille twice on future assignments.

During this period I was notified that, having passed the Foreign Service examination for career officer status, I would now have to take my oral examination. Bill Cody, the counselor for public affairs at the embassy in Paris and my boss, would be coming to Marseille for this purpose. He had asked the consul general in Marseille, Donald Edgar, to sit in as the other board member. Cody, the stout bon vivant who had eaten his unperturbed way through lunch on the Eisenhower train to Paris, had a protocol fetish. He did not hesitate to tell young officers how to dress or when it was proper to wear brown or black shoes. A homburg wearer, he had taken a marked dislike to the tweed caps I wore and did not approve of my ginger mustache or the cigars I smoked.

I was not looking forward to his visit, but I was pleased to be shedding the status of a reserve officer. I was not unduly worried about passing the oral examination. Donald Edgar, a veteran State Department career officer nearing retirement, gave me the impression that he considered my oral exam a formality to get through quickly.

I was working in my office, smoking a cigar, when I was summoned to the consul general's office for the exam. Cody and Edgar sat facing me on the other side of Edgar's desk. Cody asked most of the questions. He growled his queries from deep inside his bulky frame. Many of them had to do with diplomatic procedures and some touched on protocol. It was as if he were searching for overt signs of what he considered my nonconformism. Edgar's questions covered a broader spectrum, touching on history, general knowledge, family background, and career goals. It was soon approaching the noon hour and my two interrogators had reservations at one of the city's best seafood restaurants. The flow of questions slowed and finally stopped. I was free to go.

That evening I served Cody a Scotch and water at rue Saint Jacques and put the question directly. Had I passed? He cleared his throat and shook his head slowly in disbelief.

"You passed," he grumbled disapprovingly. "But you're probably the only officer in the Foreign Service who took your orals while smoking a cigar!" I don't think he ever forgave me for such a blatant breach of diplomatic etiquette.

In mid-May of 1960 I swung the black USIS station wagon into the driveway of the Carlton Hotel in Cannes, turned the keys over to the uniformed doorman, and proceeded to register. The doorman saw to the unloading of three cases of duty-free booze that were duly wheeled up to the luxury room provided by the French government. The room was one of the perks I enjoyed as a member of the official U.S. delegation to the International Film Festival. The potables from the embassy commissary were essential, as my representation allowance for the festival was practically nonexistent.

Two weeks earlier, John Mowinckel, Bill Cody's deputy, had called from Paris to tell me I had been named as a member of the delegation. John, who had served with the Office of Strategic Services (OSS) during World War II and had helped "liberate" the bar of the Hotel Crillon on the Place de la Concorde in 1944, had soothed my worries as a neophyte to Cannes and predicted that I'd do just fine. Jack Hedges had warned me about the upcoming festival, but the demands of settling into my new job in Marseille had wiped it from my mind.

I wasn't sure what an official delegate was supposed to do, but I called Hedges, who provided more detailed information. One heartening bit of news was that the French government not only paid for the room at the luxurious Carlton but also picked up the tab for the delegate's meals *and* wine. Gilles Daziano supplied technical details on registration and accreditation from the festival offices in Cannes.

Normally, the chief delegate would be a well-known member of the American film industry or someone the White House might decide was entitled to a two-week expenses-paid vacation on the French Riviera from services rendered. The director of the Motion Picture Export Association of America's (MPEAA) European office in Paris was the professional representative, and the USIS chief from Marseille, in this case myself, was normally the sole government representative.

I had received an unexpected and unwanted shock before leaving Marseille for Cannes. Mowinckel had informed me there would be no chief U.S. delegate that year.

"It's all yours," he'd said, with a hint of mischief in his voice. "Good luck!"

Waiting for my luggage in the Carlton's impressive lobby, eyeing the marble pillars, crystal chandeliers, and manicured fingernails of the concierge, I knew this was going to be a unique experience. The lobby was a cross between a fashion show runway and a particularly affluent old-home week for the international film world. Tubby men in shades, smoking expensive Havana cigars, greeted each other like long-lost brothers, while their young female partners in tight, bra-less summer-wear smiled vapidly, gauging their mirror-image counterparts as possible rivals. Young French directors with two-day beards and long, unwashed hair rushed for the elevators surrounded by their Left Bank, Cahiers de Cinéma disciples. Journalists and film critics prowled the premises on the alert for star arrivals while observing the movements of their professional competition.

There were a number of envelopes waiting in my room along with a classic fruit bowl . . . but no champagne for the head of the delegation. The envelopes contained an invitation to the black tie opening ceremonies and film showing that evening; a welcoming note from Robert Favre Le Bret, the festival's director; instructions on how to pick up my official delegate's identity card; and a note from Gene Moscowitz, a writer for the trade paper *Variety* suggesting we get together for a drink and a talk.

My room, on the west side of the hotel (the rooms of the front façade facing the Mediterranean were reserved for industry moguls), looked out on the palms in the courtyard of a more modest hotel. Noticing the twin beds, I made a mental note to explore the possibility of bringing my wife over for a few days of beachside relaxation.

Later, adjusting my black tie before going down to the Carlton's rococo dining room for dinner, I reviewed the still-hazy outline of my official duties. I was to keep the chief delegate happy, occupied, and trouble free. I was now the chief delegate, so that should be easy. I was to maintain liaison with the U.S. and foreign media; attend foreign delegation receptions and dinners and appear at festival functions; assist in arranging press conferences, luncheons, and receptions for the U.S. delegation; attend the screenings of specific films, particularly significant productions from Iron Curtain countries; act as adviser to visiting U.S. 6th Fleet units, seeing that captains and admirals received invitations to token screenings or receptions, but tactfully guiding the navy away from too much involvement in the proceedings; and prepare a detailed delegation report (including a classified section on Iron

Curtain participation, films, and propaganda activities) for signature by the chief delegate.

I ate in the Carlton's two-star restaurant that first night in solitary splendor, trying to identify some of the film personalities at the other tables. Strangely enough, the only sure identification I was able to make was the novelist Georges Simenon, who was to serve as the jury president of the 13th Cannes Film Festival. I recognized the pipe-puffing creator of Inspector Maigret from his book jacket photos. The maitre d'hotel was kind enough to point out the *14* members of the Soviet delegation at a large table in the center of the room. Some nagging questions crossed my mind as I worked my way through the delicious meal. Why had no U.S. chief delegate been appointed? Was it not strange that no one from the festival office had greeted me as the sole U.S. delegate? Wasn't it unusual for me to be eating alone on the opening night of the festival? Where was the MPEAA representative?

I made my way on foot to the nearby Festival Palace. It was a perfect night: the palms were etched in black against the bright moon and the sea was calm. I inched my way up the broad entrance staircase with a mass of dinner-jacketed men and breathtakingly beautiful women in low-cut gowns. Blinking at the brightness of the flashbulbs, I entered the auditorium and found my place. This was not difficult, as the national flags of the delegates were fixed to the back of their seats. The hammers and sickles engulfed my single stars and stripes. I shook hands with some of the other official delegates and settled down to watch the opening ceremonies.

Festival officials delivered platitudinous speeches, while I perused the list of jury members. It made interesting reading. The 11-member feature film jury included director Marc Allegret among the four French members; Grigori Kozintsev, a director from the USSR, as the sole Soviet member; and Gene Kelly and Henry Miller as the U.S. members. Other jurors came from Italy, Japan, Germany, and Argentina. The speeches ended, a French government official declared the festival open, and a Hollywood feature was screened as an out-of-competition, first-night attraction.

Alone on the boulevard de la Croisette after the screening, I decided to return to the Carlton's terrace for a beer. Turning away from the Festival Palace, I saw Van Johnson standing on the curb. I hesitated a moment, then walked up to him.

"Mr. Johnson," I said, extending my hand, "my name is Howard Simpson. I'm the official U.S. delegate to the festival."

"Yeah?" he said, looking down at me. "So what?"

It was definitely not the response I expected. My reply was far from diplomatic.

"Screw you," I mumbled, turning on my heel.

"Wait a minute," Johnson said, "I'm sorry. I'm in a terrible mood. So far this festival has been a disaster."

We walked back to the Carlton together, ordered some beer, and one of Hollywood's best-known stars unreeled a tale of woe. He had been invited to Cannes as a guest of the festival. Since his arrival, he'd been practically ignored. He, too, had eaten dinner alone. On arrival at the Festival Palace for the opening ceremonies, he'd been asked to buy an entry ticket! Listening to Johnson's angry litany delivered in the inimitable voice that had held audiences in such films as *Battleground*, *The Caine Mutiny*, and *The Last Time I Saw Paris*, I was convinced there was something very strange going on at Cannes.

For some reason the official U.S. delegate was being ignored, and invited American stars were not faring much better. Although it would take some time to find an answer, there was one thing I could do immediately. I could invite some of the American and French media representatives and any stars I could round up to a drinks party. At the least, this would prove that a U.S. delegation did exist; at the most, it might garner some media coverage for the attending stars. Van Johnson agreed that this was a good idea, told me that Tina Louise might be persuaded to attend, and promised to come himself.

Two nights later we had our party. It was a pale reflection of the vodka and caviar extravaganzas my Soviet counterparts were throwing, but it achieved its goal. The reception was small, informal, and intimate. It had to be: it was held in my room. The voluptuous, redheaded Tina Louise charmed even the most cynical newsmen, and Van Johnson moved easily among the guests, glass in hand, good-naturedly exchanging quips and trading Hollywood stories.

Representatives of the *Daily Mail*, the *New York Times*, *Variety*, *Figaro* and the Nice and Marseille newspapers came early and stayed late. A Canadian delegate helped to restock my fast-melting ice supply, and a Polish radio reporter conducted an interview with Van Johnson in the bathroom. The floor waiters hovered in the corridor, fascinated. They had never seen a reception conducted in such a small space.

I had just moved to the dresser that served as a bar to mix a drink when a floor waiter motioned to me.

"There is someone in the hall who would like to speak with you," he said.

Puzzled, I left my room and walked out into the hall. A husky, middle-aged, balding man was waiting there. He looked grim and introduced himself as Fred Gronich, director of the MPEAA's European office.

He wanted to know what I was doing. I told him what I was doing and why. He told me I shouldn't have taken such an initiative and asked if I was unaware of the situation. I asked him what situation. We were getting nowhere. I invited him to join the party, but he declined. I sensed he didn't want to talk with the press. Finally, he asked that I refrain from any further delegation social initiatives until he explained all to me the next day. This seemed fair enough. Gronich took his leave, and I returned to the party. Gene Moscowitz of *Variety* watched my return over the edge of his glass.

"Got your hand slapped?" he asked, grinning. Our little party didn't make any headlines, but at least I could now match some media names and faces.

The next morning, Fred Gronich welcomed me to his suite, poured me a coffee, and explained some truths about Cannes. The festival officials and the MPEAA were feuding over a number of issues and—until a truce occurred—the American film industry was "downplaying" the festival. This was why I had been named chief delegate. It also explained the coolness Van Johnson had encountered. Unfortunately, no one had bothered to brief me, and I had walked into this daggers-drawn situation like an innocent. I did learn one lesson from the episode. Never underestimate the knowledge and usefulness of a press contact at Cannes. Gene Moscowitz had known all the details of the feud. If I'd taken him up on his drink offer, I would have been forewarned.

Even though my first meeting with Fred Gronich had been tension filled, we became close friends. In the future a call from Fred suggesting that we "split a herring" over lunch was to presage our government-industry cooperation in Cannes, Paris, and Algiers on a modest but effective scale.

I eventually survived a number of Cannes Film Festivals as a member of the U.S. delegation before turning over the task to a younger colleague. I've recalled some of my experiences at the festival to present a picture of this unique and enduring international institution:

- Producer Sam Spiegel's yacht was lying off the Carlton beach, riding easily on a light swell. The buffet tables on the afterdeck were groaning under an array of delicacies, and the Dom Perignon corks were popping. I had accompanied chief U.S. delegate Allen Rivkin, a true gentleman and president of the Screen Writers Guild, to the party and was enjoying a glass of champagne and one of Spiegel's large Havanas. Alfred Hitchcock, in Cannes to promote his film *The Birds*, sidled up to me frowning.

"What," he demanded in his mock-serious manner, "is a U.S. official doing smoking a Cuban cigar?" For once, I found a ready reply.

"I've been assigned," I told the rotund director as if imparting a secret, "to destroy their overseas stock." Only a slight twitch of his mouth disturbed his deadpan countenance to indicate that I had hit the target.

- I received a message that Favre Le Bret needed my help on an urgent basis. This was indeed a first. Normally, the aloof festival director tended—if he could—to ignore the government member of the U.S. delegation. I eventually found him just inside the Festival Palace trying to reason with a bespectacled, irate Henry Miller. The author of *Tropic of Cancer* and *Tropic of Capricorn* and American member of the jury was refusing to wear a black tie to the evening showing. He had been stopped at the entry by one of Favre Le Bret's security staff.

As I arrived on the scene, Miller was telling the director where he could stuff his festival. That said, he turned and strode away from the palace. An agitated Favre Le Bret asked me to "do something" and pushed a clip-on black tie into my hand. After a slight hesitation, I set off after the lanky writer. In those few minutes of pursuit through the thick crowd I reflected on the surreal quality of the situation. I was chasing Henry Miller, the perennial rebel whose work we had venerated during our GI Bill days in postwar Paris, in an attempt to cajole him into wearing a black tie to a screening at the Cannes Film Festival.

I caught up with Miller close to the Carlton. I won't attempt to reconstruct our conversation word for word, but I do recall that he had calmed down considerably. By establishing my bonafides as a former resident of bohemian Montparnasse, we reached a common ground. I didn't appeal to Miller officially as a U.S. delegate. That would have been counterproductive. But I did mention that the festival media would like nothing better than to blow this minor misunderstanding all out of proportion.

Miller finally accepted the clip-on, and we walked back to the Festival Palace together. Favre Le Bret was all unctuous smiles.

But they were reserved for Henry Miller, the juror, not for me. I heard later that Miller jettisoned the tie once seated.

- For one chief delegate, a diplomat from the Paris embassy of General Franco's Spain, the festival proved a disaster. He and his wife seemed pleasant. They dutifully attended the screenings and represented their country at the various social events. The diplomat did not, however, appear too conversant with the world of cinema. The main Spanish entry that year was Luis Bunuel's *Viridiana*, a surrealist, sacrilegious melodrama featuring a corrupted novice nun.

  Unfortunately for the chief delegate, this fascinating but raw take on contemporary Spain won the festival's highest honor, the Golden Palm. When the announcement was made, I turned to congratulate him. His face had gone chalky white and he seemed to be sinking into his seat. Then, in a barrage of flashbulbs and the glare of TV lighting, he was forced to go to the stage and accept the award from the master of ceremonies. For the Spanish government of the time it was an unwanted honor that obviously had been brought on by a breakdown somewhere in the government's coordinating machinery. I suspect that Luis Bunuel, the old surrealist, nonconformist, and practical joker, had had something to do with it. I later learned the "*Viridiana* incident" had negatively affected the unfortunate chief delegate's diplomatic career.

- One year a member of the U.S. delegation made informal contact with a shapely Soviet starlet on the Carlton beach. He had invited her to join a number of friends for a prelunch drink in his room. When I mentioned the omnipresence of the Soviet delegation's "minders," he shrugged me off. He planned to meet her in the Carlton lobby and escort her to the gathering himself. Alas, he learned that the long arm of the Cold War reached even to the heart of the film world.

  The brief ballet in the lobby was pure Woody Allen with a touch of Keaton. Shrugging off the protests of her guardian angels, the rebellious starlet took my friend's arm as he escorted her to the elevator. The two Soviet heavies who had been escorting her blanched and looked at each other in horror. Their superiors at Dzerzhinsky Square hadn't prepared them for such an eventuality. They dashed for the broad, carpeted stairway. To their credit, they were present, puffing and wheezing, when the elevator doors opened on the third floor. With fixed smiles and apologetic nods they whisked their ward away from my friend and the vile temptations of a decadent, bourgeois Hollywood.

- There is one shock the government representative on the U.S. delegation is never prepared for. This occurs when opening the window blinds in the Carlton to a bright sunny day and finding what appears to be the entire U.S. 6th Fleet in the Bay of Cannes. Carriers, cruisers, destroyers, and attack transports lie offshore like a World War II task force, the wake of their small boats tracing lines of white froth over the calm water. The fleet's presence is soon signaled by frantic calls from junior officers seeking tickets for screenings and invitations to receptions for their admirals and captains. The delegate can also count on the inevitable heavy media humor accusing America of trying to intimidate the festival jury with a show of naval strength.

These are minor problems compared to the responsibility of keeping the U.S. Navy a respectful distance from the festival proceedings and ensuring that no cinematic con artist or public relations impresario takes advantage of the fleet.

In 1963, a few days after the fleet's arrival, an American journalist asked me whether I'd seen the bulletin board in the festival pressroom. When I said I hadn't, he suggested I should.

"Maybe I'll see you at the cocktail party," he'd said.

I didn't know what he was referring to, but I climbed the stairs to the pressroom and pushed my way past the teletypes to the bulletin board. At first I saw nothing of great interest—the arrival times of international stars, notices of press receptions, and a flutter of personal messages.

Then I noticed a large placard with a blue ink border. There was a very rough drawing of an American flag near its top. "Press cocktail," it read, "aboard aircraft carrier." I swallowed hard and continued reading. "All accredited correspondents are invited to attend a press reception hosted by...." There was an admiral's name, obviously misspelled, and the information that the cocktail party would be held aboard the carrier lying at anchor in the bay. The purpose of the "cocktail" party was spelled out in much larger letters. A Lebanese production company appeared as cohosts and promised the presence of several of their starlets, all of whom were soon to appear in a "smashing extravaganza" filmed in Beirut, *The Crossroad of the Whole World*. The notice gave the time of the cocktail party as 6:30 P.M. that day and promised small boat transportation courtesy of the U.S. Navy.

There had been points in my Foreign Service career when I had experienced a variety of sinking sensations: flying out of the narrow Lai Chau valley in northern Indochina in a battered deHavilland piloted by a completely sloshed French pilot during a tropical thunderstorm, having my vehicle shot up during the Binh Xuyen revolt in Saigon, and asking Ambassador "Chip" Bohlen for identification—prior to admitting him to his own briefing. These now faded into insignificance as I experienced a new and unique feeling of impending doom. Cocktail parties did not occur on American aircraft carriers at that time, and blatant promotional use of naval craft by foreign film producers is hardly in the best interest of the 6th Fleet or the U.S. government.

I didn't have much time. Running in search of the Lebanese entrepreneurs was out. It would only lead to useless argument and lost time. My first target would have to be the carrier. At the least, there had been a "misunderstanding." At the most, there was the possibility of an embarrassing frameup. Glancing over my shoulder, I pulled the tacks from the poster and slid it behind a nearby phone booth.

I sped to the fleet landing in a cab. It took me some time to convince the officer in charge of the shore party and the ship-to-shore radio that I did have official business with the carrier's captain. A message was finally sent, and I boarded one of the shuttling liberty boats rather than waiting for the captain's gig.

The ship's public information officer (PIO) was waiting as I climbed aboard, a puzzled but nervous smile on his face.

"I understand there is some problem...?"

"That's right. I better see the captain right away." I was led along the companionways to the captain's cabin and served the obligatory cup of watery navy coffee. The captain was in his dress uniform, and it was obvious that he was headed ashore on some protocol function. He was tanned and healthy. He settled back to hear my story. Halfway through my narrative, his tan took on a slight purple tint. When I had finished, the purple had given way to a pale quality that clashed with the brightness and warmth of the Riviera.

As I had expected, there was no party planned, nor would there be during the festival. The captain asked a circle of aides and subordinate officers whether anyone had heard of the party. He drew a blank. We thus faced the disconcerting possibility that close to 400 film writers, reporters, photographers, and cameramen, both American and foreign, would be arriving at the fleet landing for a cocktail party that wasn't. I would have liked to search the ship for an officer who just might have met the Lebanese film executives and their starlets, and, in an off-hand manner, just might have responded yes when he should have said no—but that would have been no real help.

I said goodbye with a promise to do what I could to stem the thirsty tide. I warned the PIO that he might soon have an opportunity to leave public information work for perennial duty on a small minesweeper and jumped down into a pitching shore boat for a quick run back to Cannes.

The rest of the afternoon was a whirl of typing notices, posting them throughout the Festival Palace, calling the director's office and the press office, buttonholing newsmen on the beach and along the street, leaving notes in hotel boxes, and generally carrying the message to the media—No Cocktail on Carrier!

Later, as the sun set behind the old fortress walls above the port, I stood at the fleet landing to receive the frustrated partygoers and express regrets for the unfortunate misunderstanding. I was in luck. Only about 15 newsmen appeared. No representatives of the Lebanese production showed themselves. The small attendance was due in part to my work during the afternoon but mainly because most experienced newsmen knew American naval ships were then dry. They tended to think twice before spending an hour or more sipping pineapple juice no matter how well turned out the Marine detachment might be.

The real world sometimes had a tendency to shatter the pleasant isolation of the festival. In 1963 I received a telephone call from the embassy informing me that a telegram had been received from the USIA personnel office assigning me to Laos. Prompt personal intervention by the ambassador and the consul general kept me in Marseille. In 1964, my fifth year of festival going, a similar summons—this time without reprieve—sent me back to Vietnam. I was given two weeks, including a brief period of consultation in Washington, to get to

Saigon, where I was to be an adviser to the prime minister of Vietnam, General Nguyen Van Khanh.

Although one tended to become blasé after regular attendance at the festival, I did come away with some memorable impressions. These included the unforced intellectualism and kindness of soft-spoken director Fred Zinneman; the bubbly good humor of a wisecracking Shelley Winters; the china doll perfection of Claire Bloom; director Rouben Mamoulian's jokes; sharing a bottle of champagne with the talented Peter Ustinov; the healthy, heart-stopping sexiness of Sophia Loren; the constant worried look of the security heavies attached to the Soviet delegation; the regal beauty of Anouk Aimee; chain-smoking Simone Signoret in a motorcycle jacket and black leather trousers; a huge Orson Welles, smacking his lips over a gargantuan, champagne-lubricated lunch in the Carlton's dining room; and the urgent, tongue-in-cheek telegram from former chief delegate and producer Walter Mirisch that was waiting for me at the Carlton's reception desk one year with the message, "Remember, they don't charge for wine—but they *do* for coffee!"

6

Living with Lafayette

Working in France in the early 1960s was not easy. President de Gaulle's suspicion of American foreign policy objectives was reflected in the attitude and actions of his subordinates. Our embassy and consulates in France had to deal with the usual Communist and left-wing demonstrations, media attacks, and visits of irate party delegations on everything from U.S. policy in Vietnam to the "threat to peace" posed by U.S. NATO forces in Europe. We were also under fire from the right wing for not supporting its bellicose stance on the continued, bloody war in Algeria. We had received direct threats from the bombers of the OAS, the outlawed Secret Army Organization opposed to de Gaulle's Algerian policy, accusing us—through the CIA—of supporting the liberation movement in Algeria. Worst of all, we were forced to joust with Gaullist officials, some of whom were still smarting from real or imagined slights administered by "the Anglo-Saxons" dating back to World War II.

As information officers we found ourselves attempting to counterpunch the propaganda of France's government-controlled media.[1] Doses

---

1. In October of 1997 Pierre Rougelet, a former officer of the Renseignements Généraux (RG), or Police Intelligence, revealed that the RG had 53,000 files on media representatives and had killed stories of embarrassment to the government by threatening to make public sordid details of certain journalist's lives. *Plus ça change!*

of this negative material were continual and on a national scale. A TV commentator would dwell on American errors or blunders in foreign policy. A roundtable of intellectuals on cinema would emphasize Hollywood's worship of the almighty dollar compared to the "true" cinematic culture of their country, this despite the fact that American films were then (and now) by far the most popular in France. A prize-winning documentary at the Cannes Festival on the U.S. Marine Corps concentrated on the "brutality" of its drill instructors. Extended coverage of racial discrimination in America was constant, although the callous mistreatment in France of North Africans and emigrants from France's newly independent black African colonies was all but ignored.

Fortunately, there were fair-minded media outlets and individuals willing to give us space and time to present our side of the story. The influential Paris daily *Le Monde*, ever ready to emphasize its independence, was occasionally willing to accept material of high quality or print exclusive interviews that we arranged with American officials such as Under Secretary of State George Ball. When we couldn't place articles in the French press or obtain time on radio or television, we relied on the targeted, large circulation USIS monthly *Informations Documents*, special briefings, and public appearances to put U.S. policy to specific audiences. Some of our friends in the media took exception to their government's more blatant anti-Americanism and, with our help, attempted to blunt this propaganda offensive.

In Marseille I spent considerable time in the dingy offices of newspaper editors, attempting to place our material or offering the daily services of our Washington-produced wireless bulletin. Strangely enough, I ran into more resistance and argument from the editors of the right wing *le Méridional* than from Defferre's Socialist daily *Le Provençal* and its afternoon paper *Le Soir*. The local Communists were well aware of our activities, because their *La Marseillaise* shared the same building as the right-wing publication. We occasionally placed nonpolitical material in *La Marseillaise* on science, space, and the arts. The editors ran it without crediting the source.

One of de Gaulle's prime objectives in the postwar period was to restore France's self-confidence and pride. To do this he had to convince the French people that they—through the Free French Forces and the Résistance—had played a major role in the liberation of France and the Allied victory. A secondary goal was to obliterate from the French conscience the population's support or tolerance of the collaborationist Vichy government.

That many gallant French men and women did play a key role and did die to rid their country of the German occupation forces is not in doubt. Unfortunately, in emphasizing France's role in the war, the Gaullists often downplayed the massive contribution made by their British and American allies.

As a student in 1949, I had attended a de Gaulle rally in Paris. He was naming a square in honor of General LeClerc, the commander of the 2nd French Armored Division and liberator of the French capital. Not once during his speech did I hear a reference to the Americans who had made the liberation possible. I refer to those GIs of the landings and bitter hedgerow battles in Normandy who had been ordered to halt just short of Paris to allow the recently disembarked LeClerc and his division to enter the city first.

In the summer of 1960 I had an opportunity to redress a bit of the balance. It wasn't a question of who did what in 1944, who did it better, or who might have landed on a specific beach on the first, second or fifth day after the initial assault. It was a simple case of fairness, of ensuring that those who deserved credit received it. Perhaps more important, in the context of American foreign policy and Franco-American relations, was the need to impress on a new generation of French citizens the important and costly role a distant America had played in the liberation of their country from Nazi domination.

It all began when I was invited to the annual ceremony honoring the war dead buried at the well-kept American military cemetery at Draguignan, just inland from the beaches where the Allied forces had landed in southern France on August 15, 1944. I had also received a French invitation to attend a ceremony on the same day honoring the Commandos d'Afrique, who had scaled a seaside cliff to neutralize the enemy gun positions at Cap Nègre prior to the landings.

The overall amphibious operation had first been code-named Anvil, and later Dragoon (the name change designed to confuse the Germans). The French Commandos and American Rangers had struck in the early morning hours. At 4:30 A.M. an Anglo-American airborne division (Rugby Force) of 535 transports and 410 gliders brought 9,700 troopers to the Le Muy-Roquebrunne areas to cut enemy lines of communication and block lines of retreat from the coast. The American 6th Army Corps of General Alexander M. Patch had then led the main landings at Cavalaire, La Nartelle, La Garonnette, Le Dramont, and Antheor. The battle-tested 3rd, 45th, and 36th U.S. Infantry Divisions spearheaded these assaults. Units of the 1st French Armored Division were soon ashore, and at 5:00 P.M. on August 16th the bulk of the 1st French Army under General de Lattre de Tassigny was to follow.

I had done some cursory reading on this campaign before attending both ceremonies, so I was able to conjure up images of what had happened 16 years earlier. The French commemoration was brief, modest, and moving. A postceremony inspection of the cliffs scaled by the Commandos confirmed their right to a place in the military history of World War II. When the ceremony ended, I asked a French official whether there were any monuments, plaques, or markers to indicate the American landing beaches. He told me there was a monument on the beach at Le Dramont where the U.S. 36th Division had landed. It now served as the central marker of American participation. I pondered this information as my driver inched his way through the dense summer traffic along the highway on our way to Draguignan. August is the height of the French vacation period, and the south swarms with families seeking sun, sea, and sand.

The services at Draguignan were impressive. The neat rows of 861 white headstones (many of the American dead were returned to the United States after the war), the green, clipped lawns, the cloudless blue sky, the warm breeze that stirred the trees and tugged at the flags, the 6th Fleet honor guard, a contingent of French infantry, the sound of taps, the aging veterans, and the small crowd of onlookers—all combined to form the traditional image of a classic memorial ceremony.

Later, on the way back to Marseille, I decided to stop by the beach at Le Dramont. The area was packed with vacationers in swimming gear. Passersby looked vague or puzzled when I asked for directions to the monument. It was some time before I located the bulky monolith set some distance back from the shoreline. A group of children sat at its base eating ice cream cones. I stood looking at the monument and surveying what had been Beach 264 B of Operation Dragoon. Not far away a direct hit on LST 282 had cost the 36th Division 40 dead and wounded. Considering the limited attendance of the French public at the Draguignan ceremonies and the de Gaulle government's ambivalence over our role in the liberation, I decided the monument at Le Dramont should be the centerpiece of a minor campaign of truth.

That winter Ramon Garcia and I began to put together a program for the next year. With the help of the army attaché in Paris we were promised a color guard from a U.S. infantry division in Germany. The 6th Fleet agreed to supply an honor guard and a bugler. U.S. veterans groups in Nice and Marseille were happy to participate, and French men and women who had worked with the Americans as liaison officers or members of the Résistance agreed to help. Representatives of the regional French military command promised to assist us and to supply a French honor guard. They could hardly do otherwise without creating a media scandal. It was also true that many in the French military at that time were not overly fond of General de Gaulle.

When the next August 15 rolled around, we were ready. The approach to the monument at Le Dramont was hung with French and American flags, and the U.S. Army and Navy were present, as were a French honor guard *and* military band. More important, the surrounding area was crowded with French onlookers: family groups, teenagers, young men, beauties in skimpy bikinis, and residents of Le Dramont who had lived through the events of August '44. While I was wandering through the crowd during the wreath laying, I heard a young boy ask his mother a question.

"Who are those soldiers," he demanded, pointing to the GI color guard.

"They're the Americans," she told him. "They saved us."

Many more ceremonies have been held at Le Dramont and at other American landing sites along the coast since 1960. For me, none could match that reactivation of the memorial at Le Dramont. The uninitiated might see the whole project as a dated example of flag waving or jingoism. At the time, when we were faced with a blatant attempt to alter history for political purposes, it seemed the only thing to do. It also provided those of us involved with a feeling of intense satisfaction.

Not all of our efforts on the August 15 anniversary of the landings proceeded as smoothly. Years later, while officiating at the Draguignan ceremonies as consul general, I came very close to omitting the local Catholic Church authorities from their rightful role. Luckily, an alert American veteran caught my lapse and saved me from a complete diplomatic disaster.

Following John F. Kennedy's inauguration in 1960, the U.S. Information Agency seemed to have a new lease on life. The respected broadcaster Edward R. Murrow, whose reports from London during the Blitz had brought the war's significance home to Americans, had been named as the agency's director. A contingent of young "new frontiersmen" with progressive ideas and enthusiasm now filled many of the agency's key posts in Washington. George Stevens Jr., son of Academy Award–winning director George Stevens, had taken over USIA's international film operation, and Don Wilson, formerly with *Life*, whom I had known in Hanoi, was named as a deputy director. John Mecklin, a *Time* correspondent in Vietnam during the Franco-Vietminh war, was destined to become the agency's top man in Saigon during the trying period that led to President Diem's assassination. My colleague and friend from San Francisco newspaper days, Pierre Salinger, was now White House press secretary.

Kennedy's inaugural speech promising a more active American role in foreign affairs had inspired field officers like myself. We looked forward to implementing imaginative new policies and procedures. There was definitely a change from the conservative, status quo atmosphere of the Eisenhower regime. Although the subsequent disclosure of Camelot's negative side eventually tempered my view of the Kennedy administration, those early days were filled with excitement and a gung ho attitude. They also produced a marked decline in bureaucratic stuffiness, thanks to the new administration's insistence on straight talk and brevity.

In the winter of 1960 I was temporarily assigned as the press adviser to the U.S. delegation to the 11th General Conference of UNESCO in Paris. This meant leaving the sunshine of Marseille for more than three weeks of gray, cold Paris winter and a single room in the Inter-Continental Hotel on the rue Castiglione. The assignment caught me by surprise, but I suspected that my friend Jack Hedges had recommended me for the position—and I was right. I knew little about UNESCO and even less about our delegation's objectives, but I had a few days to read the file on the last conference and to scan the telegrams and memorandum in preparation for the 1960 meetings.

Despite Bill Cody's mumbled reference to UNESCO as a "can of worms," I thought my task would be relatively simple. Alas, Cody was right and I was wrong. The can of worms became a nest of vipers as the cultural dilettantes of the UNESCO delegations played at international politics and dabbled in Cold War maneuvers. The large Soviet and Iron Curtain delegations united to vote against any U.S. initiative and posed as selfless supporters of Third World propositions with little substance or practicability.

The chief of our delegation, a special assistant to the secretary of state for the coordination of international educational and cultural relations, was not the soft-spoken cultural guru one might expect in such a position. Robert Thayer was tough, crusty, outspoken, and determined to keep the Soviets in their place. At a conference where the media suffered from a low boredom threshold, the verbal barbs he directed at the Communists served to keep the journalists awake. I too was kept awake by his unusual style of cultural diplomacy, working late into the night drafting speeches or preparing press releases as ammunition in this unique battle of Cold War one-upmanship.

The high point of Thayer's performance came one day toward the end of the conference. A heated debate was taking place on the funding to preserve the Egyptian archeological sites at Abu Simbal, soon to be threatened by the Soviet-constructed Aswan Dam. When Thayer tried to make a debating point, his outspoken manner offended the Iron Curtain delegates. They raised a mighty clamor. He waited patiently while the conference president attempted to reestablish order. When this failed, Thayer calmly bent over, removed one of his shoes, and—looking directly at the Soviet delegation—threatened to pound the lectern with it. This obvious imitation of Soviet Premier Nikita Khrushchev's recent, undiplomatic shoe-pounding incident at the United Nations in New York produced a shocked silence, broken only by a few guffaws. Our chief delegate was then able to resume talking.

Although a visit and concert by Duke Ellington marked a high spot for our delegation, I came away from the UNESCO conference with the definite conclusion that government participation in cultural projects should be limited or—at least—carefully weighed. Culture has an impetus and strength of its own that is beyond politics. Large-scale government intervention or international measures are justified only if a culture or its product is threatened. Perhaps my UNESCO experience was too negative. Recalling the army of UNESCO *fonctionnaires* producing reams of useless papers, reports, and memos, the endless politically oriented debates, and the inevitable expensive diplomatic receptions in the name of advancing world culture, I think not.

Despite suffering the pinpricks and occasional solid blows of Gaullist policies, most Foreign Service officers working in France could not help but admire *le Grand Charles* as a master politician and media magician. His lofty insouciance in time of crisis—demonstrated during the liberation of Paris, when he had walked upright toward Notre Dame Cathedral while sniper fire cracked and echoed around the square—had not deserted him.

One of his grandest moments was to come in April 1961 when the Revolt of the Generals opposed to his policy in Algeria threatened to send paratroopers from Algiers to seize Paris and overthrow the Republic. It was a touch-and-go situation. The government was scrambling to determine what army, gendarmerie, and police units remained loyal and was coping with repeated requests for arms from Communist and Socialist militants. A sobering rebel radio message had been intercepted by government monitors. It stated, "The cousins from the provinces arrive tomorrow morning at 0500 wearing light kit." This latter reference seemed to indicate that the "paras" intended to land at nearby airports rather than jump over their objectives. By now antiaircraft guns were visible on the roof of the naval ministry on the Place de la Concorde, and the guard of de Gaulle's nearby Élysée Palace had been reinforced by 70 naval commandos. The American ambassador in Paris, General James Gavin, a former paratrooper himself who had jumped into Normandy with his 82nd Airborne Division, hastened to assure de Gaulle of President Kennedy's support.

It was in this crisis environment that General de Gaulle appeared on national television. At 8:00 P.M. on April 23rd, I joined some colleagues from the consulate general in Marseille to watch the general address the nation. We had a direct stake in de Gaulle's survival as an ally and NATO partner. We also saw his Algerian policy as the only sensible exit from an impossible political situation and endless war.

I had a more personal reason to hope for his success in preventing a broadening of the revolt. In Indochina I had marched and lived with some of the parachute units and officers involved in the revolt. I could understand their isolation and frustration after the defeat in Indochina and the continuing, bitter revolutionary war in Algeria. Nevertheless, I could think of no worse end to their military careers than to be involved in a misbegotten revolt that could find them condemned to death or facing disgrace and long prison terms.

Fortunately, the "paras" were not to drop on Paris or land at its airfields. De Gaulle, wearing his old wartime uniform of a brigadier general, once again displayed his dramatic mastery of the media. Addressing the public directly as president of the Republic, the general spoke with obvious disdain of a "group of partisan, fanatic, and ambitious officers." Predicting that their actions would lead directly to a "national disaster," he called on everyone, both soldiers and civilians, not to obey the rebels' orders. At the conclusion of his address, after a telling pause, and looking directly at his audience, he uttered both a plea and a command.

"Françaises, Français, aidez moi!" ("Frenchwomen, Frenchmen, help me!") It was a dramatic moment.

Although the rebel generals were already facing grave problems in perpetuating their revolt, de Gaulle's address to the nation was rightly credited as the death blow to the three day insurrection.

Before the end of our first two-year tour in Marseille, I once again felt the long arm of the Paris embassy. Quite without warning I found myself reassigned as the assistant press and publications officer of USIS Paris. Tours of duty in the Foreign Service were usually for two or three years with a break for home leave and, if the post was not a hardship assignment, the possibility of a return tour. But, like the military, all assignments were based on "the good of the service." This could mean interim moves during the posting period. It was all part of life in the Foreign Service, and we accepted it with a minimum of grumbling. Nevertheless, such unexpected disruptions did put a strain on families and particularly on children who had to be uprooted from their schools and leave new friends for a completely new environment.

After the usual farewell reception and the installation of my successor, Sam Dieli, an army veteran, linguist, and former lecturer at Columbia University, the Simpson family left for Paris and a temporary bolthole at the Brighton Hotel on the rue de Rivoli. We were shoehorned into a large room overlooking the Tuileries Gardens. It was a short walk to the embassy on the Place de la Concorde, where I began to learn my new job. Meanwhile Mary Alice—whipping around Paris in our Volkswagen Karmen Ghia—set about finding more permanent housing and a school for Shawn and Lisa.

After several false starts inspecting unattractive apartments listed by the embassy that rented for sums far above our government housing allowance, the gods smiled on us. Mary Alice called me at the office one morning to say she "might" have found what we were looking for. It was a three bedroom apartment on the Left Bank near the Jardin Luxembourg and within our allowance. It had been rejected by a number of embassy officers because the central heating depended on a small, coal-stoked furnace in the downstairs kitchen. Mary Alice swung by the office to pick me up, and we headed for 58 rue de Vaugirard.

The apartment on the corner of Vaugirard and the rue Bonaparte belonged to the Comte de Chambrun, a direct descendant of the Marquis de Lafayette and an honorary U.S. citizen. Catherine de' Medici had once lived in the ancient building, and it was rumored to have secret underground escape routes. An aged, heavy door opened to a vaulted entrance and an interior courtyard. We obtained the keys from the concierge, walked up the wide, carpeted marble stairway to the apartment, and entered history.

The high-ceilinged rooms were an antique collector's dream. The music room, with its large piano and harp, was done in authentic Louis XV and Louis XVI, with a gold-framed mirror, chairs of gilt and red leather, embroidered settees, and a large but worn oriental rug. Antique Chinese vases stood in the corners, and a large oil portrait of a young Lafayette hung over the polished piano. Other portraits of the nobleman who fought with George Washington were placed throughout the apartment. The tall windows looked out onto the Jardin Luxembourg, a wooded children's haven where a young Ernest Hemingway had surreptitiously snatched pigeons to add to the family pot during his lean years on the Left Bank. It was also a pleasant retreat during good weather, full of bird song and leafy sun patterns, much appreciated by students, artists, and writers, including myself during the days I had spent as an art student in Montparnasse.

The apartment's dining room was furnished in Directoire and Empire. A door covered in green baize led to a small pantry, complete with dumbwaiter and a narrow iron circular stairway leading to the kitchen. We couldn't have hoped for a better location. Montparnasse and Saint Germain de Pres were within walking distance; the Métro I would take to work was not far away; and Notre Dame de Sion, a branch of the same school Shawn had attended in Marseille, was nearby.

There was one hurdle to pass before we could move into the apartment. We needed the approval of the aged General de Chambrun, father of the count, who occupied the apartment directly across the hall. The general, whose military career had included an assignment in the late 1800s as an artillery officer during the Congo expeditions of the French explorer Savorgnan de Brazza, had been described to me as "someone special." That was all I had to go on the afternoon I knocked on his apartment door, dressed appropriately for my approval-seeking mission.

A maid greeted me and led me into a salon where the general was waiting. He was seated at a small gaming table with his back to the window. It took some time for my eyes to adjust to the light. When they did, I saw an elderly man wearing an eyepatch. He was smoking a thick, pungent French cigarette. A half-full glass of red wine was before him on the table and the bottle nearby. A polished wooden stand in the corner of the room contained the regimental flags of his former commands.

"Bonjour, mon général," I greeted him, shaking hands and eager to make a good impression.

"I speak better English than you do French," he responded dryly, "so let's speak English." He indicated that I should sit down, poured some wine into an empty glass, and handed it to me. Our conversation was definitely one-sided. He posed a number of questions about my background and Foreign Service experience. He appeared interested in the fact that I had been a war correspondent, but he didn't pursue the matter. My attempts to learn more of his military career were fruitless, although he did speak with fondness of his many sojourns in the United States. When it was time to go, I had the feeling there was a good chance the apartment was ours. We moved in a few days later, sent on our way with a bottle of iced champagne by the couple who managed the Hotel Brighton.

The champagne also served to celebrate the long-delayed publication of my novel on Indochina. I had beavered away at the manuscript on my off-time in Nigeria and Marseille. *To a Silent Valley* was a fictional amalgam of the battles of Nasan and Dien Bien Phu, dedicated to "the Paras of the Indochina War." The late John Schaffner, a patient and professional New York agent, had managed to place the book with the prestigious publisher Alfred A. Knopf, and I was mightily pleased. This pleasure was compounded when Blanche Knopf, the publisher's wife, also active in the firm, took the time to call me while passing through Paris to say how much she liked the book. This fiction writing would continue irregularly during my Foreign Service career, resulting in five published novels.

Working in the frenetic environment of Paris was lightyears away from the easy, slow pace of Provence. Jack Hedges was the embassy press attaché, and I, as assistant press and publications officer, was his second. Both jobs meant long hours and considerable tension. We were always under the gun from Washington on breaking stories and at the ambassador's beck and call night and day. Jack had fit easily into his new role. The first reception we attended at the Hedge's rented apartment on the Place Saint Sulpice brought together a good mix of guests, including high-ranking French government officials, foreign diplomats, newsmen, and such well-known Paris residents as our compatriots, artist-photographer Man Ray and author James Jones.

The members of the Paris press corps—French, American, and foreign—were heavy eaters and hard drinkers. They expected us to be the same. A great deal of business with the media was conducted over three-hour French lunches that began with an apéritif of Kir, moved on to muscadet, then gigondas, and concluded with some fine armagnac or cognac. Jack's master list of target bistros included Chez Pauline, the Champs de Mars, Pierre au Palais Royal, Allard, the Fontaine de Mars, Au Petit Riche, and, for special occasions, the brasserie La Coupole. He also had a genius for finding obscure bistros in the popular quarters of Paris where such solid dishes as *boudin noir, pommes mousseline* (blood sausage with mashed potatoes) and unlabeled red wine straight from the vintners was consumed by workers and the neighborhood businessmen.

The objective of these calorie-packed encounters was to cement relations and gain the confidence of influential newsmen to ensure that U.S. policy received a fair shake in the French national media. This often paid off when the contented invitees accepted background material from us on which they could base an informed article. For others, we might arrange a program of encounters and exclusive interviews with embassy contacts or government officials in Washington, D.C. It was all aboveboard, but it didn't always work. Some of these business lunches, though a pleasant way to spend an early afternoon, were duds. Selling an idea or explaining a specific U.S. policy in the face of a French journalist's Cartesian logic when the policy itself was vague, inconsistent, or practically nonexistent was extremely difficult. Arguing our role in Vietnam with veteran French newsmen who had spent some of their working life in Indochina and were considered area experts often proved impossible.

This type of semiofficial "Front Page" atmosphere extended to the bar and grill of the Hotel Crillon, directly across the street from the embassy. During the early 1960s, the Crillon bar served as a rendezvous point, information exchange, watering hole, and home-away-from-home for a select grouping of foreign correspondents. It was no exaggeration to say that inside knowledge of what was going on in France, and misleading rumors to the contrary, were nowhere more readily available than at the Crillon bar during the prelunch and predinner apéritif hour.

The frequent periods of political crisis in France turned the Crillon bar into a journalistic hubbub, as newsmen came and went on their way to or from the president's Élysée Palace, the prime minister's residence at the Matignon, or the ministry of the interior. Political officers from the American and British embassies, on the prowl for scraps of information and trying to look inconspicuous, offered free drinks to some newshounds—until their meager representation allowances evaporated.

Through all this, Sam White, a columnist of the *London Evening Standard* and the doyen of the Crillon habitués, sat imperturbably at *his* corner of the long bar, silently signaling for a refill with an upraised finger and surveying the scene with bemused indifference. White, a tall, hatchet-faced man, had been in France for many years and boasted a network of contacts throughout Paris. While many of his colleagues rushed around the French capital in search of a story, White often remained at the Crillon, close to the bar phone to receive calls from his tipsters. A bronze plaque marking "The Sam White Corner" was fixed to the bar's wall at the time of his retirement some years ago.

Harold King of Reuters, a short, testy journalist approaching retirement age, claimed the other end of the bar. Horn-rimmed eyeglasses pushed up on his brow, he would hold forth on de Gaulle's greatness to younger newsmen, accepting their offer of drinks as his due. The two Brits, White and King, tolerated each other, but conversation definitely lagged if they happened to be the only regulars at the bar.

I had a lively falling out with King one night in October 1961. My wife and I had agreed to drop King off at his Left Bank apartment on our way home after drinks at the Crillon. A few days previously, under the orders of Maurice Papon, the prefect of police, the Paris police had violently attacked groups of demonstrating Algerians. Unofficial estimates put the death toll at close to 200. Many demonstrators had died trampled and crushed against the closed gates of Métro entrances or drowned in the Seine while trying to escape the flailing clubs and lead-weighted capes of the police. In the car, I mentioned the deaths to King, classifying them as murder, and stating my view that the guilt lay with Papon (the same Maurice Papon who, on October 8, 1997, went on trial in Bordeaux for allegedly sending 1,560 Jews to their deaths at Auschwitz while serving the Vichy regime as secretary-general of the Gironde Department).

"Stop the car!" King had shouted in a rage, as we were driving through the Place de la Concorde. My wife pulled over, and King got out and stamped off into the Paris night. He didn't speak to me again for a year.

Louis, the head barman of the Crillon, presided over this gaggle of scriveners, serving up a Kir or an American dry martini with equal skill and flourish. He also had the forethought to guide hotel guests to distant tables, far from the salty language of his journalistic customers. If Louis retained half of what he overheard, he must either have been one of the best–informed citizens of the Republic or a gold mine of disinformation.

Hedges and I, both former journalists, fit easily into this environment despite our official titles and offices in the nearby embassy. Jack often arranged to have important calls to the press attaché's office, including those from the ambassador, transferred to our "annex office"—the Crillon bar and grill.

Unfortunately, the Crillon's prices escalated faster than correspondents' wages, and the journalists pulled stakes, migrating to other drinking spots. It was just as well. The bar and grill had lost much of its clubby, masculine atmosphere following a renovation and the frothy whims of the new decorator.

One of the best shows in Paris took place at the Élysée Palace. General de Gaulle's press conferences sometimes bordered on farce—but never at his expense. Some world leaders attempt to run or dominate a press conference. De Gaulle manipulated his in the style of a master puppeteer. He sat facing and slightly above his audience of journalists on a stagelike dais. His ministers were seated to one side (André Malraux fidgeting without his steady intake of nicotine or other stimulants) and a group of newsmen favored by the Élysée occupied the gilt chairs directly in front of the general.

De Gaulle always greeted the journalists with solemn courtesy before launching into a special announcement. These were usually important policy statements that would inevitably provide the fodder for follow-up questions, allowing the general the time needed to make his point. He would then take questions from the floor, some planted previously among cooperative newsmen by his press officers. He would accept several questions at a time. This was designed to demonstrate his phenomenal memory and allow him to juggle his answers, depending on the importance he placed on the subject matter. Questions he preferred not to answer were lost in the shuffle and not mentioned again.

The general's poor vision played a role in these performances. It excused the fact that his identification of questioners from opposition newspapers lagged far behind his acknowledgments of journalists from more favored publications. Harold King, holder of the Legion of Honor and considered a Gaullist by adoption by some of his colleagues, would inevitably get the general's condescending nod.

Toward the close of a conference the general would unveil his major ploy. Haughtily scanning his audience as if searching for a familiar face, he would spread his hands and say, "Someone asked me about. . . ." Here he would insert a subject upon which he wanted to go on record or make a statement. There was no "someone" and no such question had been asked, but the journalists would smile tolerantly and dutifully note the substance of the general's response.

One morning I received a call from Ambassador Gavin's office. He had been invited to visit the set of the film *The Longest Day*, then being shot by director Darryl Zanuck. Because of my assignments to the Cannes Festival, the ambassador's assistant had recommended me as an official escort. Not that "jumping Jim" Gavin needed an escort. He had been asked to watch some interiors being filmed relative to his participation in the D-day operation. The actor Robert Ryan, who was playing Gavin, and John Wayne, portraying another paratroop officer, were involved in a briefing scene.

The cigar-chomping Zanuck, who had turned out an impressive on-the-spot documentary on the North African campaign as an army major, considered himself an expert on military matters. He climbed down from a camera platform to greet us, asked Ambassador Gavin to signal anything that didn't ring true, and led us to our seats. Nothing is more dull, after the first 15 minutes, than watching a film being made. The cuts, the pauses, the script checks or changes, the director's dissatisfaction with line delivery or movements, all are definite yawn producers.

In the scene being filmed, Robert Ryan—as General Gavin—was making a dramatic gesture with his weapon, the U.S. Army M-1 carbine of World War II, designed primarily for the use of officers. The small carbine just didn't lend itself to dramatic gestures. Watching this, the ambassador shook his head but remained silent.

During the break, as coffee and croissants were passed around, Zanuck sought the ambassador's reaction. The soft-spoken Gavin pointed out that he had carried an M-1 rifle in combat. He explained that a carbine was not always dependable and lacked the punch of a full-size M-1. Zanuck shouted for his chief prop man, took him aside, and read him the riot act. When shooting resumed, the toy-sized carbine was back on the prop pile, Ryan was wielding an M-1, and the sequence had found its drama.

Later, over lunch in an Alsatian brasserie, I sat opposite an uncommunicative John Wayne. "The Duke" had been a favorite of mine during the immediate postwar years, particularly in John Ford's epic depictions of frontier life in the U.S. Cavalry. On this day, Wayne was speaking in monosyllables and obviously was in a bad mood. It might have been because he was seated at some distance from the ambassador and Zanuck. I tried to make conversation by mentioning that I too had taken part in the Normandy campaign. This bit of information only seemed to make matters worse. I concentrated on my mug of beer and plate of *choucroute-garni* while stealing occasional glances at Wayne's hairpiece. I couldn't help recalling my friend Paul Garvey's story of "the Duke," infuriated because he had been refused further drink in Toot Shor's New York nightclub, snatching off his toupee and hurling it at the bartender. Someone in Zanuck's crew later told me that Wayne, having avoided military service during the war, did not like listening to war stories from those who had been there.

For me, the Paris embassy was like a huge, impersonal factory compared to the consulate general in Marseille. The numbing Paris winter was a purgatory and the need to switch your car from one side of the street to the other to conform with the odd-even parking regulations was a nightmare. Fourteen months into our Paris tour, I learned of Sam Dieli's unexpected departure from Marseille and requested to return there.

The four of us, with Mary Alice pregnant, were soon on our way south. Our only regret on departure was leaving the apartment on the rue Vaugirard. Luckily we'd kept it in the official family by turning it over to another USIS couple.

7

America Day

The salt tang of the sea and brisk gusts of the mistral wind welcomed us once again to Marseille. The bright sun reminded us that
we had made the right choice. We rediscovered our friends, and the
children reentered their previous school. Working visits to Aix en
Provence, Montpellier, Avignon, Nimes, Arles, Beziers, Toulon, and
Nice helped me pick up where I'd left off and confirmed my growing
fondness for the region.

In 1962, Charles E. "Chip" Bohlen, one of the State Department's
foremost experts on the Soviet Union, was appointed ambassador to
France, replacing General Gavin. Bohlen's appointment by President
Kennedy was a reversal of the usual pattern. Such ambassadorial positions had normally gone to very wealthy political appointees who
could afford the lavish entertainment expected in such capital cities.
Kennedy, bucking this trend and seeking a career diplomat to work
with the difficult de Gaulle, insisted on Bohlen's presence in Paris.

One of my first assignments for the newly appointed ambassador
rekindled memories of Cambodia. I was to deliver a two-volume
Histoire du Peuple Américain (History of the American People) by
André Maurois of l'Académie Française to Prince Norodom Sihanouk
of Cambodia as a gift from the ambassador. The prince was undergoing
one of his periodic cures at a clinic near the town of Grasse in the
Alpes-Maritime. I hadn't encountered Sihanouk since the epic battle of
the elephants on the grounds of his palace in Phnom Penh. Driving

through the gate of the clinic, I was curious to see how the prince had aged in ten years' time. An unexpected encounter with draconian Franco-Cambodian security measures quickly took my mind off Sihanouk's aging process.

Just inside the gate I was stopped by a sentry of the gendarmerie. He was backed up by a colleague armed with a submachine gun. The gendarme checked my consular card, asked me my business, and wanted to know what was in the wrapped package. Once I'd told him, he called ahead on his walkie-talkie and motioned me forward. There were two black Citroën sedans parked on both sides of the clinic's entrance. Each car was filled with French heavies in dark suits, all wearing tinted glasses.

One of these loungers left his car and crunched across the gravel to me. He was broadshouldered, had a broken nose, and had not graduated from a diplomatic charm school. He could have been from the SDECE (Service de Documentation Extérieure et de Contre-espionage), France's then-equivalent of the CIA, the DST (Direction du Surveillance du Territoire), or a diplomatic protection group from the Police Nationale. Whatever his affiliation, he radiated a certain barely controlled menace.

"Park it over there," he told me, "away from the building." I did so, retrieved the wrapped volumes, and locked the sedan. The one-man reception committee was now between me and the door. Unimpressed by my consular card with its tricolor slash, he patted me down, ran a metal detector over me, and then over the package, before allowing me to pass.

A member of the prince's Cambodian staff, meticulously attired in a well-cut Italian suit, welcomed me with a smile and led me to a seat in the clinic's spartan waiting room. He offered me Vittel, orange soda, or coffee. I accepted a black coffee, declined a cigarette, and was left to wait with the assurance that the prince would soon appear. I walked to the window to admire the umbrella pines, but my appearance produced a scowl from one of the prince's minders outside. It's strange how easily security agents can make you feel guilty. I had shifted my attention to some prints of old Nice hanging from the wall when I heard hurried footsteps.

Norodom Sihanouk entered the room smiling broadly, rushed toward me and—once more—took my hand in both of his. A husky Cambodian minder stood beside him.

"Ah," the prince said in his high-pitched voice, "Monsieur Sim-son!

We have not met for a very long time. How are you?" I doubt if he remembered me from that short meeting in Phnom Penh, but his briefers had prepared him.

We exchanged pleasantries, and I told him the purpose of my visit. I reached for the package and presented it to the prince on behalf of the ambassador, explaining that it contained a history of the American people by Maurois. The prince beamed even more widely and asked me to thank the ambassador. He did not attempt to open his gift. Even as he spoke, the package was on the move. It was a smooth, practiced, and very speedy security handoff: Simpson to prince, prince to minder, quick exit minder, minder to French security. I don't know where the package finally came to rest. I doubt, however, that the prince spent his evenings in Grasse reading about George Washington, Abe Lincoln, Teddy Roosevelt, and Harry Truman. Ambassador Bohlen smiled when I described the presentation. He suggested that such precautions were probably responsible for keeping the beleaguered prince in one piece, considering the chronic political violence in his country.

One of the joys of working in Marseille was daily contact with the cuisine of Provence. Grilled sea bass and red snapper; plates of *Aïoli* pungent with garlic; fresh langouste and langoustines; stuffed squid; rich, saffron-bright bouillabaisse; raw oysters of all kinds, *soupe de poisson*, the spicily sauced *pieds et paquets* (sheep's trotters and tripe—a Marseille classic), and young, tender spring lamb from les Alpilles roasted with *herbes de Provence*. These were just a few of the temptations that lay in wait at business lunches or official dinners. These meals were accompanied by bottles from the regional vineyards and the Cotes-du-Rhone.

This continual high-caloric intake, added to what had been my daily consumption in Paris, was bound to have its effect. The first Christmas after our return to Marseille proved to be the catalyst. My old friend Gerry Clode, the former member of the Free French Navy, NATO employee, and British diplomat, invited me to join him for some after-office pre-Christmas cheer. We adjourned to a French version of a clublike British bar on the rue Beauvau near the Vieux Port. Clode insisted that Black Velvets were the only drinks to fit the season. The rich blend of Guinness and champagne plus a steady intake of salted, roasted almonds did the trick.

Crossing the street several days later, I misjudged the distance and turned my ankle on the curb. It became swollen and I limped home that evening and called the consulate doctor. Dr. Lena, a husky, shaven-headed Corsican, with no bedside manner whatsoever, asked me a few questions, handled the painful ankle, and smiled malevolently.

"C'est la goutte!" he announced. "It's the gout!"

I argued that this couldn't be. I told him I'd had the same sort of accident in Nigeria, and the British doctor had simply bound up my ankle.

Lena nodded sagely but ignored my protestations. "It's the gout," he repeated. "A blood test will prove it to you. It comes with your profession."

He was right. When confirming his diagnosis, he pointed out that gout is easily treated. "I have it too," he confided. "All men of blood suffer from its effects."

Acting as a public affairs adviser to 6th Fleet units visiting France's southern coast had its ups and downs. I had been born and raised in Alameda, California, a maritime town on San Francisco Bay with a large naval air base. My uncle Theodore had fought at the battle of Manila Bay aboard the USS *Boston* and had actually received "prize money" for his ship's capture of the Spanish cruiser *Don Juan de Austria*. I'd always respected the navy, and there was no denying a certain thrill rolling out to one of the incoming 6th Fleet vessels aboard a pilot launch, watching a destroyer's sharp prow cleaving the waves, the ensign and signal flags snapping in the wind, the bosun's pipe trilling, and the crew manning the sides. It was also ego enhancing to be piped aboard with the honors due a consul or consul general.

Nevertheless, I'd often felt that sailors never quite adjust to the realities of life ashore. To some extent this proved true in my dealings with the 6th Fleet. If the road to hell is truly paved with good intentions, the 6th Fleet's contribution would have built a superhighway. Both officers and men seemed to have gone through a special "do good to others" course. I can't fault them for being nice human beings, but a hefty dose of acid reality would have helped them understand France and the French.

The prime problem was that most of the coastal towns had been visited by U.S. naval vessels over a number of years. To the inhabitants, such visits were routine. But, as the ships were rotated or interchanged, it was often a new experience for most of the ship's complement.

Where the Vikings had waded ashore to plunder, rape, and pillage, the U.S. Navy landed to give band concerts and ice cream parties for orphans, to paint churches, to repair roofs, and to generally lend a helping hand.

Normally, the ice cream parties and the band concerts were appreciated. No one but a scrooge would be against kindness to children, and the appeal of music is universal. Church painting, roof repair, and other projects blending charity with construction work were a different proposition. In 1962, World War II had been over for 17 years. Despite the struggles in Indochina and Algeria, France was recovering and de Gaulle had managed to rekindle some of the nation's fierce pride.

The arrival of a 6th Fleet vessel offshore and the skipper's by-the-book announcement that his crew was ready to paint a monastery, church, or orphanage or to repair the roof of a retirement home could indirectly infer that the local citizens or officials were incapable of carrying out such mundane upkeep themselves. It could spark confusion and, occasionally, resentment. This was particularly true if the town had a Socialist or Communist mayor, or if there was a strong, local anti-nuclear movement. Such initiatives could also reflect badly on the French Navy. Why, the residents might ask, doesn't our navy offer the same services?

At one point a small delegation of nuns called on me at the consulate general. The senior nun spoke softly and was obviously nervous. I tried to put them all at ease and leaned forward to better hear what was being said. It was simple enough. They did *not* want their small orphanage repainted. Over the years, successive American naval work parties had plastered and painted the exterior of their building. This meant that the pristine appearance of their façade kept them from receiving the funds they had requested for extensive internal repairs. One nun suggested with the hint of a smile that the successive coats of paint were the only reason the orphanage was still standing. Such pinprick problems were easily solved. Others had to do with a more basic clash of cultures.

Fleet messages passed to my office often had to do with luncheon or dinner invitations from the ships. Whether it was the 6th Fleet admiral or the skipper of a visiting destroyer, the message inevitably requested that we prepare an invitation list. This would include local officials—both civilian and military—and leading politicians, educators, and media representatives.

Somewhere in the world this might have been an easy task. It was not so in France. U.S. naval ships during this period were dry. This meant that the fine crystal goblets at the admiral's table were filled with water for the ritual toasts, and they remained filled with water throughout the meal.

Most of the well-padded, rose-nosed French politicians invited for a first time to luncheon or dinner aboard one of our ships sat at the table in a state of dismay. Each course came and went without the familiar pop of a cork or the reassuring appearance of wine in the crested glasses. This may seem a small thing, but, to those guests whose suspicions had already been aroused by fruit juice cocktails on the quarterdeck, it did mark a definite Franco-American cultural divide. Honored guests aboard French, Italian, and other European warships could be assured of a preprandial warm-up round or two of drinks before accompanying the food with a proud national vintage. Even our brother Anglo-Saxons in the Royal Navy proffered a jolt of whiskey or rum before eating, claret with food, and the traditional decanter of port with the cigars.

It's true that abstinence can be good for the character. But one cannot change centuries-old habits and customs. The dryness of the American ships produced what can be called the "assistant syndrome." American naval officers who had invited the prefect of the region, the mayor of the city, the president of the chamber of commerce, the ranking general of the region, and other high officials would be surprised to find them replaced by their *adjoints*, or assistants. Nor did their consternation stop there. Successive visits to the same port might find more new faces appearing as guests. These recruits came from the ranks of the *deuxième adjoints*, or the *troisième adjoints*, sent forth to do their time behind the water-filled glasses. This did not mean the coastal population and their officials were alcoholics. It usually meant that to sit through a mediocre meal without their habitual wine, listening to a language many of them did not speak, and touring a type of warship they had seen before did not fit their idea of an enjoyable outing. Today, 6th Fleet skippers have access to "exception" rules that will allow the serving of wine and beer for specific, approved, on-board social events while in port. I only hope the exceptions are pushed to the limit.

There were other more serious manifestations of Franco-American noncommunication. Americans enjoy being liked. We often expend considerable effort seeking friendship. In the 1960s many of the French, having experienced a comparatively recent war, occupation, and liberation, were chary of sudden friendships and suspicious of strangers. Although some 6th Fleet personnel formed close friendships or married into French families, others could not understand the reticence or veiled animosity they sometimes encountered.

How many American officers and sailors realized that Allied air raids had taken a heavy civilian toll along the coast and particularly in Marseille, leaving a wake of understandable resentment? How many understood that the actual, fighting Résistance movement had been relatively small in comparison to those involved in active and passive collaboration with the occupier? How many knew that inter-Résistance fighting had often been vicious and had spilled over into ongoing, postwar political violence in which some participants considered Americans the international villains? The answers to all these questions was the same: very few. This was not a shortcoming on the navy's part. It was a simple fact of life. But it did not make our job easier.

One hot summer following my return to Marseille, I had a run-in with the commander of the 6th Fleet. It was a question of fantasy versus reality. The city of Nice was planning an "America Day," and we had agreed to help. Gilles Daziano was the coordinator on the ground, and we were backing him logistically from Marseille. It was primarily a cultural effort, involving concerts, lectures, readings, jazz, and the participation of Americans resident in the Nice region. The 6th Fleet was to participate in a modest parade and band concert. The date was set and all seemed in order.

A week before America Day, I received a call from Daziano. I sensed an uncharacteristic tightness in his voice.

"The America Day committee has just had a planning meeting," he informed me. "I thought I should call you."

"Yes?"

"I think there is a problem."

"Yes?"

"The admiral..." Gilles stopped to clear his throat. "He wants to land Marines on the beach."

"He what?"

"To show the readiness of the 6th Fleet. He wants to put Marines on the Nice beach."

I couldn't believe what I was hearing! If there is one thing the French hold sacred, it is their summer holiday. They beg, borrow, and scrape throughout the dreary winter in order to migrate to the shores of the Mediterranean in search of their share of sun and sand. As Daziano outlined the admiral's plans in more detail, I had a terrifying vision of the pebbled beach at Nice filled with bronzed vacationers while the bow waves of landing craft and amtracs drew closer, each loaded with heavily armed Marines in their camouflaged gear. This nightmare imagery extended to include screaming vacationers fleeing from the grinding treads of the amtracs.

I managed to take down all the details and promised to call Daziano back. My over-the-top reaction had now been modified. The vision of amphibious mayhem had been replaced with a picture of the same vacationers being herded off the beach by the gendarmerie prior to the landing. There were no screams, only deep resentment and children weeping over their sand pails, having been forced from their beach so the nasty Americans could play soldier. I could also envisage the approaching banners of Communist demonstrators with the attendant French riot police pouring out of their vans. However I imagined it, the admiral's project would be a catastrophe.

I couldn't reach the admiral, and the fleet public information officer was no help. The admiral had spoken and that was that. A captain in the naval attaché's office in Paris listened sympathetically, but it soon became obvious he was not going to buck the admiral. I called John Mowinckel, who had replaced Bill Cody as counselor for public affairs, and gave him the details. He suggested I also discuss the matter with Ambassador Bohlen's special assistant. This was done, and I waited for results. I didn't have long to wait. The ambassador spoke to the admiral, suggesting diplomatically that a Marine landing didn't quite fit America Day's cultural format, and the problem ceased to exist.

Fate, however, plays strange tricks. A short time later a navy message confirmed that the 6th Fleet flagship would be making an official visit to the naval port of Toulon. I was to represent the absent consul general at the ceremonies and luncheon in honor of the visitors. My first duty on arrival was to board the flagship at dockside for an informal call on the admiral. He was well aware that I had been instrumental in blocking his planned landings, but he said nothing. He was icily polite while his mess attendant offered coffee. The ambiance was perfectly frigid. Once the ordeal of protocol had ended, the admiral went off on his official calls. I was glad to leave the air conditioned cabin for the warmth of the Provençal sun. If it had been the old sailing navy, I'd probably have been the admiral's prime candidate for a fully barnacled keelhauling.

The labor scene in Marseille was volatile and unpredictable. The Confédération Générale du Travail (CGT), a powerful national union run by militant Communists, dominated the city's industrial life. The CGT's politically motivated strikes, walkouts, and strong-arm tactics could shut down the port, paralyze whole sectors of the economy, and spark waves of violence between the right and left. During the early Cold War years, the American labor movement had supported the non-Communist unions in France. In the 1960s, USIS retained links in Marseille with the Catholic Force Ouvrière (FO) and the Socialist Confédération Française de Travail (CFDT), providing them with information on U.S. and international labor developments in the form of news items, publications, and documentary films. We also fed promising young labor union members into the leader grant selection machinery for working visits to the United States.

All of these unions shared office space in an old building not far from Marseille's central market. There were certain sensitivities to bear in mind when we called on our labor contacts. The CGT militants weren't above labeling us as "reactionaries," "capitalist mercenaries," and "agents of the CIA." The Communists monitored our rare visits to the FO and CFDT representatives, but we didn't skulk in the shadows or slip through side doors. The fact that I had been a member of the AFL-CIO American Newspaper Guild eased my relations with the non-Communist unions, and invitations to their evening guitar, wine, and cheese sessions followed. Despite the fact that the American embassy in Paris had long had a labor attaché, the Communists still had trouble reconciling the worlds of diplomacy and labor. That was their loss.

We rarely had direct contact with the CGT. When we did, it was in the form of vociferous demonstrations outside the consulate general or short, grim-faced visits by their delegations, bearing petitions protesting U.S. foreign policy. It was therefore a surprise to receive a call from one of the city's top CGT officials inviting me to visit him at his headquarters. Puzzled but curious, I accepted the invitation. The official and three of his lieutenants received me in his office, and we quickly got down to business.

The official was approaching retirement, and he had just received an invitation from an old friend and fellow Marseillais who now lived in the United States and wanted the official to visit him in Washington state for two weeks of fishing. A fervent angler, he wanted to go badly. But his staff had told him it was impossible, as a CGT member, to get a visa. I had been invited to the lion's den to confirm their argument— and reinforce their prejudices.

The direct sincerity of the aging labor leader and the smug, negative attitude of his staff combined to present a challenge. A strong case for a waiver was submitted and supported by considerable lobbying in the form of memos and telephone calls to the Paris embassy. In the end—despite some strong opposition (pink-tinged labor leaders were not overly popular in the Washington, D.C., of 1963)—the CGT official received his tourist visa and left for the Pacific Northwest.

On his return I was asked to his office for an apéritif. The same staff members were present, sipping their pastis in silence while he described his trip. He spoke of the pleasure of seeing his old friend but inserted the standard dialectical zingers. The United States had "many problems," he had been shocked by the "low status" of American Blacks, and he couldn't understand why the American police had to be "armed to the teeth."

When his staff drifted off to lunch, he insisted that I have one last drink. He then shut the door and produced an album of Polaroid shots demonstrating his prowess as an angler and the outsized proportions of his catches. The political jargon was set aside, and he beamed, thanking me profusely for making his visit possible. His last comment as I walked out the door was, "Monsieur, you have a truly beautiful country." In the long history of Cold War give and take, this effort counted for little. But proving his party hacks wrong had been well worth the effort.

The elegantly engraved invitation was a work of art. My wife and I were invited to a black tie dinner at the préfecture in Nice. The *préfets*, the senior government representatives in specific regions of France, are like minor kings. They see that the will of Paris is done and that the central government is informed of developments and trends throughout the provinces. The préfecture in Marseille was across the street from the consulate general, and we had always had good relations with various prefects and had been their infrequent guests. The préfecture in Nice, however, was considered a prime target by the Riviera's social climbers. For many, an invitation to the Italianate pile set back in its semitropical garden was a thing to be treasured. To me, still harboring an innate aversion to black ties, it seemed the drive from Marseille to Nice was a long way to go for a dinner. But, duty called.

We arrived at the Hotel Negresco in the early evening and were settling into our room when Mary Alice made a disheartening discovery. Somehow, between us, we'd managed to leave my cuff links in Marseille. Serious business indeed! We decided to have a drink on the terrace to consider the situation. Most of Nice's shops were now closed. Even if a few tourist traps remained open, the price of cuff links would undoubtedly be exorbitant. Perhaps I could rig replacements of some kind and keep my sleeves well down over the cuffs. I might have been able to borrow the links of our consul in Nice, but he was on leave. The clock was ticking. I stood a good chance of being the laughing stock of the party, the "little match boy" of American diplomacy.

A flash of silver caught my eye. The bar waiter was clearing a nearby table and the bright lights of the terrace had caught his cuff links. Almost instantaneously, Mary Alice and I both had the same thought. Within minutes the waiter and I struck a deal. I "rented" his stainless steel cuff links for a nominal sum and promised to return them the next morning. I was then able to escort my wife through the tall iron gates of the préfecture with renewed confidence.

I didn't appreciate the full irony of the situation until it was time to find our seats at the *préfet*'s table. I was seated beside Florence Gould, the French widow of Frank J. Gould and patroness of the arts, and across from the Begum Agha Kahn, the statuesque former British showgirl and widow of the wealthy Bombay-born leader of the Muslim Ismaeli sect, who had been pictured in the newsreels each year receiving his weight in diamonds.

These two eminent ladies, obviously deciding that I was just another government *fonctionnaire* of insignificant rank, spent most of the evening comparing the carat power of their jewelry collections, holding their huge diamond rings up to catch the light of the chandeliers and bemoaning the difficulty of finding competent servants. In retrospect, I realized I should have casually mentioned that my shiny cuff links were pure silver but, fearful that one of the *grandes dames* would produce a jeweler's glass for a closer look, I remained silent. The only kindred spirit I sensed during this ordeal was a nearby French general. He too had overheard the jewelry discussion. Catching my eye, he permitted himself a wry smile, a slightly lifted eyebrow, and an almost imperceptible shake of the head.

On March 11, 1963, our third daughter, Kate, was born in the Clinique Bouchard in Marseille. Unlike Shawn, born the night of the Binh Xuyen revolt in Saigon with wounded littering the hospital, or Lisa, delivered in a noisy nursing home on the Lagos-Ibadan road in Nigeria, Kate's clinic was a model of order and cleanliness. And so it should be, taking into account the persistent rumor that it was where the "godfathers" of Marseille's underworld chose to send their expectant wives.

The French département of Corsica fell within my jurisdiction as regional USIS representative, and my visits to that land of clans, vendettas, and the law of *omerta*, or "silence," were unique experiences. The primary goal of my first visit was to establish contact with local government and civic officials, media representatives, and educational authorities. Corsicans had long held positions of authority in France's overseas territories and colonies. They were also heavily represented in the French military, the police, and the customs service and influential as vocal, hard-nosed politicians on the national scene. In addition, there were increasing indications that a homegrown independence movement might soon cause real problems for the French government. For all these reasons I wanted to be sure Corsica received a fair share of our leader and educational grants. I also wanted to ensure that U.S. foreign policy statements and documents were promptly available to the media, officials, and local politicians. Most of all, I wanted to get the feel of the place and store away what knowledge I could gather for future reference.

I timed the visit to coincide with an invitation to the civic celebration of Napoleon's August 15 birthday in Ajaccio, Corsica's capital. A requiem Mass was celebrated in the sun-baked, palm-dotted square in front of the city hall. Most of the women wore black dresses and their heads were covered with black shawls. The men were also somberly dressed and silent. The only sounds seemed to be the click of rosary beads, the soporific, mumbled Latin of the bespectacled priest, and the wash of the distant sea on the shoreline.

Then, when the host was raised, all hell broke loose. Innocently expecting the discreet tinkle of a communion bell, I was jolted by a loud rendition of ruffles and flourishes from a military band. Each elevation of the host filled the square with a burst of martial music and sent the pigeons rocketing into the sky. They stayed aloft for some time as the drumbeats echoed back to the square from the narrow adjacent streets. An official at the *préfecture* in Marseille had told me I'd find Corsica "different." He was right.

During a post-Mass apéritif, a civic official gave me a 15-minute lecture on the genius of Napoleon while stroking an exhibited bronze death mask of Ajaccio's favorite son. He also suggested that I not underestimate the importance of the Bonapartiste party in Corsican politics. Later, at a newspaper kiosk, I noticed that some of the postcards on view lionized Corsica's bandits by reprinting old photos taken in the 1920s. The bearded denizens of the wild maquis, or bushland, were pictured in heroic poses, rifles in hand, bandoleers of ammunition crossed on their chests. They were frowning from under broad-brimmed hats at some imagined policeman or foreign invader.

To begin to understand Corsica and its inhabitants one had to bear in mind the Island's history of invasions. The Romans, Vandals, Byzantines, Lombards, Moors, Pisans, Spaniards, Genoese, French, and Turks were among the earlier unwelcome visitors. Throughout these trying and often bloody periods, the Corsicans learned that resistance and survival depended on their close-knit clan system and the law of *omerta*. In World War II the Italians and Germans were the invaders and occupiers until September 1943, when a combined effort by the Corsican Résistance and the Free French Forces liberated the island.

From Ajaccio, where I fed on lark paté and chestnut-fed wild boar—both Corsican specialities—I headed north in a rented car for the mountain pass of Vizzavona. Fall comes early in Corsica and the narrow road was buried under a thick layer of fallen golden leaves. The forests were a beautiful sight, but, with no visible white line or edging to the road, I crept over the pass and arrived late for my appointment with the mayor of Corte. He understood my problem, however, and devoted most of his afternoon explaining that Napoleon had really been born in Corte and not Ajaccio. I drove on to spend the night in Bastia, where some local journalists tried to explain the intricate web of Corsican politics over a few bottles of wine from the nearby vineyards of Patrimonio. From there it was off to the beautiful port of Calvi, where locals claim their city—and not Genoa—is the birthplace of Christopher Columbus. Little did I realize at the time that I'd be returning to Calvi in 1995 to spend a month with the 2nd Parachute Regiment of the French Foreign Legion to complete a book on that unit for my current publisher. The drive from Calvi to Ajaccio skirted an untamed, rugged shoreline scented with the wild flowers and herbs of the maquis. I knew my short visit had not accomplished much, but I was returning to Marseille with some definite impressions. These included the confirmation that the Corsicans on their home ground were as much a race apart as those I had known in Indochina, that French officialdom was not particularly welcoming to U.S. diplomats snooping around their island département, and that Corsica would be receptive to only limited USIS activities.

Late in the evening of November 22, 1963, I received a puzzling telephone call at rue Saint Jacques. I was the consulate's duty officer that week, so all after-hours calls were being transferred to my number. The deep-voiced male caller was obviously in a noisy café. He had to shout twice for silence before I could hear him.

"Is this the American consulate?" he demanded in a Marseille accent. I told him it was.

"Is it true?" he asked. From the tone of his voice I knew this was something serious, but I didn't know what he was talking about.

"Is what true?"

"President Kennedy! Is he dead?"

I was speechless for several seconds. "Who told you that?" I finally croaked.

"It's on the TV here in our docker's cafe. Is it true?"

"Give me your name and number. I'll call you back." I was turning on the TV as I spoke and preparing to call the Paris embassy. My wife had run to get the radio. The first black-and-white images from Dallas were flickering on the TV screen accompanied by vague reports and rumors. The line to the embassy was jammed. I used *priorité d'état* (official priority) and got through. The embassy duty officer was engulfed in queries and could tell me nothing. Finally, the French radio and TV confirmed President John F. Kennedy's assassination. A follow-up call from the embassy put an official seal on it. Someone was already talking about opening books of condolences for signature by local officials, the consular corps, and the French public.

Still stunned, I picked up the telephone and dialed the number the earlier caller had left. He must have been close to the telephone, because he responded immediately.

"*Alor?*" he asked hoarsely. "Is it true?"

"Yes," I told him. "I'm afraid it is."

There was a moment's silence before I heard him confirm the news to those around him. Then, this unknown Marseille dock worker broke down and wept.

On-the-job training in diplomacy. The author *(second from right)* conferring with Vietnamese and French officials in the Vietnamese prime minister's Saigon palace in 1952.

The author *(right)* at an official French government reception talking with Nguyen Van Tam, the French-installed prime minister of Vietnam, and Jean Letourneau, French minister for the Associated States of Indochina.

Above: The author *(at right in shorts)* in 1953 at a French command post at Phu Ly in northern Vietnam while he was a U.S. Information Agency war correspondent.

Right: Governor Adlai Stevenson is surprised to find an American with the Franco-Vietnamese forces during his visit to the Tonkin battle zone in 1953.

In the field with French and Vietnamese officers of a Vietnamese infantry battalion in 1953.

Left: With T'ai partisans near Dien Bien Phu in December 1953 as the Vietminh encircled the French stronghold.

Below: The author photographing victorious Vietminh troops as they enter Hanoi on October 9, 1954. For several hours he posed as a Polish press officer before leaving the communist-occupied city.

A photo by the author shows Vietnamese paratroopers counterattacking Binh Xuyen rebel forces attempting to overthrow the Diem government in Saigon in the spring of 1955.

In the northern Nigerian bush near Kaduna with the Queen's Own Nigeria Regiment in 1958.

USIA

An impromptu jam session, complete with "talking drums," while crossing the Niger River in November 1958.

The author and his Lagos staff at his going-away party in the spring of 1959.

The author *(center)* anxiously awaits the reaction of French wine growers and officials to California vintages during "America Day" at the Montpellier Wine Fair in the fall of 1959.

As press adviser to the U.S. delegation to the 1960 UNESCO Conference in Paris, the author tries to signal to chief delegate Charles Thayer that he is straying from the official policy line.

USIA

Exchanging memories of the Indochina campaigns with two French colonels following the author's decoration as an *officier* in the Order of French Combat Engineers at Angers in 1961.

The press office of the prime minister of South Vietnam in February 1965, with the author at center front. Nearly all of the men were military officers or noncoms.

The author shares a joke and a book signing with Olivia de Haviland *(left)* at Versaille in 1965. He had just published his second novel.

The author, in his capacity as an adviser to the political warfare section of the South Vietnamese army, on an operation near My Tho in 1965. The West Point-educated American adviser on the right has just complained about the Vietnamese propensity to call in artillery on "suspect" villages.

USIA

Lecturing on the French experience in Indochina to senior U.S. military officers at the Naval War College in 1969. The author also taught a course on the psychological aspects of guerrilla warfare and served as faculty adviser and consultant to the president of the college.

DEA

Consul General Simpson with officials of the U.S. Drug Enforcement Administration in 1974 at the site of a major heroin-producing laboratory outside Marseille. Large quantities of heroin and hashish were being trafficked through southern France, and the U.S. consulate general included a DEA contingent that worked closely with the French police.

Gaston Defferre *(left)*, the longtime mayor of Marseille, Resistance leader, and Socialist deputy in the National Assembly, receives U.S. ambassador Kenneth Rush and Consul General Simpson in December 1974.

Consul General Simpson is welcomed aboard a U.S. Navy vessel at the port of Sète in southern France in 1975.

The author and his wife, Mary Alice *(in striped dress)*, host a reception for visiting U.S. Naval officers and their French counterparts at the Marseille consulate general in 1976. Due to constant social events, U.S. diplomats joke about having but one liver to give for their country.

The author places lighted joss sticks on the tomb of Col. Pham Ngoc Thao, with whom he had shared an office, at the Patriot's Cemetery near Ho Chi Minh City in March 1991. This visit had two purposes: to prove to himself that Thao had been honored as an enemy agent and to remember him— whatever the ideological differences—as a friend.

8

Protocol Wars

Vietnam was like sticking plaster. Once you'd touched it, you couldn't shake it off. This applied both to one's personal nostalgia for that country and to the entry in your file that flagged any knowledge of it. My three years' previous service there made me vulnerable on both counts. In early 1964 Foreign Service personnel specialists were pouring over the files attempting to find officers needed for a major American buildup in South Vietnam. The White House called this "sending in the first team," a phrase more fitting for a football game than a grim guerrilla war.

President Lyndon Johnson could not understand the inability of the South Vietnamese to form a viable working government and perform well on the battlefield. Most of all he wanted the U.S.-financed and -trained Army of the Republic of Vietnam (ARVN) to cease the intolerable round of military coups that were sapping its strength and resolve. The Texan tended to see things in the black and white of "down home" politics, where deals were made, pressing the flesh paid dividends, and those whom you backed did what they were told.

Johnson's frustrations with the South Vietnamese soon spread to his own diplomats and generals on the spot. When they argued that they could push the Vietnamese only so far, he decided whatever the Vietnamese couldn't or wouldn't do, a team of American experts should and could. In sum, we were going to save the Vietnamese from themselves. This presidential initiative was heeded, but the State Department and other involved agencies were less than enthusiastic. The understanding was that it was to be implemented as discreetly as possible.

My sudden summons to return to Vietnam reached me at the Cannes Film Festival, where my wife was staying with me in the temporary luxury of the Carlton. I was advised to return to the consulate general as soon as possible. Within hours we had loaded our luggage, said our goodbyes, and were driving through the mimosa-covered hills west of Cannes on our way to Marseille.

Once back in my office, I read the classified telegram twice to be sure there wasn't some mistake. There was none. I had two weeks to arrive in Saigon, and my family could follow at a later date. The 14 days would include a short period of consultation in Washington and attendance at a high-level conference on Vietnam at CINCPAC (Commander-in-Chief Pacific) at Pearl Harbor. I was to be an adviser to the new prime minister, General Nguyen Van Khanh, and to the political warfare section of the ARVN. General Khanh had put himself in the catbird seat thanks to a military coup, and we were now going to base our "nation building" on his regime.

In his book *The Lost Revolution*, Vietnam expert Robert Shaplen described the decision to seed American specialists into the Vietnamese government at high administrative levels to assist the Vietnamese in the fields of foreign relations, economics and finance, public affairs, and psychological warfare. I was to be involved in the last two categories. According to Shaplen, we were to form a "shadow government of non-military advisers" who would formulate and implement "a national campaign plan...beyond the competence of the Vietnamese government." The Vietnamese were understandably cool to the idea from its inception but were still paying lip service to the project when I received my orders. As it turned out, I would be the only member of this supposed "brain trust" to arrive in Saigon.

My primary concern at the time was the safety of my wife and daughters. Foreign Service officers' families were still being allowed into Saigon, but increased Viet Cong (VC) attacks, the constant coups, Catholic-Buddhist hostility, and the general instability of the Saigon regime were causes for worry. No small part of my unease had to do with my previous Vietnam service. I had been labeled a "spy with a sly smile" by the official Communist Party newspaper in Hanoi and, as mentioned earlier, had been featured with other Americans on a death list published by the Binh Xuyen rebels during their attack on the Diem regime. The Binh Xuyen had then claimed, when two officers and myself were evacuated to an Air Force hospital in the Philippines with hepatitis, to have poisoned a number of us. This had all happened nine years ago. In Asian time measurement and memories, this was the equivalent of an American 24 hours.

The fact that we were expecting another child did not ease my mind. To her credit, Mary Alice was preparing to follow me with the girls once I'd arranged housing in Saigon. She had already been exposed to violence there when I'd been medically evacuated in 1955. We comforted ourselves with the truism that things usually looked worse from a distance than they actually were on the ground.

That year was to be a unique experience. The "first team" concept disintegrated shortly after I was installed in the prime minister's office as an adviser. General Khanh had accepted me under pressure from Ambassador Henry Cabot Lodge, but he was not happy at having an American on his doorstep and had no intention of following my advice. The ARVN generals accepted me more readily, mainly because I'd experienced the previous war, often the same campaigns they had. Unfortunately, none of them seemed to have the slightest idea what their "political warfare" section was supposed to do, if it wasn't to plan coups and countercoups.

I worked under Barry "Zorro" Zorthian, the savvy USIA officer in charge of the civilian-military Joint U.S. Public Affairs Office (JUSPAO) in Saigon. I was also allowed to report directly to Ambassador Lodge and later to the ambassadorial duo of General Maxwell Taylor and U. Alexis Johnson, depending on the crisis situation and developments at the prime minister's office.

A few months after my arrival, the rumors of coups intensified and the waltz of the colonels and generals began. The embassy security nets were filled with reports of military movements within the city or on the outskirts of Saigon. The coups, demicoups, and coupettes did come, pitting one ARVN unit against the other while the VC consolidated their hold on the hamlets and villages.

The first Vietnamese staff member I worked with in the prime minister's office had been a member of the Vietnamese Ministry of Information under the French and had had direct links to French intelligence. The second, Colonel Pham Ngoc Thao, is now buried in the Patriot's Cemetery near Saigon as a "hero of the Revolution" and one of North Vietnam's best agents. It was a time when even some of the old Indochina hands, including myself, learned the hard way that no one could be trusted. I did my time in the field with ARVN units and armed propaganda teams and recalled what it meant to be in a "hot zone," where the villages were empty, the dogs silent, and the bodies unburied.

On October 18, 1964, our fourth daughter, Maggie, was born in the clinic of Dr. Dé, an American-trained obstetrician who had been minister of health under President Diem. It was indicative of the topsy-turvy atmosphere in Saigon that Dr. Dé, under house arrest in his clinic, had to be summoned from his daily rollerskating session on the clinic's parking lot to assist at the birth.

Things continued to heat up in Saigon. Suddenly Nguyen Van Khanh was out, and a shaky civilian government attempted to take over under the critical eye of Khanh, who had retained command of the armed forces. In December 1964 Generals Khanh, Thieu, and Ky deposed the short-lived civilian government of Tran Van Huong in another coup, and Ambassador Maxwell Taylor dressed down the young generals—thus alienating them permanently.

The VC got bolder, attacking U.S. installations at Bien Hoa Air Base on November 1, destroying six U.S. aircraft and killing five Americans. On Christmas Eve they struck in the heart of Saigon by planting a powerful bomb in the basement parking area of the Brink's BOQ that killed two Americans. On February 7, 1965, the VC hit Pleiku airstrip in the central highlands killing eight Americans and destroying eight U.S. aircraft. Within hours of the Pleiku attack, President Johnson had ordered reprisal airstrikes against North Vietnamese targets. A short time later the order came through to evacuate all American dependents from Vietnam.

The time between my family's departure and the end of my one-year tour of duty went mercifully fast. My efficiency curve—never very high—plunged with each coup-fueled change of government. My last foray into the green reality outside of Saigon included a short stopover at the sandbagged, heavily armed CIA field office in Tam Ky and a subsequent rough C-47 ride through a tropical thunderstorm. The aircraft swiveled and plunged all the way back to the capital, and I decided my days in the field were over for good—or so I thought.

Mary Alice had been waiting for me in Marseille. We'd thought it would be best for the girls to return there, to the same schools and the same friends. It also preserved the continuity of the French education they'd received in Marseille, Paris, and Saigon. The family met me at

Nice airport with a bouquet of roses and a temporarily hired car and driver. For old times' sake, we all spent the night at the Carlton in Cannes. This time the French government did *not* pick up the tab.

I was notified of my next assignment during home leave in California. Lee Brady, the senior officer who'd interviewed me as a recruit and had been my first boss in Saigon, managed to have me assigned to his staff in Paris as the embassy's information officer. This was a choice slot, and we immediately began making plans for our return to the French capital: preparing the girls' reentry into their previous schools and writing to the Comte de Chambrun to see whether the apartment on the rue de Vaugirard happened to be available. By a miracle it was. When we dragged our bags through the front door, Lafayette's patrician portrait appeared as an old friend.

Although I had left Vietnam behind for the third time, it was not through with me. Because of my recent service there, I was shackled to events in that unfortunate land as an in-house embassy "expert," this at a time when the French government and most French political parties were opposed to U.S. policy in Southeast Asia.

My first command performance took place before the embassy's country team. I had resolved to tell the truth about my experiences, so American officers leaving the briefing would have at least a whiff of reality to balance the propaganda about "progress" and "light at the end of the tunnel" emanating from a Washington so far removed from Vietnam. I also tried, perhaps with too much force, to make it clear that those who had never served in Vietnam could not possibly understand the complexities of the situation. I made the point that those of us who served there were often at a loss to explain certain developments.

I talked of the coups, the state of the ARVN and the corruption in its upper ranks, the continued military infiltration from the North, my own negative opinion of the overdependence on airpower in a guerrilla war, the omnipresent VC and their hold on the people, and the questionable procedure of pulling inexperienced officers from their posts around the world to be thrown into the crucible of Vietnam on short notice.

The faces at the conference table had tightened as I spoke. When I asked for questions, some were posed in a clipped manner bordering on hostility. I had pulled back a curtain to reveal a Vietnam that didn't match their steady diet of positive, bureaucratic thinking. Strangely enough, it was the military attachés who were nodding their heads in agreement with some of my points.

But the real difficulty of explaining U.S. policy in Vietnam lay beyond the embassy. It was easy enough to accept a speaking engagement from a conservative, pro-American organization or a veterans' group. They would clap no matter what I said. The difficulty was reaching those wide strata of French citizenry and youths who were shocked by the violence of Vietnam and America's role in the war. Nightly television was introducing a new generation to the realities of another war in Indochina, where all the strength and power seemed to be on our side. Thanks to a rolling barrage of propaganda from the French Communist Party and France's romantic, historic attachment to Vietnam, the North Vietnamese and the VC were often seen as valiant, barefoot freedom fighters, Third World Davids facing the mighty U.S. Goliath. The fact that the powerful North Vietnamese Army (NVA) was now infiltrating the South along the Ho Chi Minh Trail(s) with modern heavy weapons soon to be followed by light tanks did little to shatter this image.

More than once I fell into a well-prepared ambush. At one evening appearance not far from Paris, I was told at the last minute that my debating opponent would be a member of the local Communist Party. He proved to be articulate, suave, and very well prepared. He played directly to the audience's emotions, reciting figures on civilian deaths, bomb tonnages dropped, and ARVN atrocities. Ironically, much of his material came directly from American publications and most of it was true. In traditional Marxist fashion he had also brought along his own support group, carefully dispersed among the audience.

I tried logic and reason, speaking from my own experience about the ARVN units that *had* fought well, the Vietnamese officials who risked their lives daily attempting to administer their provinces, and the clandestine assassination methods used by the North Vietnamese and the VC against anyone opposing their political objectives. But here I was at a disadvantage. My opponent, by delving into the material on Vietnam openly available in the Western media, was privy to a wealth of information that could be credited to known and respected sources. My figures, background material, and personal experiences were considered tainted, coming from government sources and from me, a government official. It did no good for me to state that an efficient province chief and his family in the Mekong Delta had been ruthlessly murdered at 3:00 A.M. by a VC assassination squad if I couldn't quote the source of the information as the *New York Times*, the *London Observer*, or *Le Monde* of Paris. To argue that I knew such events to be true or even to have been on the spot drew only murmurs of disbelief and hostility. When I left the hall after the debate, I knew how General Custer must have felt at Little Big Horn. At least I had been able to walk away.

To many in France, the selfless, black pajama–clad VC had taken his place beside Che Guevara as a symbol of progressive revolution. Others secretly relished Uncle Sam's distress in Indochina, particularly as they had considered us only too eager to replace them in their former colony. Another Vietnam debate that ended as an uneasy draw in an atmosphere of ill-feeling convinced me that such appearances were counterproductive. I researched each invitation carefully and eventually abandoned the lecture circuit. For the moment, the printed word and one-on-one conversations with influential media contacts would have to do.

Well settled into my office overlooking the Place de la Concorde in the embassy annex that once belonged to the French statesman and diplomat Talleyrand, I was pleased to find that Vietnam didn't occupy my every working hour. I was now listed on the masthead of our monthly magazine *Informations et Documents* (I&D) as directeur de la publication and, although the veteran French staff did an excellent job, I was ultimately responsible for the publication's contents. Fortunately, we were allowed considerable leeway in selecting material. A small print disclaimer stating that "the articles published in *I&D* do not necessarily reflect the views of the American government and are the sole responsibilities of their authors" allowed us to include the occasional controversial piece and broach subject matter seldom seen in a government publication. This streak of independence appealed to the French, and *I&D* had a faithful readership. We covered everything about the United States: politics, sports, industry, culture, racial and ethnic matters, history, the arts, the military, conservation, space, labor, and law. We may not have won many hearts and minds, but I believe we did cause many readers to pause and reflect.

In the fall of 1966 an old friend dropped by my office for a visit. Pierre Schoendoerffer and I had first met at the French strongpoint of Nasan in northwest Vietnam. He had been a combat cameraman with the French Army and I had been wearing my shoulder flash as a *Correspondent de Guerre USIS*. We had subsequently met on various military operations. He had been captured at Dien Bien Phu and endured the hell of long marches and Vietminh prison camps. Once liberated, he had turned to writing and film directing. His *317th Section*, a realistic depiction of the arduous withdrawal of a small French unit from Laos, had won a number of prizes, including one at the Cannes Festival. It still stands as one of the best films to come out of the Vietnam wars.

Pierre wished to spend adequate time in the field with an American combat unit to produce a worthy documentary on *our* Vietnam war. I was wholly sympathetic, but his project was a tall order. Although Barry Zorthian remained the director of JUSPAO in Saigon and U.S. media policy in Vietnam was still in its "full disclosure" mode, representatives of the French media were not exactly welcomed with open arms. A team from French National Television had recently done a hatchet job on America's role in Vietnam, and some French journalists—all attentive and unctuous on the ground—often turned highly critical and vituperative once they were back in Paris.

I knew I could trust Schoendoerffer, and I also knew the inherent quality of his work. His proposal was particularly interesting as his footage was scheduled to be shown on *Cinq Colonnes à la Une*, one of France's most prestigious television programs, somewhat in the style of America's *60 Minutes*. On these counts, I approached both Washington and Saigon for project approval. In principal, under the prevailing rules, any accredited journalist, cameraman, or photographer could cover the Vietnam war and could take advantage of airlifts and chopper trips to the action, courtesy of JUSPAO. But there were subtle methods of denial if a specific visitor was considered bad news. A jeep might be too late to make a scheduled chopper flight, an operation touted as action-filled might turn out to be a dud, a "special" briefing could be boring and filled with dross. I knew these truths because—inserting "Dakotas" and "Beavers" in the place of choppers—I had endured them when the French were in charge. I didn't want Pierre to risk the same fate.

Lee Brady backed me, we sent an eyes-only telegram to Zorthian at JUSPAO, the Schoendoerffer project was approved, and he was guaranteed full cooperation once in Vietnam. The two months of filming, most of it spent with a combat company of the 1st Cavalry (Airmobile) commanded by a Lieutenant Anderson, a Black West Pointer, produced *The Anderson Platoon*.

Schoendoerffer had been lucky in his choice of subject matter. The men of Anderson's platoon had been active during the period of his visit, and his camera had followed them on chopper-borne assaults and into a confused but deadly firefight. One of the documentary's most memorable images was that of a Black trooper gripping the hand of a wounded White comrade while awaiting a medevac chopper. If a Hollywood director had slipped that sequence into a contemporary war film the public would have cried "phony." But the urgency and reality of that filmed instant caught the onlooker by the throat.

The Anderson Platoon won raves from French TV critics; was sold to a number of European networks, including Yugoslavian TV; won several prizes as an outstanding documentary; and had an even wider international distribution. Perhaps its greatest contribution to prevailing attitudes was that it presented a true picture of the Vietnam War without the taint of propaganda. It did not sanitize the war or preach, but it did present the American troopers as human beings, not mercenaries or "baby killers." It showed them as brave, frightened, professional, and caring. I had pushed for the project not because I saw it as a policy vehicle but because I knew we could count on Schoendoerffer's integrity and professionalism. I made no editorial contribution whatsoever and saw the final product only days before it appeared on French television. In sum, *The Anderson Platoon* made John Wayne's *Green Berets* look like a child's fantasy. Pierre Schoendoerffer went on to produce more prize-winning films and novels of literary merit. In 1991, he wrote and directed the film *Dien Bien Phu.* Schoendoerffer arranged for serving French paratroopers to jump over North Vietnam as their predecessors had done 38 years earlier. I had been able to watch some of the filming during a visit to Hanoi, but the role of war correspondent "Howard Simpson" was played by the late Donald Pleasance. I pointed out that I had been 28 during the period of Dien Bien Phu, and Pleasance, although an excellent actor, was in his 70s! Schoendoerffer heard me out, shrugged, and remarked, "Well, he does speak French." Schoendoerffer is now a member of the revered Académie Française and hard at work on another novel.

Working at the embassy under Ambassador Bohlen was a considerable pleasure. He kept a steady hand on the wheel of command and, despite various crises and demonstrations of Gaullist pique, remained calm. His work with the Soviets had been a hard school of diplomacy.

He had been there and seen it all when it came to antagonism, both official and unofficial. Suggestions from overzealous staff members that the embassy lodge official protests or dispatch diplomatic notes to the French government over media comments or speeches criticizing the United States were quickly scotched by the ambassador. He patiently explained that such reactions had to be saved for *real* crisis situations and that overreaction to every pinprick attack was exactly what our antagonists were seeking.

Another plus of Paris during this period was the opportunity to work with Nicholas King, the embassy press attaché. He was a tall, portly New Englander with a dry, cutting humor. A graduate of Harvard and independently wealthy, he was very much at home among ambassadors and the upper strata of French society. Nevertheless, as a former newsman, he had many friends among the French and foreign media in Paris. Nick was unflappable under pressure. His normal speaking voice—somewhere between a mumble and a drawl—would sometimes become indecipherable in a crisis situation. I suspected that this was a protective gambit to give him more time to think. His deflating asides murmured during the boring perorations of colleagues made it difficult to keep a straight face. King was the perfect press attaché to work with Ambassador Bohlen. He and I operated smoothly together and perpetuated—when we could—the use of the Crillon bar as an embassy adjunct.

The autocratic wives of certain ambassadors and senior colleagues were sometimes the bane of Foreign Service life. These uncrowned "Queens of the Castle" or "Dragons" seemed to think the wives of lower ranking officers were in place to serve as their secondary servants. Some of these harridans expected the American wives to remain behind following a dinner party to help with the dishes even though their residences were fully staffed.

Early on in my career I had clashed with a senior officer's wife who had complained at the lack of a photographer at a meeting of the American Women's Club of Saigon. I'd explained that our photographer was covering a military operation in Tay Ninh Province and suggested she call a commercial photographer. Hours later I had a call from her husband. He was obviously telephoning on his wife's instructions. He hemmed, hawed, and wheedled to the point of embarrassment but was careful not to pull rank. The essence of his message was, "Won't you please try to send a photographer the next time." In deference to his discomfort, I promised to do what I could. I suspect a psychiatrist would find ample material for study in the fact that the husbands of these "Dragons" often proved to be comparatively weak men.

A minor incident during our 1965–67 tour in Paris showed the extent to which these ridiculous charades can develop. My wife received an invitation to an informal coffee morning at the ambassadorial residence to introduce the embassy wives to Mrs. Bohlen. The invitation, issued by a French woman employed as a social secretary, stated that hats and gloves would be worn. My wife had never worn a hat to a diplomatic function and, with my full backing, she wasn't about to start. Lee Brady's wife, Mary, was duly informed. Without batting an eye or attempting to influence Mary Alice, she passed the word to the social secretary. Thus, the secretary's choice was Mrs. Simpson without a hat (as most chic French women would appear at the time) or no Mrs. Simpson.

Mary Brady soon received a hurried call from the flustered social secretary. She obviously couldn't understand why my wife would not comply with the by-the-book requirements of protocol.

"Is it a question of money?" she asked.

"No," Mary Brady replied, "it's a question of principle." The ambassador's wife, learning of this minor skirmish in the protocol wars, made it clear that, as far as she was concerned, hat wearing was a matter of personal choice. My wife attended the function *sans chapeáu*, and *l'affaire Simpson* ended without further repercussions.

Despite the leadership of a professional ambassador and the company of competent colleagues, the embassy remained a foreign affairs behemoth. There were staff meetings on staff meetings and a seemingly endless flood of paperwork: drafts, revised drafts, clearances, memos, dispatches, field messages, telegrams, diplomatic notes, aide memoirs, and biographic sketches. I had recurrent fond memories of Marseille, but I knew that a return there was not in the cards.

Fortunately, a quiet family weekend at our rented apartment on the rue Vaugirard and walks through my old student stamping ground of Montparnasse cleared my mind of the embassy's bureaucratic tangles. Winter in the Jardin Luxembourg, particularly after a light snowfall, was a magic time. The trees and bushes seemed to belong in an Alsatian forest, tiny animals had left their tracks in the virgin snow, and the bronze statue of Balzac seemed to glower under its mantle of white. The windows of nearby cafés were impenetrably steamed, and the street lights, switched on early due to the winter darkness, were surrounded with glowing, frosty halos.

Time was passing quickly and I was approaching the end of my two-year tour when retired Colonel Lucien Barret, president of the National Federation of Sapeurs Combattants, or Combat Engineers, called on me in my office. Gray-haired, ramrod straight, and with a command voice that could shatter crystal, Barret had come to thank me for our assistance in facilitating contacts during a U.S. visit by members of his organization. Since his return, this former member of the Résistance had done some personal research, through embassy friends and some old Indochina contacts, into my brief military experience and early Foreign Service career. He'd found that I'd been trained as a combat engineer during World War II, that I'd served in three European campaigns, and that I'd spent some time as a war correspondent with French assault engineers during Operation Hautes Alpes on the Day River near Ninh Binh. All this, said the colonel, in addition to the help I'd provided to his organization, made me eligible for some form of recognition.

He then announced that his governing body had decided that, because of "services rendered and zeal for my arm [the combat engineers]," I should be awarded the rank of *officier* in the order Honneur et Fidélité of the French Combat Engineers.

Speechless for several seconds, I finally muttered something about my inability to accept foreign decorations. But the colonel had been thorough in his research. He assured me that accepting a decoration from a friendly foreign power or official organization was possible "with the permission of your commanding officer" or, in my case, the American ambassador.

Thus it was, in the spring of 1967 and with the approval of Ambassador Bohlen, that I traveled to the headquarters of the French Military Engineers at Angers to receive a medal from Colonel Barret followed by the traditional kiss on both cheeks before a convivial gathering of serving and retired officers. Wearing the small black, red-striped rosette of an *officier* in my lapel was a new experience, and it was interesting to see how a bit of colored cloth could arouse the interest and, in some cases, respect, of the man on the street. But, as much as I appreciated the honor, I had to be honest with myself. It wasn't the Medaille Militaire or the Legion d'Honneur, nor should it be. There was, however, a certain poetic justice in the award. After I had covered a number of military operations in Indochina, a French liaison officer had told me that I was being considered for a Croix de Guerre. Instead, the decoration went to an American correspondent who had covered the war from the Hanoi press camp, filling his copy with material from the official communiques of the French High Command.

Considering that Barret and some of his friends were fervent anti-Gaullists, I had a sneaking suspicion that, in addition to honoring me, they obtained considerable pleasure in presenting a military decoration to an American official during a rocky period of Franco-American relations. Regardless, I was grateful for their gesture, and unbeknownst to me at the time, that small rosette was to fit perfectly into the environment of my next assignment.

The official letter was waiting on a pile of papers in my "in" box. A cursory glance and the designation "Per" on the return address told me it was one of those periodic missives from the USIA Foreign Service personnel office that decided our posting for the next few years. I walked to the window, watched the speeding traffic on the Place de la Concorde for a few seconds, and ripped open the envelope. I was assigned as the USIA student to the School of Naval Warfare, for the academic year 1967–68 at the Naval War College (NWC) at Newport, Rhode Island. The next paragraph explained that the School of Naval Warfare was the navy's leading academic institution and that I'd be joining senior officers of all the services as well as those from State, CIA, DIA (Defense Intelligence Agency), and NSA (National Security Agency).

I was late for a meeting so I stuffed the letter in my pocket and hurried over to the main embassy building. I was cautiously elated but puzzled, my mind full of questions. When the meeting ended, I hurried to the press attaché's office in search of Nick King. He was a New Englander, perhaps he could enlighten me. Nick was standing near his desk when I rushed in, waving the letter.

"Do you have a map?" I demanded. "Where the hell is Newport, Rhode Island?" Drawing himself up to his full six-foot-plus, this worthy scion of the Kings of Newport—one of the first families of that historic town—eyed me with scorn and disbelief.

Finally, making allowances for the fact that I was only a westerner, he gave me a quick briefing on his birthplace. Later, a naval officer in the defense attaché's office congratulated me on my good fortune, ignoring his army colleague, who labeled the Naval War College a "country club."

A few days before our departure from Paris, a bulky manila envelope arrived by diplomatic pouch from Washington. It contained my Medal for Civilian Service in Vietnam, featuring an Annamite dragon coiled around a torch of freedom. Another mail-a-medal.

9

Escaping State

The destroyer heeled slightly to come on course, plunging into the summer swell. The tow aircraft was barely visible astern as it closed the distance on our ship. It was a perfect day. The sun shimmered on the surface of Rhode Island Sound and several inquisitive gulls were hovering overhead when general quarters sounded, summoning the crew to battle stations. I had joined a group of my war college classmates on the destroyer's afterdeck to watch a demonstration of antiaircraft firing.

It was only the first week of our course at the School of Naval Warfare, a week of orientation and getting to know the navy. The military and naval students would soon change from uniform to civilian attire for the duration of our studies. For the moment, their being in uniform was useful. It allowed us to read their service history and experience through their insignia and ribbons. We were still strangers and each service was hanging together in small groups. The civilian students, too few to form a group, were dispersed among their uniformed colleagues.

The destroyer lurched into the trough of a particularly large swell, and we grabbed for stanchions, lines, or the nearest solid metal for support. The tow plane was above our stern, the yellow target sleeve visible a safe distance in its wake. A flurry of bells and indecipherable commands over the loudspeakers, and the firing began. The rapid-fire guns thumped into action, jolting the deck with their hammer blows. Black puffs appeared high in the sky, trailing behind the target.

The racket continued for an overlong time, but the shell bursts appeared no closer to the target. A thin, tanned Marine colonel stood beside me, the Purple Heart among his decorations. He sighed, glanced up at the dirty smudges in the sky, glared at the naval gunners, and shook his head.

"They still can't hit their ass with a banjo!" he complained. "C'mon," he suggested, pointing belowdecks. "Let's get a cup of coffee."

My family and I had arrived in Newport, Rhode Island, on a quiet Sunday in the summer of 1967. It had been a headfirst plunge into New England Americana. Temporarily established in the Viking Hotel, we'd walked along the sun-dappled sidewalk of Bellevue Avenue and paused to inspect the newly washed fire engines parked at the open door of a red brick fire station. The lounging firemen had invited our daughters in for a closer inspection, lifting them into the high driver's seat and letting them try on the heavy fireman's helmets—a Norman Rockwell painting come to life.

In the days prior to enrolling at the war college I'd explored the historic streets of the city built on "slaves, rum, and molasses"—a city known for its early religious tolerance, where Quaker, Jew, and Christian lived side by side and worked together as merchant princes to bring prosperity to one of the leading colonial ports of the eastern seaboard.

I'd also paused before the statue of Lieutenant-Général Comte de Rochambeau overlooking Narragansett Bay. It was here on July 9, 1780, that Admiral de Ternay had landed Rochambeau and his 5,000 French regulars. These troops and their general, along with the young Lafayette, had participated in a number of battles beside George Washington's Continental Army, including the final victory over the English at Yorktown.

But more practical matters than those reflecting on Newport's history demanded my attention. We were lucky in finding "Eastcourt" on Bellevue Avenue, an 1880s villa near "The Elms," a 1901 mansion modeled after an 18th-century French chateau. Eastcourt had been built in "Carpenter Gothic" style. Normally we wouldn't have been able to afford Eastcourt, but many such homes remained empty during the winter. Dependable war college rentals at reduced rates kept money coming in for the owners and kept the premises occupied. Mary Alice placed the girls in a school with links to their previous institution in Paris, and I was able to concentrate on my studies.

The School of Naval Warfare is not—as some people believe—an institution limited to naval tactics, where students push tiny ships around on a flat surface, reliving the battles of Santiago or Jutland. It is, in fact, an intense course designed to expose senior officers to the history and contemporary trends in political-military matters and maritime strategy, international affairs, economics, international law, maritime history, physical sciences, and social and political philosophy.

This isn't to say that the navy didn't indulge in a little benevolent brainwashing. During our first weeks in Newport, we learned more about the historian and naval officer Alfred Thayer Mahan than we ever wanted to know or could absorb. This erudite president of the Naval War College in the late 1800s had influenced many statesmen and naval strategists, including Teddy Roosevelt, with his books on sea power and history. It was a bit difficult, however, to convince an infantry colonel newly returned from Vietnam that control of the seas would have much affect on the North's infiltration of the South.

The courses, taught by civilian professors and qualified officers, equaled 15 semester hours toward a masters degree in international affairs, and an intensified program run by the George Washington University Center at the war college allowed enrolled students to obtain their M.A. degrees upon graduation. In addition, a succession of eminent lecturers, some opposed to U.S. policy, occupied the podium and later submitted to a drumfire of questions from their audience.

The more we got into the course, the more we enjoyed these sessions. They allowed us—captains, commanders, colonels, and civilian officers—to throw questions at admirals, generals, ambassadors, high administration officials, pundits, politicians, and scholars while under temporary protective cover as students. Some of us took full advantage of this new status, rising to state our name, arm, or agency and playing to our audience of fellow students. What could have bordered on insubordination in other circumstances was now forgiven as participation in the search for knowledge and truth.

At one point I rose to ask the army chief of staff, General Harold K. Johnson, about the effectiveness of the long-range patrols then operating along the Laotian border. A press dispatch a few days earlier had moved that classified operation into the public domain. Momentarily taken aback, the general asked whether the hall was completely secure before responding. Later, a war college staffer suggested I had pushed things a bit close to the line. "Open to questions," I'd reminded him, "means just that."

I found those months as a late-blooming student fascinating. One of the reasons for seeding civilian officials into the war college was to expose us to the military and to their methods and thinking. It was a two-way street that allowed officers of the services to mix professionally and socially with State Department, USIA, and CIA representatives. They discovered that labeling Foreign Service officers as "cookie pushers" perpetuated a myth, and we soon understood that a tough Marine "burrhead" could be well read and could seriously engage in the study of international affairs. I looked forward to prelunch drinks at the officer's club, where we could compare notes on the morning's study session and carry out ruthless critiques of our professors.

Christmas in Newport resembled one of those clichéd seasonal cards full of snow, candlelight, and holly that I used to wonder at in sunny California. The snow scrunched underfoot, the air was pure and crisp, and the pitch pine logs in the fireplace sizzled and spit. Membership in the 18th-century, Palladian style Redwood Library and time spent in its cozy reading room allowed us to feel a part of Newport and its history. Later I'd stand, swinging my arms on an icy dock, waiting for the snow-mantled fishing boats to make fast before selecting some live chicken lobsters for the Christmas pot.

Once the holidays were over, the Class of '68 returned to its studies with added vigor. We were all tasked to deliver a thesis or research paper before the end of our term, and participation in various study projects kept us busy. The NWC was proving to be far from a "country club."

On January 30–31, 1968, the entire college—and the country—received a sudden shock. The North Vietnamese and the National Liberation Front (VC) had launched their Tet offensive. The first reports were sketchy, but it was soon obvious that a major Communist effort against most of South Vietnam's major cities and towns was under way.

I recall walking into the war college canteen the morning after the news reached us. The normally noisy atmosphere had become silent except for the sound of transistor radios as students and faculty listened to the latest news reports. Many of these officers had recently left Vietnam or were due to go there after their time in Newport. Most had friends or acquaintances on the spot.

The North Vietnamese Army (NVA) was pressuring the Marine base at Khe Sanh, the enemy was inside the city of Hue, and there was fighting around the U.S. embassy in Saigon. I wondered how Barry Zorthian and his JUSPAO crew were faring. A faint touch of the "fire horse" syndrome had me wishing I was there. At the same time I realized how lucky I was to be in Newport. There was a lot of swearing that morning as more disastrous news arrived. The cursing was neither loud nor bombastic. It was the quiet, personal expression of frustration and regret.

The first days of the Tet offensive produced considerable anger among my fellow students. Some of this anger was directed at the enemy, but a portion of this largely unspoken wrath was reserved for the faceless officials in McNamara's Pentagon and the more identifiable top brass—those professional optimists who had been speaking of a light at the end of the tunnel and a war as good as won, right up to the moment the first VC sapper's charge exploded in the grounds of the Saigon embassy.

Over the following weeks, the updated news from Vietnam produced a veiled division in the ranks of faculty and students alike. The Johnson administration and General Westmoreland's headquarters in Saigon were rushing out the news that the NVA and the VC had been badly damaged during the heavy fighting. The high casualties suffered by the VC were said to have wiped out whole units that had been in action since the start of the war. Much of this proved to be true. But, such was our cynicism that many of us suspected that it was an attempt to fuzz the hard fact that we'd been caught criminally unprepared for the Tet offensive. This too was largely true. Thus, some of us considered the Tet offensive a tactical victory for the United States and others saw it as a disaster in psychological terms, particularly regarding public trust in the administration and the military. My experience in Vietnam and shock at our unpreparedness for Tet put me firmly in the latter camp.

The whole episode left us all in a serious, pensive mood. It was in this environment that I pulled together the elements of my research paper, "The Guerrilla and His World: The Psychological Aspects of Guerrilla Warfare." It was my first experience with this form of writing, and I soon discovered that producing novels did not necessarily prepare one for extensive research. Fortunately, the college library was a goldmine of material, and my bibliography was soon growing.

But we weren't allowed to spend every day buried in the book stacks.

A field trip took us to Quantico, Virginia, where the Marines put on an impressive live-fire demonstration, proving that a combat commander's hoarse voice was still an effective communications tool. One morning we boarded a submarine and quickly found that the order "Dive! Dive! Dive!" meant just that. When the submarine went bow-down, some of us ended up in an undignified tangle at the base of the periscope.

But it was not all studies and gung ho games. Every class at the war college, including the 18 visiting foreign officers in the Naval Command Course, had to experience a New England clambake. I am not sure how the officers from Thailand, Venezuela, Germany, Brazil, and other nations really reacted to this traditional seaside event. As a San Franciscan, my own taste for shore eating ran to the tasty Italian fisherman's stew, *cioppino*, dungeness crabs with homemade mayonnaise, and well-purged clams steamed in white wine and garlic, all consumed with crisp-crusted sourdough French bread and chilled Chablis in a comfortable, sheltered spot.

Our long-heralded clambake took place on a bare, windswept beach under a gray New England sky. The smoke rose in billows from the sand pit where the seaweed-covered crabs, chickens, potatoes, sausages, and clams were cooking. We clutched our cold cans of beer, our backs to the wind, and made conversation. When the feast was served, we found that the chicken tasted like clams and the clams like sausages. All the ingredients had one thing in common. They were liberally sprinkled with gritty sand. It was definitely a unique experience, and one I have not repeated.

My research paper was finally finished. I had covered the guerrilla fighter as an individual, the importance of environment, the role of the political officer, guerrilla morale, the importance of the outside world, and targeting the enemy. A substantial section on terrorism covered terror and its effect, reactions to terrorism, selective terrorism, the individual terrorist, and counterterrorism. It was followed by the role of the counterguerrilla, the patience factor, American attitudes, and the misleading lessons of counterinsurgency in Malaysia, where success often ignored the fact that the majority of rebels were ethnic Chinese and not Malayan Communists. I had closed with a look to the future to include the urban guerrilla and coastal, delta, and riverine war.

Shortly after handing in the paper, I was approached by Colonel W. F. Long, the army adviser to the college, who suggested I might consider staying on in Newport as a member of the faculty. This possibility hadn't even occurred to me, but it had its appeal. The tall, avuncular Colonel Long, an infantryman who had done his time in Asia, was a doer. Within weeks the college president, the secretary of the navy, and the director of USIA had agreed to my remaining at the NWC as faculty adviser and consultant to the president. Long suggested that I put together two proposals outlining courses I could teach during the 1968–69 academic year. This was definitely unmapped territory for a man lacking even a B.A. degree.

In the rush toward the end of term, I was informally notified that my research paper had been rated "outstanding" and that I had been selected as a "distinguished graduate of the School of Naval Warfare." Admiral John T. Hayward, president of the NWC, wrote to the director of USIA to express his delight at having me on his faculty and commented, "In the navy he would be prime material for flag rank." For someone who had been rejected by the Marine Corps in 1942 for color blindness and was prone to seasickness in rough weather, this was high praise indeed.

Moving into my new office across the hall from the president, I thought of my Uncle Theodore and wondered what that old "man o' warsman" would have thought of it all. He'd sailed with the Great White Fleet, fought at Manila Bay, run a waterfront "tavern" in Cavite, and bombarded Naval Intelligence in the 1930s with letters warning of Japanese plans to use "exit planes" and "small submarines" for suicide attacks on capital ships in the "coming war." Fortunately, he died in 1939 and was spared the sight of "exit planes" in the form of kamikaze attackers wreaking such havoc on his beloved navy.

Rank or a title in the Foreign Service does have its privileges, but it does not have the same day-to-day actuality and utility as military rank. I learned early on that Foreign Service officers were entitled to equivalent military ranks. Discharged from the Air Force Hospital at Clark Field in the Philippines in 1955, I'd had to spend two days in the BOQ on the base before returning to Saigon. The helpful staff sergeant checking me in had referred to his equivalent rank sheet and informed me I'd be roomed as a captain. In that particular instance there wasn't much difference between a lieutenant's bunk and a captain's cot, but it was a lesson to be remembered.

In the summer of 1968, returning to Newport from leave in California, my navy flight was forced to land in the Midwest because of bad weather. I soon found myself checking into another BOQ. This time equivalent rank paid off. I occupied the quarters of a rear admiral (lower half) or a Marine brigadier general, complete with air conditioning and a well-stocked fridge. I underline these experiences, because many Foreign Service officers still appear unaware of their military equivalency status. In a profession where the perks are constantly diminishing, this is one that should be utilized.

My advisory and teaching role at the NWC was a completely new experience and one I thoroughly enjoyed. I taught two courses: the first, "The Psychological Aspects of Guerrilla Warfare" was based on my research paper. "The French Experience in Indochina" was the second. Both courses drew a respectable number of students, but the latter was, by far, the most popular. As I explained in the course description, it would be "a study of the Franco-Vietminh War, with emphasis on the political, psychological, and military aspects of the conflict and their effect on Vietnam, Laos, and Cambodia today."

Many American officers had not had time to study the contemporary history of Vietnam. Some were aware of the French defeat at Dien Bien Phu and had read Bernard Fall's books on Indochina, but few had a detailed knowledge of the French war and the early U.S. involvement in that conflict. An extensive reading list and lectures detailing the various campaigns of that war, the clash of guerrilla and conventional tactics, the psychological outlook of the opposing forces, and the lasting effect the struggle had on the armies involved was designed to provide a basic understanding that I hoped would be timely and useful.

I was fortunate in having Colonel W. S. Hathaway as a backup in both of these courses. An army battalion commander with the 1st Infantry Division in Vietnam in 1966, Hathaway had refused to use artillery and air on a Vietnamese village he knew to be filled with civilians. He and I had been classmates in the School of Naval Warfare, and we formed a good working team.

We operated in a relaxed academic atmosphere to say the least. Where else could a lecturer puff on a cigar while wielding a pointer indicating Lai Chau or Nam Dinh on a wall map? Where else could a "professor" join with "pupils," who had also experienced Vietnam, over a few jolts of the hard stuff after class?

Despite this surface ease, we were dealing with serious subject matter important to all of us. One afternoon, as I discussed a Vietminh ambush of a French road convoy, I'd been interrupted by a Marine colonel.

"Excuse me," he'd said, "but where exactly did that take place?" When I told him, he'd shaken his head.

"Son of a bitch," he'd murmured, "they did the same thing to us at almost the same spot!" We were dealing in living history.

There were other duties for the USIA adviser to perform. I assisted with the college's public affairs seminars, lectured to the School of Naval Command and Staff, took part in the ten-day counterinsurgency study, and acted as a thesis adviser to six students going for their M.A. degrees in the George Washington University program. I was also asked to assist in the presentation of a wargame in the War Gaming Center.

This latter project had to do with the hypothetical rescue of an elected chief of state from coup plotters in a West African nation. The rescue was to be carried out by a U.S. Navy Task Force. Because of my familiarity with West Africa and firsthand knowledge of coups, I was given carte blanche to insert any reasonable scenario, when I thought it timely, into the wargaming computer.

The day of the game, I spent the morning as an observer, watching the earnest young officers entering their jargon-filled scenarios, heavy with detailed planning and by-the-book procedures. So far, all had gone well, and the operation had a clockwork quality that only orderly minds could conceive.

By mid-afternoon I was ready, and in went my imaginary contribution. An urgent message I'd drafted was received by the task force commander from the Marine officer in command of the landing party. The prime minister of the country in question was holed up, drunk, in his villa and refused to leave without his three mistresses. In addition, he intended to leave his wife behind. The appearance of that message created a momentary silence. The mouths of both faculty and students dropped open. The task force commander was now struggling with a *real* problem.

It was to the credit of the student gamers that they recovered quickly and entered into the spirit of the thing. They soon had the U.S. chargé d'affaires distracting the prime minister with a number of Jack Daniels' toasts to his nation and his beneficent rule. Meanwhile, the Marines, using a two-chopper lift, had ferried the wife and "secretaries" out to separate ships of the task force. The prime minister followed in a very happy state, falling asleep before a chopper delivered him to the flagship.

Later, during the postoperation critique, I assured the gamers that my submission was not a far-out attempt to add spice to the proceedings. It was, I explained, the kind of thing that could easily happen under such circumstances, and they should damn well be prepared to handle it. The new president of the Naval War College, Admiral Richard D. Colbert, thanked me for my "realistic" contribution to the wargame.

My research paper had been published in the Naval Institute *Proceedings* and the Naval War College *Review*. The State Department's Foreign Service Institute was using it as a training aid in its Vietnam orientation program. A few personal letters from military officers and civilian officials involved in counterinsurgency informally welcomed me into their circle of "experts."

But time was passing fast. I had been in harness long enough to know that such minor notoriety would fade and that the glowing accounts of one's performance submitted by outsiders would soon be buried in an overstuffed personnel file in a barlock cabinet. Although I had begun to badger the agency about an ongoing assignment, I did want to leave my mark in some way at the Naval War College. The most practical and sensible way to do this was to ensure that the advisory slot I'd occupied would be maintained by USIA in the future. Admiral Colbert and his staff, with the concurrence of the Navy Department, were all for it. Alas, Frank Shakespeare, the Director of USIA, signed a letter—undoubtedly prepared by his personnel office—asking for a delay in decision time because of an officer shortage. A short time thereafter, CIA filled the vacancy.

I did leave a small token of my passage through Newport. For several weeks after I'd begun my studies, I'd been constantly troubled by the small wine glasses in the dining room of the officer's club. They were slightly bigger than a sherry glass. This might have been acceptable if the manager had stocked his cellar with rotgut. To his credit, this was not the case. To see a robust Chateauneuf-de-Pape or fine Bordeaux being poured into these tiny glasses, unable to breathe, with their aroma stifled, was indeed painful. Over a short period of time, with the help of my classmates, innumerable complaints, and demands for water glasses, we prevailed on the manager. The small glasses disappeared, and a selection of capacious globes soon treated the wine with the respect it deserved.

The fatal phone call finally came. After 15 years of overseas assignments I was ordered to do my time in Washington, D.C. The argument that I'd just spent two years in the United States during my Newport duty cut no ice. USIA wanted me in Washington—period. Most Foreign Service officers spent a few years in the nation's capital after two or three foreign assignments. It was considered necessary to recharge your professional engine at the source, widen your understanding of the home base, and re-Americanize yourself. It was also seen as a smart career move. Some of my colleagues looked forward to their Washington tours. They settled in, obtained a mortgage, bought a house in suburbia, and became commuters, reading the *Washington Post* on the bus trip in and dozing on the bus trip home.

I had an altogether different outlook. I'd joined the Foreign Service to do just that—serve overseas—and not vegetate in a company town filled with bureaucrats. But duty called. Dan Oleksiw, USIA's assistant director for the East Asia and Pacific Area informed me that I was being assigned as the deputy director of the State Department's East Asia/Pacific Bureau of Public Affairs. I'd be working for Paul Neilson, a senior USIA officer I'd known for years. Oleksiw suggested that it was a choice assignment. I knew that the EA/P Bureau supplied the secretary of state and the department's spokesman with daily briefing papers and background on subject matter of media interest in the East Asia and Pacific region. I also knew that Vietnam dominated the majority of the department's press briefings.

Moving to Washington in the summer allowed us time to settle in before I had to report for duty. We rented a small house on Klingle Street in Wesley Heights, and the children were once again inserted into new schools and an unfamiliar environment. Klingle Street ran through an attractive wooded neighborhood with a skittering, inquisitive squirrel population. Good friends and colleagues lived nearby, and a brisk morning walk would bring me to a bus that deposited me near the State Department. Mary Alice, who had previously worked on Capitol Hill and who liked Washington, quickly felt at home, as did the children. I was the problem.

My first official act was to inform Dan Oleksiw that I'd be willing to consider any overseas assignment, anywhere in his area, with the exception of Vietnam, that might suddenly become available. It was not the best way to approach a new job, but he duly noted my request.

The next few months justified my negative approach to Washington. I spent long hours churning out or editing bureaucratic babble. Much of it had to do with Vietnam and our policy there. It seemed that every other day produced a crisis, and we worked on hard deadlines as the clock moved closer to briefing time. The lights in EA/P burned late, well after the other bureaus had shut down. My distaste for the bureaucracy at State was palpable. Some of the diplomatic mandarins in the upper strata still did not grasp the importance of "public diplomacy." In other words, they had not understood how a badly prepared, delayed response to a legitimate media query or a clumsy coverup could torpedo official policy or leave them with egg on their faces. This was part of the battle we were fighting in EA/P, and we often lost.

One day, boarding an elevator on the way to my office, I came face to face with my old nemesis, the acerbic pundit Joseph Alsop. Joe and I had known each other since Indochina in the 1950s, when the French were giving him VIP treatment as a visiting correspondent. In Saigon he had once demanded that I supply him with a car and driver so he could file his copy. Instead, I had suggested that he hire a taxi. That affront to his *amour-propre* had never been forgiven. Now, it appeared, he had another bee in his bonnet.

"What are you doing here?" he demanded.

"Working in EA/P," I told him.

"You belong in Vietnam," he snapped. "They need people like you out there."

"Joe," I said, shaking my head, "I've done my time."

"We'll see about that," he mumbled as I got out on my floor, intimating that his influence in high government circles was undiminished. But my disenchantment with Washington did not go so far as another tour in Vietnam. Regardless, I heard no more from Mr. Alsop.

Approximately four months after arriving in Washington, I had a call from Dan Oleksiw. He had an urgent matter to discuss. We met over lunch and he laid it on the line. Would I be willing to take over as counselor for public affairs at the American embassy in Canberra, Australia?

"How soon?" I wanted to know.

"Soonest," he told me. A newly appointed noncareer ambassador was due to leave for Canberra within two weeks, and I was to be on the ground when he arrived. The family would have to follow. I had 48 hours to decide.

I met Mary Alice for lunch to tell her the good news. She was not overly enthusiastic and suggested that we have a family meeting. Later, we all gathered in the small library of our rented house. With a world atlas by my side I announced that Daddy had been offered a job "down under" and, in all probability, we would soon be leaving Washington.

Never had I read the desires and hopes of my family so badly. Within seconds Shawn (14), Lisa (11), Kate (6), and Maggie (5) were in tears, and I felt like a confused but obvious villain. If I'd paused to think before blundering ahead, I might have been prepared for their reaction. They had just been uprooted and moved from Newport to Washington, D.C. They had settled once again into a new, temporary home, been enrolled in a new school, and—most important of all—made new friends. Apart from their evacuation from Vietnam, they had been accustomed to at least a two year stay in any one overseas location. Without warning I'd now disturbed that cycle after only four months.

I have never ceased to wonder at the resiliency of women no matter what their age. Within two hours of our crisis, Shawn was scanning a map of Australia and Kate was asking me about kangaroos. Later, over a quiet drink, Mary Alice informed me that, if she had to go to Australia, she and the girls would be traveling by ship. It wasn't an ultimatum, just a statement of fact. It seemed that I was the only family member still affected by the previous, dramatic outpouring of tears.

Those fleeting four months in State proved to be the only Washington assignment of my entire career.

10

The Outback and the Papua Payback

There it was in black and white. The Australian Department of External Affairs had published its 1970 diplomatic list cataloging the staff of each foreign embassy in Canberra in order of diplomatic precedence. I was listed as number five among the ambassador and 21 American officers. But a slight error had been made. Rather than presenting me as the counselor for public affairs, I was identified as the counselor for *pubic* affairs.

Colonel John Newman, the defense attaché, had tipped me off. He'd called to suggest that I take a close look at the diplomatic list. I bellowed with laughter on seeing the typo. A short time later, the Department of External Affairs was on the line. A hesitant official, assured that I was Mr. Simpson, extended the apologies of the department and ruefully explained that it would take some time to insert a correction page. I accepted his apologies and requested that he supply me with five extra copies. For several weeks, my entry into diplomatic receptions or official functions produced guarded smiles and a murmur of comment. It was the only amusing happening I'd encountered since landing in Australia.

I'd arrived alone at Canberra in late 1969 after the long trans-Pacific flight via Hawaii. Despite an overnight in Honolulu, I had been jet-lagged on arrival in Sydney. A subsequent flight in a turboprop through the turbulent skies over New South Wales had raised havoc with my stomach. The landscape we'd skimmed reminded me of the hills and trees in the children's book *Millions of Cats*. Canberra airport was in the process of graduating from a semisophisticated "bush strip" to the status of an international airport. The Australian sun was high, bright, and invasive. The sticky, ubiquitous flies bid me welcome. But these first impressions had been fleeting. What I'd needed was a bed and some solid hours of sleep. Bill Dietz, the cultural attaché and my second, deposited me at an empty government-leased house on residential Mugga Way, and I promptly crawled between the sheets.

The American embassy in Canberra, a red brick, colonial-style building that wouldn't be out of place in Williamsburg, Virginia, sat on the high ground looking out on Capital Hill and the blue waters of Lake Burley Griffin. A Marine guard checked my credentials and directed me to my office. I found it, left my briefcase there, and went upstairs to meet the ambassador.

Ambassador Walter L. Rice was an elderly political appointee and former businessman who worshipped President Nixon. A photograph of the president was placed on the mantlepiece of the ambassador's office. The proximity of candlesticks suggested an informal shrine. Ambassador Rice was new to the world of diplomacy and had a limited view of international politics. Nevertheless, he was basically a kind man who was determined to do his best in an unfamiliar job. I was not sure he knew exactly what my embassy function was during our first meeting, but he did seem disappointed when he discovered I was not a golfer. I explained that I would be acting as the embassy spokesman as well as the chief of the USIA operation in Australia. Unfortunately, I was soon intensely occupied with the former function.

The telephone rang early in the morning as I was preparing a solitary breakfast. An Australian newsman greeted me with the customary "G'day." He'd been put onto me by the embassy duty officer, and he wanted a statement about "the drugs case." My silence amply demonstrated that I was not going to be a great source of information. He elaborated, hoping to squeeze some copy out of me.

"The son of one of your diplomats," he explained. "The coppers have picked him up. Dealing in cannabis, or such like. What's the embassy say about that?"

"I can't comment until I have more facts. Give me some time. Call me later at my office."

"Right, mate. But I've got a bloody deadline. Oh, welcome to Australia!"

The next 48 hours were pure hell as I scrambled for information, convinced the ambassador that we should be as outgoing as possible with the Australian media, and fielded a constant barrage of queries. Customs had found cannabis in a bongo drum belonging to the son of our newly arrived deputy chief of mission (DCM). Welcome to the 1970s!

The Australian tabloids were having a field day, particularly since the Nixon administration was taking such a hard line on drugs. The more extreme journals were attempting to paint this minor drug seizure as the tip of a decadent iceberg, the discovery of a major American move to corrupt Australia's youth using the cover of diplomatic immunity.

I quickly learned that such terms as "off the record," "background only," and "not for attribution" were useless down under. Some Aussie journalists went for the jugular and woe to any official who didn't protect himself. Telephone interviews were a particular danger. Radio journalists might well forget to inform you that your conversation was being recorded. One protective measure was to invite newsmen or women to my office at the embassy. A face-to-face discussion was much more satisfactory than an impersonal phone call. It forced the questioner to "break cover" and established a direct relationship. Despite the ambassador's misgivings (he was obviously worried about how the White House might react), our full-disclosure tactics paid off.

When the dust finally settled and the unfortunate DCM and his family had left the country, I realized that this particular dark cloud had a streak of silver lining. Within a period of one week I had gained a working knowledge of the Australian media and made contact with a number of its representatives that otherwise would have taken months. I also guessed—correctly—that some of those contacts would become good friends.

Canberra was a beautiful city, with wide avenues, broad lawns, and planted parkland shaded by oaks, elms, poplars, and tall gum trees. My temporary housing on Mugga Way was not far from the bushland. A short walk would take me to a vista of rolling hills. Black-faced sheep grazed tranquilly, while passing clouds threw fleeting shadows over the grass. Flights of parrotlike, rose-breasted galahs—a bird the Australians consider useless, noisy, and "as silly as a square wheel"—swooped overhead. At sunup the blue-winged kookaburra's call sounded like a madman's laughter. The sunsets were filled with streaks of molten gold against ominous curtains of dark cloud stretching to infinity.

Mary Alice and the children arrived in Sydney aboard the liner *President Wilson,* and I took the pilot boat out to greet them. Later, during a dockside wait for baggage, the girls cooled off by eating some ice cream from a portable cart. We returned to Canberra and within 24 hours six-year-old Kate was seriously ill. Isolated in a hospital ward, she underwent a number of tests while a young specialist in internal medicine attempted to identify the responsible virus. For the next few days it was touch and go as Kate was wracked by high fever and recurrent diarrhea. Her weight loss was horrific. We'd never been so frightened in our lives. Finally, backed by a Sydney laboratory specializing in tropical medicine, the doctor found the culprit. It was a rare strain of dysentery that had affected GIs in the South Pacific during World War II. We'd almost lost Kate, but antibiotics and the proper treatment soon had her out of the hospital and recovering, reveling in the doctor's pet sobriquet for her of "sausage."

The ordeal of Kate's illness was matched by another negative experience at roughly the same time. A White House advance team descended on us to prepare a visit to Australia by Vice President Spiro Agnew. The objective of this visitation was to underline Australian-American friendship and cooperation in Asia and the Pacific. No small part of this gesture was a show of gratitude for Australian government support for our policy in South Vietnam. The Aussies had sent military advisers to Vietnam in 1962. By 1969 there were close to 8,000 Australian fighting men in-country.

In all my experiences with advance teams, this was to be the most difficult. Although some of these officials did their job properly, a few others were pompous, difficult, insensitive, and rude. They seemed to revel in their lack of knowledge about Australia, Australian-American relations, or the function of an embassy. Their prime interest lay with Spiro Agnew, his political future, and their role therein. Their horizons were limited to the banks of the Potomac, American public opinion, and the next political convention.

One of their top men, undoubtedly out to make a name for himself and using the symbol of the White House as a club, treated the entire embassy staff—including the ambassador—with contempt. This attitude was quickly recognized by the Australian officials with whom we worked. They let it be known that they would take no "bloody guff" from these visitors, White House or no White House.

This simmering diplomatic crisis came to a head during a joint U.S.–Australian meeting. The obnoxious advance team honcho announced without warning and with no prior consultation with me that there would be room only for the accompanying White House press corps when the vice president laid a wreath at the Australian War Memorial. The thought that a jumped-up American political appointee was telling the Australians that they wouldn't be allowed to enter their own war memorial was so preposterous it was almost laughable. But no one was laughing.

The Australians exploded, and the meeting came to an abrupt halt. For a few minutes physical violence was an outside possibility. It was now time for the embassy fence-mending brigade to go to work. An equal number of Australian and American journalists were finally permitted to attend the ceremony, but the resentment remained. I am not sure whether the vice president ever knew how close his crew had come to creating a public international incident and negating the entire purpose of his visit. I do know that all of us on the ground breathed a deep sigh of relief when the entire Agnew entourage was airborne and homeward bound.

In addition to Bill Dietz and myself in Canberra, our small operation in Australia included one-man branch posts at the consulates in Sydney, Melbourne, and Perth. I thus had carte blanche to travel to those centers as well as other destinations in what Australians call their "Big Country."

In many ways Australia had a "last frontier" quality to it. The "bush" began on the outskirts of Australian cities. The small bush towns and scattered sheep stations had the somnolent appearance of semiabandoned settlements in the American West. That was until the bars opened and filled. Most of these hop-impregnated outposts of the Aussie beer culture, with their sagging corrugated iron roofs and tiled walls, were the last outposts of macho man. Few "sheilas" (women) braved the swinging doors.

On my first official visit to Sydney I took some time to explore the city on my own. Dropping into a watering hole not far from the waterfront for a beer and some shade, I was introduced to the Aussie bar game of "fall down." I'd no sooner taken my first sip of the tooth-chilling lager when five laughing men at the far end of the bar fell to the floor in a tangle of arms and legs.

A broken-nosed, freckled good samaritan, spotting me as an outsider, beckoned me away from the bar. He explained that, unless I wanted to play fall down, it was better to stand in the center of the room. The game, he told me, was basically simple. One man or a team of two would decide to fall against drinkers to their right or left. Their victims would then become players and be obliged to go with the flow, tumbling to the floor with the instigators. The secret was to catch the others unaware so that they spill their brew. I suggested that broken glass could make the game dangerous. My interlocutor shrugged and classified the participants disdainfully as *nongs* before wiggling his empty lager glass. "Your shout, mate," he announced, claiming recompense for his short briefing.

But I had more pressing concerns than deciphering why grown men enjoyed beery pileups on unswept barroom floors. A telephone call from Tran Kim Phuong, the ambassador of South Vietnam, reminded me that his country was still fighting for its life. I had known Ambassador Phuong in 1965 when he was an official at the ministry of foreign affairs in Saigon. Now he was asking for my help in countering pro-VC propaganda in Australia and obtaining publications and printed matter to support his nation's cause. I promised to do what I could, but I knew that material produced by the U.S. government and distributed by his embassy in Australia would only confirm suspicions that the South Vietnamese were our puppets. Having been wrong-footed and hoodwinked often enough by some of our Vietnamese allies during my time in the prime minister's office in Saigon, I knew this was hardly true. But, in the cut and thrust of international propaganda, appearances were everything.

Phuong's call did underline Australian concern over Vietnam. Despite Australia's pride in its fighting traditions, as exemplified by the military trappings of the annual ANZAC Day, participation in the Vietnam War had become even less popular among the public than it was in the United States. Antiwar spokesmen were comparing Australia's past sacrifices in "Britain's wars" to its "subservient" role in supporting U.S. policy designs in Southeast Asia.

Delegations were calling regularly at the embassy to deliver petitions filled with signatures demanding an end to U.S. involvement in Indochina. The relatively small Communist party was active behind the scenes in organizing antiwar demonstrations and encouraging nonparty efforts from fringe groups. The My Lai massacre and the Kent State shootings had supplied abundant visual aides for the protesters' placards. Many members of the influential Labor Party were against Australian participation in Vietnam and argued forcefully in parliament for a withdrawal of their troops.

The agency was supplying us with material in support of our Vietnam policy for placement with the Australian media. Unfortunately, some of it was lightweight propaganda, churned out by government wordsmiths with little or no knowledge of Vietnam. It would have been an insult to the intelligence of any professional journalist to have passed it on. Instead, I found that straight facts and figures from our wireless file and reprint rights to well-reasoned, balanced articles from American publications were more effective even if the authors did not entirely agree with the administration's views.

I was particularly surprised to learn how little the widespread killings in Hue by the VC and NVA at the time of the Tet offensive had impressed so-called thinking Australians. Close to 3,000 Vietnamese in Hue who had been connected to the South Vietnamese government or had been known to be sympathetic to the Saigon regime had been shot, buried alive, or beheaded. This slaughter had been attested to by neutral observers, but many non-Communist protesters visiting the embassy dismissed the facts as U.S. propaganda.

My role as a lecturer at the Naval War College caught up with me in Canberra, and I was asked to lecture on the subjects I'd taught in Newport before the senior officers at the Australian Joint Services College. A brigadier at the college suggested that I visit the Australian contingent in Vietnam, but I told him such a trip was impossible. How wrong I was.

Mary Alice and I had leased an airy, rambling, one-story home on Dominion Circuit, closer to the embassy. But distancing ourselves from the bushland didn't mean we'd left Australia's wildlife behind. We were soon invaded by a possum. It foraged in the attic and used the inner walls as runways. Our unwanted marsupial visitor had an eerie habit of pushing a sliding door shut each time it was left open.

The local SPCA loaned me some nonlethal traps that I baited with banana and placed in the attic. A successful trapping was signaled by an overhead banging. I climbed into the attic expecting to find a frightened, docile animal. Instead, a beady-eyed, hissing, razor-toothed possum launched itself at me with such force that it overturned the metal trap. I recoiled quickly, cutting my head on a roofing beam. The possum was duly turned over to the SPCA, driven out to the bush, and released. For ten days the sliding door stayed open. On the 11th day, at breakfast, the door slowly shut. Our lodger had returned.

Sitting in my ground floor office one morning, I heard a loud crash and the sound of shattering glass. Ever alert to terrorist action or violent demonstrations, I rushed toward the embassy coffee shop that seemed to be the source of the racket. A Marine guard was there ahead of me, hand on his holster. Two secretaries were sheltering behind some tables, a large barred window had been smashed, and there was frantic movement outside. A wandering wallaby had panicked in the parking lot and attempted to escape a moving automobile by jumping through the coffee shop window. Badly cut, it was now struggling to escape. I followed the Marine outside just in time to see the wallaby bouncing its way down the hill in the direction of the South African embassy.

Nature in Australia could be amusing and colorful. But it could also be unforgiving. A blue, tranquil sky could suddenly fill with menacing clouds and flashing lightning. Not too long after our arrival, a number of motorists were drowned in a residential area of Canberra by a flash flood. A bush fire crackling through a sun-dried forest could devastate many miles of territory, leaving the charcoaled remains of kangaroo, wallaby, and koala in its path. Occasionally, humans who took the wrong turn or were careless met the same fate.

Australia was still a distant land for many travelers and we did not have too many visitors. Those who did come to Canberra were usually there for a short stay, preferring to spend more time in Sydney, Melbourne, or Perth. James Michener was one who passed through the capital, gathering material to update his files on Australia. After helping him with some press and government contacts, we invited the dour Michener and his charming wife to have dinner with us. Mary Alice had made a special effort, and the dinner was particularly tasty, drawing praise from Mrs. Michener. The famous author remained silent. The next day I hosted a small, stag press luncheon for Michener at our house. The food had been prepared by my wife, but she did not join us at the table. She did emerge to say goodbye to my guests as they departed. At this point Michener spoke up.

"My wife tells me," he said, "that we had a very good dinner here last night."

Needless to say, it was a comment that Mary Alice did not forget—or forgive.

The Friday luncheons of the press club in Canberra were very special occasions and often an unexpected ordeal for the international and national newsmakers invited to appear as guest speakers. The boisterous members did not hesitate to ask indiscreet or downright hostile questions. Fueled by strong Australian lager as an apéritif and constantly replenished bottles of red and white wine from the best

Australian vineyards with their meal, the media bloodhounds gave many a visitor a rough time. This was particularly true when they scented phoniness or pretension. The well-known novelist and lecturer Han Suyin, repeating her anti-Western platitudes and denigrating the U.S.–Australian effort in Vietnam, had come under particularly heavy fire. It was not that the newsmen approved of their government's role in Vietnam. It was the fact that they recognized blatant propaganda when they heard it. One could not deny Han Suyin's courage in facing such an audience, but you had to question her judgment.

The territory of Papua New Guinea, just to the northeast of Australia, came within the scope of our diplomatic responsibility. But, aside from leader grants, educational exchanges, and limited media contacts in Port Moresby, the territory's primitive remoteness and lack of a communications infrastructure made it an unlikely area for USIS activities. Nevertheless, in five years this land, richly endowed with natural resources and occupying a strategic location in the South Pacific, was due to pass from a UN trusteeship administered by Australia to full independence. For this reason alone it was essential that I visit Papua New Guinea to get a feel for the territory and make preliminary recommendations on the eventual establishment of a USIS operation there.

The Australian government had not been particularly enthusiastic about my proposed visit. They wanted considerable advance notice and details of my prospective itinerary and activities. I suspected that this was largely due to the sensitivities of the Australian Security Intelligence Organization (ASIO) regarding the growing pains of their soon-to-be independent territory. A quick call on my counterpart in the Australian Information Service helped convince the antipodean spooks that my intentions were honorable.

Nothing can prepare the uninitiated for exposure to Papua New Guinea. A flight of approximately 2,000 miles with a stop at Brisbane put me down at Port Moresby airfield. The territorial capital had a certain ramshackle charm, with its residential neighborhoods of stilted homes screened by generous tropical growth. The downtown area's sagging wooden shops and offices lined a street that rolled down a hill to a deep natural harbor. It looked like a set from a down-market production of *South Pacific*.

It was evening, and a magnificent jumble of sunset-crowned clouds were drifting north toward the distant heights of the Owen Stanley Mountain Range. It was this spine of rainswept jungle and the desperate resistance of the ill-prepared Australian infantry that had slowed the Japanese advance from Buna and saved Port Moresby in the early days of the Pacific war. The town itself had suffered a number of Japanese air raids. I didn't yet realize it, but echoes of World War II were to be a constant of this visit.

Later that evening, after dinner in the hotel, I took a brandy and my cigar out onto the balcony to listen to a night serenade of insects and small animals. But I didn't linger long in the nighttime cool. My travel schedule had been put together in Canberra with the assistance of the Australians. I had a busy two weeks ahead of me.

Our light aircraft banked steeply before a rollercoaster descent to the Mount Hagan airstrip. The carefree pilot, in shorts, wool sweater, and bush hat, aimed us toward the windsock, and we were soon bumping over the tarmac toward the low terminal building. The jungle-covered mountains rose high around us, and shrouds of brushfire smoke puffed through the open cockpit window. A hand-lettered notice hanging in the terminal warned passengers and gawkers not to enter a restricted area where petrol was stored. "No ken Goinsaid," I read, puzzling over the message until I realized that it was my first exposure to pidgin English ("no can go inside"), the lingua franca of a territory with over 400 languages, not to mention regional dialects.

The Highlands of Papua New Guinea were—and still are—one of the most primitive zones of the world. The warlike tribes of the Highlands were not discovered until 1933. By 1962 the Australians still listed 4,528 square miles of Papua New Guinea as "restricted" or not under administrative control. I had been surprised before leaving on my trip to learn that only six years earlier an Australian patrol officer, or KIAP as they were called by the local people, had first penetrated the land of the Biami tribe. He'd found these reputed cannibals busy bleaching the skulls of raid victims "before they are put on permanent display in communal houses."

At Mount Hagen, the administrative center of the Western Highlands, I was given a detailed briefing by the district officer, introduced to a bush-jacketed patrol officer with the look of a young Gregory Peck, and sent off in his care to a distant post.

A long, arduous drive in the patrol officer's Land Rover took us along winding, dirt tracks high into the mountains. We were seemingly at the top of the world. Clouds sifted down jungle ravines like slow-moving waterfalls, and brilliantly colored birds flitted through the thick foliage. Finally, we could see the post: a small grouping of one-story buildings in the center of a wide, green meadow; a tall radio mast with an Australian flag sagging on its pole; and a line full of colorful washing.

Later, sipping from a frosted "tinnie" of Foster's lager while a kerosene refrigerator hummed in the background, the patrol officer spoke of the Highland "payback system." The isolated tribes, he explained, lived in semifortified villages on the mountain peaks. Although they might be able to look across a valley to a distant village, it often took days to cover that distance on foot. Given this separation, the territorial imperative, and the warrior tradition of the tribes, the intervillage relationships were often hostile. This hostility manifested itself through raids and random killings. These in turn called for revenge action and killings that produced the payback system. Some mountain feuds had gone on for so long that it was impossible to trace their exact beginnings. In certain cases the feuds could develop into full-scale war-fare, with warriors in paint and feather finery facing each other armed with spears, bows and arrows, clubs, and finely honed hatchets.

"And it's your job to keep the peace?" I asked.

"We do what we can," the patrol officer replied. "I have a small detachment of armed, native constables. But we seldom have to use force. The KIAP is still a respected figure up here." It seemed some tribal confrontations were largely ceremonial, involving the exchange of insults, sudden rushes stopping short of physical contact, and a cessa-tion of the confrontation once wounds had been suffered on both sides.

"The hatchets you see the Highlanders carrying," the patrol officer sighed, "are not carpentry tools." Regretfully, he told me, many pay-back killings were aimed at the easy targets of women and children, struck down as they worked in an isolated taro patch or while seeking water at a mountain stream.

"What about cannibalism?" I wanted to know. "I understand it's been stamped out."

"Officially, 'long pig' is a thing of the past," he said, before changing the subject.

That evening the patrol officer hosted a small dinner party in my honor. I contributed a three-quarters-filled bottle of gin to the cocktail hour. A young couple, the regional doctor and his wife, made up our foursome. As the KIAP was a bachelor, the doctor's wife supervised his Papuan cook. The blond wife was attractive, and my antenna picked up some sexual tension that evening. Perhaps I'd read too much Maugham and Greene. For all concerned I hope I was wrong.

One morning, driving with the KIAP and one of his constables to defuse a dispute over pig ownership, I experienced an unusual and frightening experience. It was still cool and misty when we stopped the Land Rover on the narrow road to relieve ourselves. We separated slightly, walking some yards into the dense undergrowth. I halted and felt a sudden, spine-chilling presence. Looking around me I saw the cause. We had unwittingly walked into a gathering of crouching warriors. They were dressed in breechclouts and wore round headdresses of possum fur topped with macaw and bird of paradise feathers. An old man only 12 feet away had circles of ochre paint around his bloodshot eyes and wore sharp-ended wild boar tusks curling from the nostrils of his broad nose. The younger men had beards painted on their faces with a shiny, blue-black substance darker than their skins. All of them were smeared with pig grease as protection against the cold, and shiny steel hatchets were stuck behind their hips in rafia belts. They were also armed with throwing spears, bows, clusters of long arrows, and crude "killing picks," the points of which were fashioned of cassowary claws.

I turned my head toward the KIAP for guidance. He gestured that I was to stand still and keep quiet. The silence was eerie. None of the tribesmen looked at us. They were treating us as if we didn't exist. Perhaps in their world, at that particular moment, we didn't. Then, responding to some unspoken signal, they rose and moved off into the jungle. I swallowed hard and took a deep breath. "What was that all about?" I asked.

"I'm not sure," the KIAP responded, but he looked concerned. He never did tell me who the tribesmen were or where they were headed, but he spent time behind closed doors in radio contact with his base after we'd returned to the post.

A few days later, at the coastal town of Wewak, a government driver with steel wool hair and a pleasant smile took me to a small Japanese World War II shrine high on a hill overlooking the tall palms edging the Pacific surf. The shrine was impressively simple in the best Shinto/Buddhist tradition, featuring a large, square monument in the center of the narrow, unobtrusive tombstones. I stood there, reflecting on the fact that in 1943 at Buna, some 600 miles to the southeast on the same coast, George Strock had photographed dead American soldiers half buried in the surf-washed sand. Those photos, among the first to be released by the censor of our battlefield dead, had created a sensation in the United States and brought the reality of the war to the American public.

I was shaken from my reverie by the arrival of a bus filled with Japanese tourists. I shouldn't have been surprised by this, but somehow I was, as if after their defeat the Japanese had gone, never to return. The tourists were mainly elderly or middle-aged couples. Some of the men bowed a brief greeting as they passed. Others made straight for the shrine to offer prayers for the dead. I suddenly felt like an intruder and decided to leave. My driver tossed away the skin of a papaw he'd been eating and held the door open for me. Driving back to the hotel, he made some comment I thought alluded to the Japanese but I couldn't fathom his pidgin. When we arrived I asked one of the room clerks to translate for me. The driver had told me—more or less—that "Siapan wanpella he kam planti taim na crai planti", or "the Japanese come often and cry a lot."

That evening, looking over a pidgin English dictionary, I came upon some pidgin phrases. These included such useful household standbys as:

What is the time?–*Haumas kilok?*

I don't want to eat. I will only have tea.–*Mi no laik kaikai. Mi dring ti tas'ol.*

Put out the light–*Mekim dai lam.*

There are ants in the food safe.–*Bokis kaikai i gat anis.*

No doubt about it. It would take much more than my short stay to even begin to master pidgin. I closed the dictionary and smiled to myself, imagining a course in that colorful language being taught at the Foreign Service Institute.

Flying to Rabaul on New Britain in a racketing bimotor, I marveled at a most unusual cloud formation. The billowing white mass had formed into an ethereal version of the head of Balzac from the Rodin bronze in Montparnasse. I turned in my seat, tracking the clouds, surprised that the formation could hold for so long. Then I pondered why I had made such a strange comparison while flying over the blue waters of the Bismarck Sea. Had I turned into a collector of clouds? Was I suffering from too much breakfast papaw, a surfeit of Papua pork and sweet potato, a maximum of whiskey ginger and Australian lager? I finally put it down to too much time spent studying art in Paris. Then I allowed the drone of the engines to lull me to sleep.

Once again the Australians played the perfect hosts, sending a car to pick me up at the airport, along with an envelope containing my tentative schedule while in Rabaul and a few invitations for drinks or dinner. The Aussies were being cooperative with a representative of a close ally. At the same time they were monitoring and guiding my activities in a sensitive, potentially volatile trust territory then moving toward independence. In other words, they didn't want anyone to rock their boat, particularly in New Britain, where a militant independence movement had become active.

Rabaul had been the capital of German New Guinea from 1910 until World War I. Following its capture by Japanese imperial forces in January 1942, it had become the principal naval and air base for the projected invasion of Australia. The American-Japanese clash at the Battle of the Coral Sea in May of the same year had blocked Japan's southern march. Rabaul and the shipping in its harbor had then become a prime target for Allied air raids until its liberation in 1945. The harbor was still the graveyard of numerous warships and transports, as well as a rich breeding ground for tropical fish. A driver took me to see the Japanese gun positions dug into the side of a cliff. But all this WWII tourism was designed for time-killing. It dealt with the past, and my job was to think about the future.

I returned to Canberra with the firm conviction that educational exchange and travel to the United States by Papua New Guinea's potential leaders should remain priorities. I also came away with the idea that training grants for local media, particularly in radio, which served as a prime communications link, should be considered in cooperation with the Australians. I certainly did not recommend opening a USIS post in the territory. That could wait for independence. I was sure of one thing: none of us should make any decisions or pontificate on Papua New Guinea until we'd spent more time on the ground. It was only after my return to Canberra that I realized I'd had a week's vacation from the Cold War.

The invitation was very formal. "The A.D.C. in Waiting is desired by Their Excellencies The Governor General and Lady Hasluck to invite Mr. and Mrs. H. R. Simpson to Dinner on Wednesday the 23rd of June at 7:15 o'clock. Black Tie; Long Frock. Government House, Canberra. An answer is requested to the A.D.C. in Waiting." We duly informed the aide de camp in waiting of our acceptance. On the appointed evening, we set out for Government House and a dinner at which we were unwittingly to play the role of the Marx brothers.

My wife hates to arrive early at a social function. Psychologically, this probably stems from the Foreign Service imperative that junior officers and their wives arrive early at embassy functions and the fact the Mary Alice was, and remains, a born rebel. Whatever the cause, there we were, parked on a side street not far from Government House, waiting to make sure we wouldn't be the first to arrive. Alas, my watch proved to be slow. We were thus the last couple to arrive, to the obvious displeasure of the "A.D.C. in Waiting."

The guests formed a select group, including some media and cultural personalities. When we entered the drawing room and were announced, Mary Alice took a step backward and a low coffee table caught her behind the knee. Only some wild gyrations avoided a fall. It did make for an impressive entrance.

A white-jacketed steward offered us champagne, vermouth, whisky and water, or gin and tonic. I took the latter, but Mary Alice hesitated. "Do you have a beer?" she asked.

The sudden silence was deafening. The steward rushed off to find the plebeian beverage. The wives of government bigwigs and captains of industry eyed us as if we'd just left some bush shebeen. The governor general, Her Majesty's representative, seemed amused by my wife's request. He was, after all, an Australian, and beer was like mother's milk to his compatriots. Later, at table, he made a special effort to put Mary Alice at ease.

But another incident lay ahead. At a formal ambassadorial dinner at the residence my wife struck again. When dinner was announced and the guests were paired off to enter the dining room, Mary Alice trod on the long train of the designer gown worn by Lady Fairfax, the wife of one of Australia's leading press barons. The material wasn't ripped, but my wife's firm tread had brought the stout lady up short and produced an irritated frown that took an exceedingly long time to fade.

After a year and a half on Dominion Circuit, we found a California ranch-style home with a swimming pool on Mugga Way, arranged a government lease, and moved back to the edge of the bush. The pool was a dream come true for the children and ourselves. A fox came early in the morning to drink his chlorine cocktail, and cockatoos perched on the roof admired themselves in the still water. There was no better place for diplomats to let their hair down, and I made a point of adding a healthy dollop of media representatives to any swimming party. Some Australians tended to become a bit wild at these functions, and we had to be on our guard. I had to rescue a male journalist from an attractive but husky, rough-handed wife from a sheep station. She was holding him underwater, sitting on his head, and he was actually drowning. They play rough out in the bush.

A Sunday children's party was going fine—or so I thought. Then I noticed a young boy at the bottom of the pool. He seemed relaxed, almost motionless. I dove in, lit cigar and all. When I brought him to the surface he spluttered, coughed, told me he couldn't swim, and asked if he could go in again. Miraculously, my cigar was still lit.

One crisp, sunny Canberra morning in March 1971 I found a priority telegram waiting on my desk. I was to participate in an "orientation" tour of Vietnam. These tours for senior officers at USIA posts were designed to provide an up-to-date exposure to the U.S. effort in Vietnam so that America's overseas spokesmen could better explain American policy in their host countries. My initial reaction was disbelief. Surely someone had made a mistake. I was in no need of any orientation on Vietnam! I called the agency to make this point and was overruled. Australia was an ally in Vietnam, antiwar feeling was spreading down under, and I *would* take part.

This return to what was now known as "Nam" was detailed in *Tiger in the Barbed Wire*. To summarize, choppers and Air America fixed-winged Fokkers took our small group to Nha Trang, Da Nang, Hue, My Tho, Rach Gia, Chau Doc, and Hien Hung. We visited isolated fire bases near the Cambodian border, Revolutionary Development projects in the Mekong Delta, and a division headquarters in the central highlands. My visit to the Australians then became a reality. I was greeted like an old friend and listened while the Aussies criticized General West-moreland's large-scale operations as unnecessarily destructive and counterproductive.

A briefing from 77-year-old Ambassador Ellsworth Bunker at the fort-like embassy building in Saigon did not raise our spirits. The curmudgeonly Bunker lectured us as if we were troublesome newsmen. We were *winning the war* and that should be the message we carried back with us. Unfortunately, most of what I had seen during the orientation tour indicated the opposite. It was doubly worrying when one realized that our group had been aimed and guided toward positive projects and subject matter. If what we saw was positive—God protect us from the negative realities! When I left Bunker's office, I wondered whether we had been the targets of a psychological warfare campaign by our own people.

I came face to face with reality at an informal dinner for two at the fortified Cholon villa of South Vietnamese General Pham Van Dong. We had first met in 1952 at the battle of Nasan in North Vietnam and later during operation Hautes Alpes near Ninh Binh in the Tonkin Delta. He had been a major then, one of the first combat commanders of the Vietnamese National Army. A member of the Nung warrior tribe, Dong had seen more action over a longer period of time than any surviving ARVN officer. During my 1964–65 Vietnam service, he had been commander of the Saigon-Cholon Military Sector. At the time of the Tet offensive he and his Nungs had ambushed an infiltrating company of North Vietnamese sappers and had wiped them out as a unit.

When we had finished our dinner and said goodbye, Dong looked me in the eye. "Simpson," he said, with a toss of his head to indicate the city in general, "it is *not* good."

11

Cool in Bukavu,
Undiplomatic in Algiers

The agency must have thought I was mad. There I was, a counselor of embassy, living in a California-style Canberra villa with a swimming pool, well established in my work, with a number of Australian friends and contacts—and I wanted out after only two years! What the people in personnel failed to comprehend was that suburban living in Canberra wasn't much different from its counterpart in San Diego or Flagstaff. When we'd arrived in Australia's capital, I'd discounted the complaints from diplomatic colleagues that Canberra was boring. Now, after two years, I was moving toward their way of thinking. I suppose it wasn't *foreign* enough. A secondary reason was a desire to return to Europe, and France in particular.

The ambassador was not pleased, but he accepted the argument that my future career objective was Europe. The bureaucratic machinery in Washington began to grind, and there were soon no dearth of candidates to take my place in the Australian sun. My prospects for the future, however, did not look too bright. The slots I might have filled in Europe were occupied, and I could sense a certain edginess in my telephone conversations with the USIA personnel office. They didn't relish my return to Washington to join the "corridor commandos": those unassigned officers who shared empty offices, drank endless cups of coffee, read the *New York Times* from cover to cover, and haunted the Foreign Service lounge hoping for a summons presaging an onward assignment.

In 1971 there was a definite danger in returning to Washington as a corridor commando. It meant that you were putting your fate in the hands of people who would do anything to find you a temporary, stop-gap position. These could range from a re-Americanization stint in a senator's office on Capitol Hill to the post of escort officer (tour guide) to a group of South Korean businessmen interested in the fishing industry.

If I learned one trade secret early on in government service, it was to manage your own career as much as possible. Personnel officers were only human. They were continually searching for solutions and usually willing to listen if you could come up with the answer to their problem. I had to think of something to suggest before leaving Australia. As often happens in a husband-wife team, it was the wife who came up with the solution.

"How much leave do you have coming?" Mary Alice asked one evening as the sun set over the bush.

"Why?"

"Depending on your accumulated leave," she explained, "we might go back to Newport and stay there until your next assignment."

A quick calculation in the office the next morning produced some good news. My combined unused home leave and annual leave came to approximately six months. My third novel, *The Three Day Alliance*, set in Marseille, had recently been published. I'd begun another, *Rendezvous Off Newport*, but it was far from finished. The proposed stay in Newport could not be better timed. It also meant our daughters would be going back to an environment and the schools and friends they knew. I was already looking forward to renewing friendships at the Naval War College and perhaps contributing a lecture or two.

A quick exchange of telegrams sealed the proposition. Personnel was obviously pleased to have me out of their hair for six months and proceeded to authorize the leave. I put through a call to Nick King informing him of our return to *his* town. Within weeks he'd arranged for us to stay in an 18th-century colonial house a short walk from the Redwood Library. Things were working out as planned.

I said goodbye to Ambassador Rice, the embassy personnel, and my own small staff. A very liquid Press Club lunch provided an opportunity to bid adieu to my Australian media contacts before I turned the post over to Jim Pettus, previously a press attaché at our London embassy and a former colonel in the U.S. Air Force.

After the endless space of Australia, returning to Newport was like stepping onto a miniature movie set. Everything seemed compressed and a gray sky hovered low to the ground. We missed the sunsets, the cockatoos, our fox, and even the dimwitted galahs. But Newport was definitely better than sweating out an assignment in Washington, and we were determined to make the most of it.

I went to work on the novel that featured local detective John Shea solving the mysterious murder of a British naval officer attending the Naval War College. On the surface it promised to be easy writing, thanks to the readily available atmosphere and details. In reality, it proved much more difficult. Although I should have been luxuriating in my temporary freedom and open writing time, I was subconsciously waiting for the telephone to ring. Ego had something to do with it. It was hard for me to understand why the agency hadn't found an urgent need for my services. It was difficult not to reach for the phone myself. I did succumb to that temptation several times, to the chagrin of the personnel office and the consternation of my colleagues in Washington who had promised to keep me informed of any overseas position coming open.

A few months had passed and I had almost finished *Rendezvous Off Newport* when the agency did call. It was an assignment of sorts. I was asked to lead an inspection team of five officers and a "public member" (a nonagency, civilian representative) to carry out a routine inspection of our post in Zaire. I did not take long to make my decision. In fact, with my leave seemingly stretching on to infinity, I jumped at the chance.

The majority of Foreign Service officers don't welcome the periodic arrival of inspection teams. It isn't because they have something to hide. It's because inspections throw any post into neutral over a period of weeks while the staff scrambles to fulfill the inspection team's requests for documents, financial data, personal interviews, in-country trips, and meetings with the post's local contacts. Add to this the inevitable social events, and the normal day-to-day operation grinds to a halt.

I have never been overly fond of inspectors myself. Some were part of the agency's small inspection staff, but the majority were temporarily appointed officers with only a passing knowledge of the inspection procedures. Now I was suddenly acting the role of chief inspector and trying not to be too officious. I'm not sure I succeeded. There is something very tempting but inherently unfair about judging someone else's operation and writing performance ratings after only a limited time on the ground.

In sum, our job was to judge the efficiency of the USIA program in Zaire, to see whether it adequately supported the current U.S. policy objectives, and to evaluate the performances of those involved.

Our inspection took place while Zaire was one of our Cold War strongholds in Africa and President Marshal Mobutu Sese Seko Kuku Ngbendu wa Za Banga could do no wrong. Our small team didn't have time to delve deeply into policy questions. We were more involved in nuts-and-bolts appraisals covering everything from the appropriate use of the post's annual budget to relations between the American and local staffs. In retrospect I believe our final evaluation was fair, but I do recall a certain amount of nitpicking. The official judgments and final submissions have long faded from memory. In any case, they have no place here. What does remain are certain memories that come to mind when the Congo is mentioned.

- I traveled within Zaire with the public member of our team and his wife. He was a young educator from the West Coast, and they were new to Africa. They were, however, fast learners. At the airport at Kisangani (formerly Stanleyville), after a two-hour wait in oppressive heat, our aged Junkers transport was ready to fly us to the cooler climate of Bukavu. Perspiring heavily, we climbed aboard to find the interior temperature of the metal fuselage a few degrees below that of a slag furnace.

  The grumpy but well-proportioned hostess offered us a choice of warm cola or warm bottled water. I took the bottled water and a plastic glass. Guessing correctly that our takeoff would be delayed, I rummaged in my handbaggage to find the bottle of Scotch I always carried for such emergencies. This was a lesson learned in Indochina, where I found a dram or two useful in bringing smiles to the grim faces of obtuse officials or in staving off hypertension in difficult situations.

  I offered the educator and his wife a slight jolt to go with their water, but they refused politely, explaining that they didn't drink. Twenty minutes later two pilots arrived, unhurried and casual. After another 15 minutes one of the elderly radial engines coughed into life and the fuselage began to shimmy. Then the second engine turned over, the aircraft went into its shake-and-bake mode.

  The constant shaking had now begun to loosen the overhead panels, and one came away from its fittings in a cloud of dust and exposed wiring. Then *they* began to drop. I have seen cockroaches in various varieties: the black, quick-moving species of Vietnam; the more sluggish, flying fatsos of Nigeria; and the greenish, pack-traveling denizens of the Marseille drains. But I have never seen anything to equal those Congo behemoths. They began to fall on us, jarred loose from the aircraft's ceiling. I'll give the doughty insects credit. Some of them held on as long as possible—often with one leg—before plummeting down onto the passengers.

I quickly covered my glass and flicked one of the unintentional invaders off my trousers. An African businessman across the aisle shook a roach to the floor from his newspaper without interrupting his reading. The educator and his wife, after a few moments of shock, reacted well. She put on a soft sun hat; he extended his half-filled water glass toward me and nodded wordlessly in the direction of my whiskey bottle.

- At Bukavu I dined with an American consul at his small residence on the shores of Lake Kivu. This was indeed the type of Foreign Service assignment that the average American seldom matches with the diplomatic life. No champagne receptions, black tie dinners, or protocol-ridden ceremonies there. Not a cookie-pusher in sight. Just a competent young American officer in an isolated post in the heart of an uneasy, strife-torn Africa. No Hollywood tom-toms or animal shrieks, but a subtle sense of danger all the same. A short distance to the northeast was Uganda. Rwanda was across the lake, and Burundi to the southeast. Tribal clashes were frequent, foreshadowing the future massive intermassacres of Hutus and Tutsis. That evening, sipping our after-dinner coffee, we were not sanguine about regional peace and order in the near future. But neither of us would have predicted that six years later Moroccan troops, flown to Zaire by French military aircraft, would be blocking an invasion from Angola by the Congolese National Liberation Front backed by the USSR, its Iron Curtain allies, and Cuba. Nor would we have foreseen that paratroopers of the French Foreign Legion would be dropping on Kolwezi seven years later to rescue European and African hostages caught up in another invasion by the "Tigers" of the same Front de Liberation Nationale Congolais. If someone had told us that evening that the bloodbaths would continue into the late 1990s—and probably beyond—we would have considered the speaker lost in a negative fantasy land.

- The Belgian hotel owner outdid himself for our last dinner in Bukavu, insisting that we sample heaping plates of sweet, local strawberries as dessert. Later, when the educator and his wife retired, the owner poured me a prune liqueur and spoke of the

European mercenaries he had known during earlier Congo conflicts. Some of them had used Lake Kivu as an escape route when their cause had failed. Outside, the full moon was as bright as a stadium light, blotting out the stars and throwing jagged shadows of the tall trees onto the ground.

I'd been back in Newport over two months when the long-awaited call finally came. Once again I was offered a choice: Madagascar or Algeria, the latter qualifying as a hardship post. Personnel was willing to give me some decision time, but it was obvious that sooner would be better. I requested and received the post reports. We read them carefully, and it didn't take long to decide. Madagascar looked interesting but isolated. Algeria, on the other hand, was a country I had been associated with through its proximity to Marseille and the fallout from the Algerian conflict in France.

The Algerians, along with other Arab states, had broken relations with the United States at the time of the 1967 Arab-Israeli conflict, when our air force had been falsely accused of joining in the Israeli attack. We still had no diplomatic relations with the Democratic and Popular Republic of Algeria. Houari Boumedienne of the FLN Party, a dour military man, was now the president. His administration, with Russian help, was following the path toward heavy Soviet-style industrialization, despite the fact that Algeria's climate and location had made it a prime agricultural producer under French rule.

The United States was represented in Algiers by an American Interests Section in its own embassy building under a Swiss flag. The situation sounded unique and intriguing. What finally clinched our decision was a careful look at the map. Marseille and its Vieux Port were only a short flight or ferry trip away.

All bureaucracies have their glitches, and the Foreign Service is no exception. After breathing down my neck for a hurried decision, the personnel office then informed me that the incumbent officer in Algiers would, for personal reasons, be staying on a bit longer than planned. In other words, a looming time gap threatened, once again, to propel me into the ranks of the corridor commandos. It was essential for me to quickly provide personnel with a reasonable and mutually satisfying alternative.

Fortunately, I recalled that the University of Aix-Marseille had a center for North African studies. It seemed logical that an officer with no experience in North Africa on his way to a sensitive posting in Algiers, and with time on his hands, should absorb as much knowledge as possible en route. This tentative project sparked a number of telephone calls to the agency and to Ramon Garcia at USIS Marseille, who was in close touch with the rector and other officials of the university. I then sent a hurried special delivery letter to the director of the North African Study Center, who duly replied that he would be glad to accommodate me for a brief period of research. USIA agreed to cover my expenses at the center. Garcia's wife Dominique arranged for the rental of a small family farmhouse near Aix and, after a short consultation in Washington, we were once again under the warm Provençal sun.

My brief sojourn in Aix was useful, providing me with sorely needed information on Algeria and Algerian history not readily available in Washington. I was able only to sample some of the rich source material in the center's holdings. I also encountered the French government's draconian rules regarding the release of "sensitive" material, including most references to the Algerian War. But the time in Aix did increase my knowledge of a country that would be our home for the next two years.

It was also amusing for me, as someone who had served in French Indochina, Marseille, and Paris, to note the suspicion-tinged curiosity of certain faculty members and visiting specialists from the French government regarding my assignment to Algeria. Although I am a confirmed francophile, I have learned from long experience that some French *fonctionnaires* will detect dark designs and seek hidden meanings in the most innocent of "Anglo-Saxon" procedures. Nevertheless, before leaving Aix I addressed a detailed memorandum to the agency's training division recommending the center as a working stopover for officers on their way to posts in North Africa.

The "White City" rose ahead of us out of a low sea mist like a dream metropolis in a children's book. Our boxlike ferry swung wide past the northern breakwater toward the entrance to the harbor of Algiers. The entire Simpson family was on deck to see what Algiers looked like. The first rays of the morning sun illuminated the heights of the Casbah and the tall minarets of the principal mosques. We could see a park with a traditional French wrought-iron bandstand surrounded by palms as we neared the Mole Al-djefna. I would soon become accustomed to such colonial landmarks in many Algerian towns. City traffic was heavy, with motorbikes darting through the cars while overloaded buses belched black smoke from their exhausts.

Unsmiling Algerian officials cleared us through customs. An embassy driver picked us up and agreed to show us a bit of the city. We passed some unpleasant-looking port security police at the dock gates. Already, I had a premonition that I'd be earning my hardship pay. I suffered an attack of déjà vu as we drove slowly along the streets. I craned my neck toward the Casbah, remembering Charles Boyer as Pepe le Moko in Walter Wanger's *Algiers* and the gritty depiction of counter-terrorist action in Gillo Pontecorvo's more recent and realistic *The Battle of Algiers*.

We reached the Place du Forum and the balcony of la Delegation generale, where in 1958 de Gaulle had told the cheering crowds of *pieds noirs*, the French population who had been in Algeria for generations, that he "understood" them. Three years later the same location had witnessed the revolt of the French Army generals against de Gaulle, who they felt had betrayed them and the *pieds noirs* by offering self-determination to the Algerian National Liberation Front. Ahead of us now was the Milk Bar, where a heroine of the Algerian rebellion had planted a bomb that killed and maimed a number of French and Algerian customers, men, women, and children.

The déjà vu was not because I had personally experienced these happenings, but because I'd lived with their results in Marseille, a short physical and political distance from Algeria. Over two million embittered *pieds noirs* had fled to France with the advent of Algerian independence in 1962, and most of them had passed through Marseille.

The one impression I was not prepared for was the number of young men congregating at street corners or on the café terraces. I knew Algeria had a high unemployment rate, but this physical display of aimlessness was disconcerting.

We were driven to a recently completed and airy beach hotel at Sidi Ferrouch, west of Algiers, designed by the French architect Fernand Pouillon. From its exterior the hotel exuded modernity and expense. Once inside, there were premature cracks in the walls, missing tiles, and broken glass on the stairways. Pouillon, whom I was to meet later, described the series of expensive tourist hotels he was building on the beaches and at selected Saharan oases as "instant ruins."

It was soon obvious that the hotel staff considered the guests fortunate at being allowed to enter the establishment, much less be entitled to any service. Unfortunately, the hotel and its management were symbolic of this comparatively new popular republic, a presentable façade that on closer inspection suffered from cracks and fissures.

The American embassy that housed the American Interests Section, and my office were located within a walled compound on a high, pine-planted hill with a magnificent view over the city and Bay of Algiers. The white-painted building was of Moorish design, with domed cupolas, decorative mosaics, and a tiled inner court with an upstairs inner balcony. The principal officer's residence next door was a gem among government housing. It too was Moorish in style, high ceilinged with graceful arches and tiled floors. The Moorish reflecting pool on the outside patio had been deepened to provide a swimming pool, and a tennis court was nearby.

Arriving at the embassy for the first time, I experienced a definite feeling of incongruity. I was entering an edifice out of the Arabian Nights over which a Swiss flag, with its white cross on a red field, designated the official protector of the U.S. Interests Section in the capital of a revolutionary nation with which we had no diplomatic relations. Add to this the fact that this sunlit haven, complete with swimming pool and tennis court, high above the sparkling Mediterranean, was classed as a hardship post—and the word "curious" came to mind.

Bill Eagleton, the 46-year-old chargé d'affaires and senior officer of the Interests Section, was an Arabist. He had served in a number of Mideast posts, including Damascus, Baghdad, and Aden. He spoke both Arabic and Kurdish in addition to French and knew the Arab mind and culture. Our first meeting was cordial but slightly cool as we sized each other up. I could understand Eagleton's reticence. He was being saddled with someone with no experience in the Arab world or North Africa, who had automatically become the second-ranking officer in his mission. In addition, I was there to run an information program on a reduced scale, but "information" of any kind was a very touchy subject in Algeria. If handled in the wrong way, it could have had a negative effect on the already precarious links Eagleton was maintaining with the Boumedienne regime. In the weeks following our first meeting, we worked well together and soon became good friends, as did Eagleton's beautiful wife Kay and Mary Alice. This may seem an unimportant personal footnote, but in a small post such as Algiers, where the frustrations of work and living were constant, such friendships were important.

I had been forewarned that our USIS operation in Algiers was basically a holding operation. In fact, considering the state of U.S.– Algerian relations, it was a miracle that we "capitalist propagandists" were able to operate at all. Although the Communist Party had been banned since 1962, this was a nation that supported revolutionary movements throughout the world. A brass plaque on a modest building a few minutes' drive from our Interests Section marked the home-in-exile of the American Black Panther Party, and renegade groups from other countries had found a safe haven in Algeria. The official Algerian media reveled in attacking the United States and its policies on a daily basis, with our role in Vietnam providing a ready-made target.

At the same time, I soon learned that many educated Algerians— traveled professionals, students, and some government officials—took this propaganda barrage with a grain of salt. Although Communist countries were providing economic aid ($2.7 billion between 1970 and 1989) and advice to Algeria, the Algerians were fortunate in their natural resources, particularly crude oil and natural gas. To exploit this bonanza, destined to form the backbone of their economy, they required Western business contacts and technical assistance. Thus, behind the façade of revolutionary jargon, the realities and pragmatism of world trade were bringing Americans and Algerians together.

Togetherness in Algiers, however, was a rare thing. My first round of pro forma calls on government radio and TV officials was marked by long periods of waiting for substitute, secondary officials to appear for polite but brief meetings. The official press service director and newspaper editors were a bit more relaxed, but I quickly got the picture. My presence in their offices made them uneasy. It was a matter of "don't call us, we'll call you."

When John Melton, the newly assigned cultural officer, arrived, he encountered the same frustrating situation, although to a slightly lesser degree among the Algerians he was to work with. Even a hardline regime found it a bit hard to argue with an exchange of culture, particularly the arts. But the messages they deciphered, or imagined as negative, in our literature and films was a different matter.

In this environment the one thing we could do was ensure that the Algerian government and media received our output of presidential speeches, policy statements, and White House and State Department press conference transcripts and backgrounders. The Algerians might not agree with our policies, but it was our job to see that the proper texts were in their hands and not some rewrite or commentary from

Moscow or Havana. I didn't expect them to print our material, but it was important for them to be privy to the exact official texts and know what had actually been said.

I could see that personal contact with Algerians was going to be a long-haul procedure. With this in mind, I made a special effort to establish friendly links with Algiers-based correspondents of foreign news agencies such as Agence France Presse, *Le Monde*, Associated Press, and Reuters. These professionals were paid to know what was going on in Algeria, and most of them usually did.

There was no doubt about it—despite urban decrepitude and the lack of upkeep, Algiers was still a beautiful city. I soon learned that a visit to the Casbah was a must for official visitors—but only in daylight. After a stop at the Museum of the Revolution, we would descend the narrow, steep stairways that snaked down past the ancient white-washed dwellings, their low doorways marked with the imprint of the hand of Fatima, the daughter of the prophet Mohammed. Sullen adult faces peered from small Arab cafés serving mint tea and strong coffee, the curious children and skinny cats watched us pass, and the heavy air was pungent with the odors of spices and sewage.

A visit to the narrow street where French paras had blown up Amar Ali, otherwise known as Ali la Point, in his Casbah hiding place was de rigueur. Ali, who had run the Groupe Choc of the Algerian Liberation Army in the city under the command of Yacef Saadi during the Battle of Algiers, had become a national hero and martyr of the Revolution.

Hot and thirsty, the visitors would breathe a sigh of relief once out of the Casbah's claustrophobic maze and back on the boulevards. They would then be taken off to an al fresco lunch at Sid Ferrouch to eat spicy, grilled *merguez* sausages on French baguettes and drink Algerian rosé or Beer 33.

Favored visitors would be introduced to the Algiers Yacht Club, one of Algiers' better-kept secrets. Colleagues from Paris, Tunis, or Rabat expecting to find us suffering in our "hardship" status were astounded to discover this replica of the Cote d'Azur on the Bay of Algiers. A slow drive along the narrow road leading through Algerian Naval Head-quarters, where the sentries were casual and the security lax, would take us to the concrete club building. It looked like a fragment of a Busby Berkeley set from the 1930s. A stairway curved upward past porthole windows to the open terraces and parasol-shaded tables. Shrimp, lamb, and red snapper were cooked on open grills, Cuvée du

President, a full-bodied Algerian red wine, was available, and the pastry chef was known for his lemon pie. The Yacht Club of Algiers in the mid-1970s, with its clientele of Algerian businessmen in three-piece suits, government officials, and foreign diplomats, was hardly a stronghold of revolutionary socialism.

The Soviets and their Eastern Bloc surrogates were well established in Algiers. The Algerian army was equipped with Russian tanks, and Soviet fleet visits brought schoolchildren and gawkers down to the docks. The Iron Curtain diplomats based in Algiers eyed our small operation with disfavor and suspicion. I had met the director of the Soviet Cultural Center at a diplomatic reception. He was a bearded, seemingly affable giant with a slight knowledge of English. After the usual exchange of pleasantries, he hit me with some heavy questions. How many were we? Where had I served before? How long was I going to be in Algeria?

I referred him jokingly to the diplomatic list for our strength in Algiers, reeled off my former posts, and told him I had no idea how long my tour would last. A week later I accepted the director's invitation to drop by his center for a prelunch drink. The center was celebrating some anniversary of the Great Patriotic War, and, while I waited for my host to appear, I examined the enlarged photos of Soviet armored vehicles hanging on the walls. Not exactly what one would expect to find in a cultural center.

When the director arrived and ushered me into his office, it soon became obvious that I was to endure the standard "trial by vodka," a typical Soviet ploy. Although it was only 11:30 A.M., a secretary appeared bearing a tray of open-faced sandwiches of pork paté and smoked sturgeon. She then returned with three bottles of vodka. There was vodka with pepper, vodka with flecks of gold, and pure unadulterated vodka. I am not sure what my host wanted to know, but he appeared fascinated by the miniscule size of our staff and intrigued by my three tours in Vietnam. My comment that the continual war in Indochina was a tragedy seemed to discomfit him.

The vodka flowed freely throughout our conversation. I first became aware that the Algerian heat and the vodka were affecting the director by the strange angle of his spectacles. He then began to complain about his past assignments and grumble about life in Algiers with a vehemence that (1) proved we were not being recorded or (2) that he was a very good actor. By 1:30 P.M. his glasses were dangerously askew, and he had a sprinkling of breadcrumbs on his beard. It was time to go.

This proved difficult. His staff had left for lunch as we knocked back the vodka and munched the salty sandwiches. They had also locked us in, and the director could not find his own set of keys. The full import of being locked into his own center with an officer of the U.S. Interests Section appeared to have a sobering effect. My host was particularly grim-faced when he was forced to call the security office at his embassy for assistance in freeing his American guest. I tried to treat the accidental incarceration lightly, but the young, crop-haired security man who unlocked the doors for us saw no humor in the situation, nor did the perspiring director. From that moment on, he made a special effort to avoid me at official functions.

12

Time for Dissent

The fact that so many Iron Curtain diplomat missions flourished in Algiers as favored nations made us particularly cautious regarding social contacts. If invited to a Communist function, we discussed it beforehand and reported on it later. Any experienced American officer was well aware of the "honey-trap" sexual ambushes favored by Soviet Bloc intelligence services. We were always on the alert for "swallows," the KGB's attractive seductresses, often recruited from the ranks of Soviet or East German actresses. Alas, it seems they were concentrating on more productive targets.

This was still the period when the Soviets were living up to their Cold War image: very serious, slightly edgy, short top and sides haircuts, and wearing badly cut suits with wrinkled stovepipe trousers and clumpy, thick-soled shoes. The exceptions to this rule were the occasional Russian diplomatic visitors sporting Italian suits and elegant footwear. An educated guess put them in the ranks of the KGB.

Mild teasing of our serious Soviet colleagues often relieved the daily tedium of dealing with uncooperative Algerian officials. My opportunity came when I was introduced to a newly arrived Chinese general at an Algerian government function. He was to serve as the Chinese embassy's military attaché, and he was accompanied by a young, French-speaking, Chinese interpreter. This was a period of chilled relations between the Chinese and Russians. The latter considered Algeria their zone of influence and were not happy with recent manifestations of Chinese interest there.

My conversation with the general was stilted by the lag in interpretation. But his meaningless smiles and chuckles in responding to whatever I said quickly changed to "Ah!" and a series of quick questions when he learned I had been at Dien Bien Phu. He then insisted that we drink a toast together. The interpreter told me we were drinking to Chinese-American friendship. I had a sneaking suspicion the general was toasting the Vietminh victory at Dien Bien Phu in which his Red Army had played a significant role.

Some weeks later, Bill Payeff, the assistant deputy director of USIA for the Near East and North Africa, arrived in Algiers on a routine visit. Payeff, a World War II veteran who was still carrying some shrapnel from the campaign in Europe, had spent considerable time in the Far East and France. He was rotund, short, and blessed with a keen sense of humor. We agreed that he'd best get the feel for life in Algiers during his short stay through some social exposure.

We rounded up the usual suspects for a drinks party, including a few Russian diplomats. We did not tell them, or the other guests, of our little surprise. And it *was* a surprise. The smiling Chinese general arrived, uniformed and bemedaled, with his interpreter. There was a momentary silence during which I observed our Soviet guests. Watching their puzzled expressions turn to frowns was like observing the passage of a dark cloud over an uncertain sun. The frowns only deepened when Bill Payeff, a Chinese speaker, began chatting with the general in his own tongue.

The unsmiling Russians left early and together. The general stayed on to polish off his second glass of Scotch. A few of the other diplomatic or media guests had watched the Soviet-Chinese encounter with veiled amusement. A French newsman asked me if I had purposely planned the uncomfortable face-to-face meeting. I smiled but vehemently denied such undiplomatic complicity.

My spy thriller *Rendezvous Off Newport*, with a KGB agent as the heavy, had just been published in the United States and was soon to be republished by Gallimard in Paris in their *Serie Noire*. I've often wondered whether KGB researchers were among my readers and whether they enjoyed the book.

Although I left most cultural functions and contacts to John Melton, the cultural affairs officer, I did take a particular interest in Mouloud

Mammeri, a Kabyle writer whose *l'Opium et le Baton,* a prize-winning novel on the Algerian war as seen from the Algerian side, had been praised by critics in France. The Kabyle Berbers had always been fiercely independent, and Mammeri's novel had reflected this virtue through its honesty. He had not hesitated to speak of cowardice as well as courage, or of the contradictions of vice and virtue that are part of any conflict. His realistic descriptions of the revolutionary struggle had not pleased the incumbent government, which preferred to have all members of the FLN and the ALN pictured as heroes or martyrs.

When I decided to meet Mammeri, I was still fairly new to Algeria. I had not realized that the government's distaste for his book and his outspoken championing of Kabyle rights had put him under the type of close, official observation that bordered on house arrest. But my telephone conversation with him requesting a meeting—as one novelist to another—was normal, and he invited me to come to his home not far from the presidential residence.

Our conversation was cordial and innocent enough, but at midpoint in our short meeting I realized how stupid I had been to impose my presence on such a cultured and courageous person. I had selfishly thought that my few published novels would establish an instant link between us. In my eagerness, I had failed to realize that the Algerian security police would not see one novelist calling on another. They would only record the visit of an officer from the U.S. Interests Section, the officer responsible for information—a suspicious word in their lexicon—on an author they considered a possible dissident. In Mammeri's place I would probably have refused the meeting, particularly since his phone was undoubtedly tapped.

On leaving, I spotted some mustached heavies across the street. Like plainclothesmen in most tropical countries, they wore their sport shirts outside their waistbands. They took a sudden interest in a nearby flowerbed as I got in my car. Or were they cab drivers waiting for a fare? That was the kind of paranoia that flourished in the White City.

Despite this environment, we did manage some personal contacts bordering on the normal. We were invited to informal dinners or drinks hosted by foreign correspondents based in Algiers where we were able to meet and talk with Algerian journalists without government "minders" in attendance. The Algerian government allowed John Melton to hang an extensive show of American contemporary art in downtown Algiers that drew an enthusiastic audience of university students and artists. Many Algerian youths were interested in modern American music and jazz and would do their best to attend any lecture or rare concert we might sponsor.

Not all of our contacts with Algerians were work oriented. I was invited to an Algerian wedding celebration at a neighbor's house, where the men sat in one room, the women in another, and huge plates of lamb and chicken couscous were served with soft drinks and mint tea. A portable radio blasted out Algerian music with a rhythmic drumbeat that encouraged loud ululation from the women. Periodically, one of the women would dance through the hall, all swinging hips, clashing tambourine, and a swirl of voluminous red and yellow skirts. My presence had drawn a small circle of curious teenagers who questioned me not on Vietnam or the Near East, but on Hollywood.

I had been spared the task of arguing our Vietnam policy in Algeria, where no one would have been allowed to listen. But I had followed the reports of North Vietnamese and Viet Cong attacks on the northern provinces, central highlands, and Saigon region in March 1972 with the uneasy feeling that General Dong's pessimism was fully justified. I had also been monitoring the Paris peace talks and the on-again, off-again American bombing of North Vietnam. I had no great faith in the effectiveness of airpower in such a war. I knew it was being used as a powerful political tool but, although I could hardly be classed as a "bleeding heart," the image of B-52s dropping their loads over North Vietnam bothered me more than I cared to admit.

This suppressed disapproval finally erupted in late December 1972 when President Nixon ordered an intensification of the air offensive that became known as the "Christmas Bombing." For 11 days, with the exception of Christmas Day itself, three thousand sorties were flown over the heavily populated Hanoi-Haiphong zone and close to 40,000 tons of bombs were dropped—all this while we were celebrating Christmas in sunny Algiers before an overdecorated, scraggly pine.

The day after Christmas I drove to the Interests Section and drafted an eyes-only telegram to the director of USIA, Frank Shakespeare, and my immediate boss, the assistant director for the Near East and North Africa, Mike Pistor. The message detailed my experience in North and South Vietnam and stated that

I CANNOT, IN GOOD CONSCIENCE, SUPPORT PRESENT POLICY OF B-52 RAIDS OVER HEAVILY POPULATED AREAS NORTH VIETNAM.

Reassuring the recipients that I was not absorbing Algerian propaganda or grandstanding my dissent, I concluded,

HAVING BEEN UNDER DIRECT FIRE BOTH VIETNAM WARS, WITNESSED MUCH CIVILIAN
SUFFERING NORTH AND SOUTH AND AWARE INEVITABLE SPILLOVER B-52 BOMBING
INTO NON-MILITARY ZONES MUST GO ON RECORD WITH MY FEELINGS.

I didn't realize it at the time, but the "Christmas Bombing" had
already put the White House under a barrage of disapproval from both
the United States and abroad. But, as Machiavelli knew only too well,
force has its effect. On December 27, 1972, the North Vietnamese signaled their willingness to resume talks once the bombing stopped.

The official reaction to my cable came in the form of a letter from
Mike Pistor, relaying Director Frank Shakespeare's response that he
fully respected "the integrity" of my position and would "pass along"
the substance of my views. Months later I heard that once word, or
rumors, of my demarche had spread, there had been some gung ho,
desk-chair commandos in the agency out for my scalp. Years later,
when the truth about the vindictive atmosphere in the Nixon White
House at that time became public knowledge, I considered it a miracle
that I'd escaped with my career intact.

As we approached the mid-1970s, Secretary of State Henry Kissinger
decided to include Algiers as one of the stops on his route of Middle
East shuttle diplomacy. He had promised to keep the Algerians
informed of developments in ongoing negotiations with the Arabs and
Israelis. For their part, the Algerians, known for the skill of some of
their diplomats, were willing to assist in the search for peace, particularly since it involved them as players in important international
developments.

The cable advising us of Kissinger's pending arrival in Algiers came
as a bombshell. The U.S. secretary of state visiting Algiers, home of
exiled revolutionaries, one-time haven of the Black Panthers! If it had
been April 1, we would have accused someone in the message center
of playing a bad joke. But no, it was only too true. Our sole consolation
was that the news had probably been an equally surprising shock to
our Algerian counterparts.

The Kissinger visit accomplished one thing immediately. It forced
the Algerians and Americans to sit down together at a conference table
to plan the visit's details. A general meeting soon broke down into separate conferences: political, security, administration, and arrangements
for the press. Suddenly, some of the names of Algerian information

officials I had never met were matched with flesh and blood individuals sitting across the table from me.

The bloody war for independence from France and the subsequent unrest and coups d'etat had made all Algerian officials security conscious. Since they did not consider the media a privileged national institution, they were not overjoyed when informed that at least 50 newsmen and women would accompany the official party. We worked together as best we could, hopeful that the chemistry of continued personal contact might smooth any rough edges.

Things looked fairly good. Buses provided by the Algerian government would take the press to their quarters on arrival. Vehicles would be available to rush journalists to the central post office for filing copy or phoning in radio reports. A small press pool would follow the secretary to report on his activities. It all looked fine on paper.

Reality was different. Only one bus arrived at the airport, and the driver, frightened by what appeared to him an assault by gesticulating, frantic journalists, refused to open the bus doors. Meanwhile, Algerian plainclothesmen led the press pool to an empty villa in town, locked them in, and held them there until the secretary had finished his official calls. Vehicles did show up for the post office run, but the careful arrangements reserving teletype facilities and voice booths had somehow fallen apart. Broadcast correspondents had to shout their reports over public telephones, and writers had to take turns at the public cable desk, sharing teletype facilities with local citizens sending birthday greetings to Uncle Ahmed in Oran or wiring funds to daughter Farah in Paris. The journalists covering the State Department were not happy, but most of them understood our dilemma.

When the Kissinger caravan had flown off to another diplomatic rendezvous, we held a postmortem review with our Algerian colleagues. Both sides of the table agreed to learn from past errors and to prepare a foolproof scenario for the next visit. We had endured together. Surely the experience had formed a bond of some kind. Many of us were now on a first-name basis. But not all.

The chief of President Boumedienne's security detail, a young redheaded Algerian, would have fit perfectly into the role of a "hard man" on the streets of Belfast. It was he who had sent the press pool off to their temporary lockup. It was obvious that he did not like the media, and I was obviously included in this blanket dislike. But I decided that he was a problem for our security people, not me.

Weeks later, as the secretary's aircraft once again circled the Algiers airport, we were ready. I felt confident as my driver let me out on the steps of the VIP lounge. I shook hands with the Algerian officials I had come to know so well. Then I noticed someone waving to me from the fringe of the crowd where he was being held back by Algerian security police. He was a member of an American television network team that had flown in from Paris that morning. He looked desperate. I hurried to him. He explained the problem as Kissinger's jet settled into its approach run.

He and his team had arrived at the airport early, as instructed, to set up their cameras and recording equipment. The Algerian security chief, my least favorite redhead, had kept them confined to the parking area. Their French cameraman, unused to the ways of a revolutionary Arab republic, had made a whispered comment on Algerian efficiency. As a result, the entire network team, minus my informant, was now locked in the airport men's room, where they were to remain until the official party left for the city.

With minutes to spare before the secretary of state set foot once again on Algerian soil, I tried to reason with the security chief. I was informed forcibly that, diplomat or not, I could join the television team in the men's room if I so chose. The huge jet was now taxiing toward the VIP lounge, where other networks had managed to set up their cameras. I ran for the tarmac and arrived as the engines were being shut down.

A State Department security officer pushed his way forward through the officials, trying to take up his position at the foot of the debarkation ramp. His path was blocked by a husky Algerian. The American applied a bit of force. It was a mistake. He had laid his hand on one of Algeria's top security men and karate experts. The Algerian's elbow swung backward like a lethal piston. As Kissinger left the jet to be greeted by the official reception committee, our security officer was bent double, clutching his stomach, gasping for air.

Shunting the hapless agent aside, we prepared for the usual hand-shaking ritual. From the corner of my eye I saw a television news per-sonality known to thousands of American viewers. His hair was metic-ulously combed, his broadcast notes, rich with incisive comment, were clutched in his hand. He was prepared for his on-camera narrative but there was no camera, no soundman, no sign of his team.

I pushed through the crowd to his side. "Ah... your people..." I began amid the confusion. "A misunderstanding...." My words were drowned out by the revving engine of a nearby aircraft. I continued when the roar diminished. "They're locked in the men's room." Never before—or since—have I seen a man age so quickly.

Nor was this the end of our troubles. When the official cortege prepared to leave the airport and I was directing Kissinger's top press adviser to my sedan, the secretary's vehicle suddenly sped off toward town with its police escort. This completely destroyed our plan for an orderly airport departure. Instead of vehicles number 1, 2, 3, etc., it was drag race time, with the drivers being urged to catch up with the secretary. The speed of each departure depended on the senior passenger's lung power, self-importance, and certainty that his presence was indispensable to the secretary of state. My passenger was no exception. He shouted and cursed, urging the cowed driver on. But it was all to no avail. It turned out that the secretary had been rushed to a special meeting with President Boumedienne, where the bulk of his entourage was not welcome.

For my part, I stayed well clear of the secretary. Granted, he was on a high level, dealing with serious matters of international import, but his somber, imperious, and aloof manner seemed to generate high tension and rivalry among his staff. Although available for any chore needed during his visit, I had no desire to become unnecessarily involved with America's Metternich.

Relations with my redheaded nemesis never did improve, but the Kissinger visit did allow me to make a few contacts with other, more approachable security and police officials. Some time later, Bill Eagleton decided to name me chargé d'affaires of the Interests Section in his absence. Although Robert Pelletreau, the political officer, continued to handle direct contact with the Algerian government on political and diplomatic matters, I occupied Eagleton's office, cleared and signed all communications, conducted staff meetings, and, in addition to my own duties, generally acted as the Interests Section's front man. This added exposure was to serve me well during an unexpected family problem.

Our 17-year-old daughter Shawn was attending the Lycée Descartes, the last remaining French-run lycée in Algiers. Supported by French government funding and occupying a large section of choice real estate, the lycée had a mixed student body of Algerian, French, and other foreign students. It was here that Shawn met Malek Djabali, a young Kabyle student who was to become her future husband.

Like most youths in the 1970s, those at the Lycée Descartes were rebels looking for a cause. But, paradoxically, causes are not easily come by in a revolutionary republic unless you join a government rent-a-crowd. Unofficial street demonstrations are particularly frowned on, so the lycée students had to find another way to express their dissatisfaction with the world.

Not unsurprisingly for a French lycée, the catalyst was sex. A large, wooded park adjacent to the lycée had long been used by the students for smooching, canoodling, and more serious sexual experiments. This situation was frowned on by school authorities, parents, and Algerian education officials. Orders were finally given to fence off this park, making it off limits. This action provided the cause the students had long sought, and they promptly declared a sit-in occupation of the lycée.

It was not long before we realized that Shawn was not only involved in the sit-in, but that she, along with Malek, were among the rebellion's leaders. Shawn had always been a rebel, and her action came as no great surprise. It was troubling nevertheless, particularly when you saw the lycée's occupation from the Algerian viewpoint. Here were a group of privileged youths defying authority (in an authoritarian state) and risking the closure of the last French lycée in Algiers over a cause that was dubious at best. In addition, this minor whiff of student defiance could possibly spread to the underprivileged youths in under-funded and overcrowded Algerian schools with dire consequences.

I reasoned with Shawn when she slipped out of the sit-in to return home in search of food and bottled water. But she was adamant, a real *passionara* of the park. Television clips and news reports on student demonstrations elsewhere in the world had contributed to this bizarre sit-in. I expected it to be over in 24 hours. It wasn't. The director of the lycée called me to underline the seriousness of the situation. He was not sure the Algerian government would allow his institution to survive.

The call that finally got me moving came late on the second day of the sit-in. It was an Algerian security officer whom I'd met during the Kissinger visits. He stressed the fact that his call was personal and not official.

"I would advise you, Monsieur Simpson," he said, "to remove your daughter from the Lycée Descartes as soon as possible." I had begun to bridle at his dictating what I should do, but his next words silenced me.

"If the sit-in does not end this evening," he told me, "we are sending in our riot police. Heads will be broken. I tell you this as a father."

I was at the lycée within 20 minutes. I warned the director, found Shawn and Malek, and ushered them out of the lycée grounds as word spread about what might soon happen. By this time the sit-in had run out of steam. The riot police stayed in their barracks, a compromise was reached on the park, and the Lycée Descartes survived. But that brief flame of student power in Algiers had come very close to filling some hospital beds.

⁓

The powers that be in Washington had decided that personnel serving in Algeria should have a couple of weeks of European R&R in addition to their normal annual leave. We tended not to think about this until the time came. Suddenly, it was our turn and we had to make a decision. Where to go? We knew England, France, Spain, and Italy. The problem was to choose a country we didn't know that would appeal to the girls. Then we remembered a brief offshore stop at Cork, Ireland, when we were traveling to a Paris assignment aboard the SS *United States*. In those days the government allowed you to travel minimum first class by ship if there was no urgency to your arrival at post. The secret was to wait until the last minute before booking a cabin in the hope that the minimum first class accommodations were filled and you'd be upgraded to more luxurious quarters.

Now we remembered that cool, crystal-clear day with our ship riding easily offshore and the rosy-cheeked, laughing women who had come aboard from a rolling launch to sell hand-knit fisherman's sweaters and tweed caps. We recalled the landscape, the rolling hills and fields that formed a misty tapestry of varishaded green. Most of all, despite the distant sound of waves on the shoreline, we remembered the silence and peace that seemed to blanket the land. We decided that Ireland would be our target.

Within weeks we were participants in the rent-an-Irish-cottage scheme and temporarily established in Ballyvaughan, County Clare, on the shores of Galway Bay. The wind was fresh, the oysters plentiful, and authentic folk music readily available at the nearby village of Doolin. Although unused to cows sticking their muzzles over a half door to observe the customers, I took easily to the local pub culture and its veneration of the creamy-headed "black stuff."

Our Irish sojourn sparked some serious thinking about the future. Mary Alice and I had four growing children and no home anywhere in the world. It was time we dropped anchor somewhere, and Ireland appealed to both of us. We had seriously considered France, but a brief house-hunting experience with officious notaries and auctioneers had been off-putting. Prices were comparatively low in Ireland and we began to house hunt. Within a week's time we had begun the process of buying "Folly House," an 18th-century farmhouse on a hill overlooking the Bandon River at the small, historic seaport town of Kinsale in County Cork. We had found those green fields we'd seen from the sea years earlier. Despite the warning from a Ballyvaughan publican that Kinsale had been "Englished," Folly House became our family home.

Periodically, either through some administrative form or an entry on their yearly efficiency reports, Foreign Service officers are given an opportunity to suggest or request future postings that fit their qualifications and desires. I had brought one of those post preference forms home during our stay in Canberra. If I recall correctly, there was space for three choices. Mary Alice and I had pondered our future, suggesting and rejecting various options. Then, with that blend of common sense and zeal that is her trademark, Mary Alice had suggested a first choice.

"How about consul general, Marseille?" she'd asked.

I'd told her that she was being unrealistic, that State would never appoint an agency officer to fill the post, and that we'd never be allowed still another return to France. In the end I acquiesced and Marseille went down as my first choice. What did I have to lose? The identity of the other two choices have faded with time, but I believe they were London and Rabat.

By early summer of 1973 my two-year tour in Algeria was coming to an end, and I was seized with the onward-assignment jitters. Mary Alice and the girls were in Ireland for the summer, and I was acting as chargé d'affaires and preparing to host a 4th of July party at the residence under the Swiss flag. I was also being stuffed with couscous, *chorba* soup, and *merguez* sausages on a daily basis. Harem, our cook and housekeeper, thought any man without an ample and expanding waistline was in danger of being blown away by the sirocco winds. When she wasn't chasing our terrified cat through the house with a broom, she was preparing a heavy culinary treat for Monsieur.

Late one evening a call came through from a friend in USIA personnel. He told me I was under consideration for the consul general position in Marseille but it was far from decided and I should not count on it. I knew that State and USIA trade positions from time to time, and I presumed that was now going on in regard to Marseille. I was warned to await his next call and not discuss the matter. I didn't. The fact that the family was in Ireland made it easier to remain silent.

Four days later, my friend was back on the line to inform me that I would shortly be named as the next consul general in Marseille. I was surprised. I'd been pretty sure the "Christmas Bombing" cable had killed my chances. Normally cynical when it came to government, I had to admit to a certain pride in a Foreign Service that could accept dissent while moving the dissenter onward and upward. I knew the Marseille assignment could mean a minimum tour of three years or possibly four, broken with an interim home leave. Once off the line with Washington, I quickly dialed Mary Alice in Ireland.

"*Bonsoir*, Madame le Consul General," I greeted her in a bad imitation of Yves Montand.

13

Chicago on the Mediterranean

In late August 1974 my wife and I stood on the wide, second-floor terrace of the consul general's residence in Marseille and looked out over the Mediterranean toward the Island of Endoume and the legendary Chateau d'If. The sun was setting, veining the sky with gold. Two fishing boats from the Vallon des Auffes were heading out to sea for a night of squid fishing, leaving wakes like ink lines on the calm water. From this terrace we'd be able to watch the distant white ferries departing for Corsica and Algiers, the varicolored, ballooning spinnakers on regatta days, and the approach of visiting warships from the U.S. 6th Fleet. For us it was a dream come true. For our daughters the return to Marseille was like coming home again.

We had been to the impressive, stuccoed villa many times as guests but never as occupants. The villa and its hillside gardens, high above the Corniche President Kennedy, had belonged to a local newspaper publisher who had succumbed to the infection of collaboration during the war. The U.S. government had later purchased the property and turned it into the principal officer's residence. With it came a housekeeper, who served a demitasse of black breakfast coffee that would burn the paint off a tank turret; her gravel-voiced, cigarette-puffing husband, who performed odd jobs; and a Spanish gardener, who indulged in inordinately long siestas.

My elation at returning to Marseille and moving into the villa was somewhat tempered by my uncertainty in a new, unfamiliar assignment. I was counting on my former tours in Provence, my knowledge of the region, and a number of local friends, both official and unofficial, to cushion the transition.

My first official call on Député-Maire Gaston Defferre was unfettered by unnecessary protocol.

"So, Hemingway," Defferre greeted me with a broad grin, referring to the ginger beard I'd grown since last seeing him, "you're back!" He had remarried since our last meeting; his new wife was the novelist Edmonde Charles-Roux, an outspoken intellectual who had served in the Free French Forces as an ambulance driver. The député-maire promised me his cooperation and assured me that the door to his office was always open.

Defferre was not the only one surprised at our third return to Marseille. Some of the consulate staff, not quite sure how a USIA officer could metamorphose into the principal officer of a State Department post, were a bit confused. I too was feeling my way in an altogether new situation. The consular jurisdiction of Marseille included the French departements of the Aude, Aveyron, Bouches-du-Rhone, Gard, Hérault, Lozère, Pryénées Orientales, Tarn, Var, and Vaucluse. These were indeed some of the choice regions of France, but I wondered how my consul and I could possibly cover such a wide territory. The answer was simple enough: we couldn't. In addition to the two of us, four special agents of the Drug Enforcement Administration (DEA) occupied third-floor offices inaccessible to the public.

When I'd first come to Marseille from Nigeria, the post was staffed by six American officers: a consul general, a consul/political officer, a vice consul/economic officer, a vice consul/consular affairs officer, and two USIS officers with consular titles. The subsequent major reduction in staff had not signaled a diminution of the region's importance; it was more a result of our own retrenchment, budget reductions, and involvement in other parts of the world. My predecessor, Phillip Chadbourne, a career Foreign Service officer who had parachuted into France as a member of the OSS during World War II, had retired prior to my arrival and was busy preparing for a move to Monaco. We were thus both spared an official handover.

Entering my new office brought back a number of memories. It was there, sitting before the large desk flanked by the American flag and the blue, white-starred flag of a consul general that I had taken my oral examination puffing a cigar. It was where Consul General Dan Anderson's telephone call had convinced Ambassador Bohlen to block my unexpected transfer to Laos; where I had joined other officers to pool our impressions of Nikita Khrushchev's official visit to Marseille; and where I'd escorted Communist delegations delivering petitions to the incumbent consul general to protest U.S. policy in Europe, or Asia, or Africa, or South America, or reproaching us for racial repression in America.

In addition to renewing acquaintances with the consulate staff, I had to make a number of protocol calls on local officials and the consular corps. I was also briefed by the consul, Marsha Von Durkheim, who familiarized me with consular procedures and the operation of our communication facilities. Although USIS Paris had withdrawn its American officers from the consular posts in France, I was pleased to see Ramon Garcia, now a senior national employee, in charge of the regional program in Provence.

While reviewing administrative matters, I was sidetracked by some old records and a booklet titled "General Instructions to the Consuls and Commercial Agents of the United States," dated 1838. The records confirmed that the consulate had been in existence by 1795 but could have been established prior to that date. The "General Instructions" included a Department of State circular of August 8, 1815, prescribing the "consular uniform." It consisted of a

> single breast [*sic*] coat of blue cloth with standing cape or collar, and ten navy buttons in front... the front, cuffs, cape, and pocket flaps, to be embroidered in gold, representing a vine composed of olive leaves, and the button holes to be worked with gold thread... vest and small clothes of white and navy buttons... with this dress a cocked hat, small sword, and shoes and knee buckles, are to be gold; otherwise gilt.

Fortunately, such costuming was no longer required. A business suit, rep tie, and comfortable oxfords had become the consular uniform of the day.

I also noted a Navy Department circular dated June 22, 1833, stating, "Where a Consul General resides, it shall be the duty of a commander of our ships of war (commanders of squadrons excepted) to visit the consul general and offer him a passage to the ship of war." Squadron commanders were spared the call but did have to provide the consul general with "passage to the flag-ship." All this was to "promote harmony and concert of action between the commanders of our ships of war and Consuls of the United States residing in foreign ports."

A few weeks into my new job, I began to realize the true extent of the workload and responsibilities involved. Although the overworked consul supervised the visa and passport offices, as well as services to American citizens and visiting merchant ships, I occasionally had to step in to help. Fielding after-hours phone calls from stranded Americans, rushing off to visit Americans in French jails, and organizing the return of deceased citizens were new experiences.

In a city famed for the 1971 film *The French Connection* and its ongoing prominence as a key processing center for the international heroin trade, our consular section was often called upon to assist Americans arrested for smuggling drugs into France from North Africa. For years, our embassy in Paris and the consulate general in Marseille, in coordination with the DEA, had been pressuring the French authorities to get tough on drugs. Now that they had, we often found ourselves trying to explain to imprisoned, weeping, and often criminally naive Americans that we were powerless to free them. We could recommend lawyers, contact their families, monitor their cases, and visit them periodically, but, if they expected the arrival of the U.S. consular officers to end their troubles, they were badly mistaken. We were *not* the 7th Cavalry. My introduction to consular matters increased my respect for the officers involved—and convinced me I would never want to specialize in that "cone" of career development.

The consulate general in Marseille was still considered a political reporting post, and well it should be. Marseille, along with Lyon, was vying for the title of second city of France. It was France's busiest seaport; an opening to North Africa and the Middle East; and home to a strong, well-entrenched Communist party as well as a large Russian consulate general, which was considered a Mediterranean listening post for Soviet intelligence. It was a city and region bubbling with strong political rivalries and racial tensions. This all fit well into my interests and capabilities. I was destined to concentrate on political reporting, to the point that the Paris embassy would remind me that economic reports could be equally important. As principal officer I was able to send cabled reports direct to the department in Washington, with an information copy to the embassy in Paris. Nevertheless, to avoid overkill I had to control my enthusiasm for this new-found freedom.

My previous tours in Marseille had introduced me to the city's reputation as a crime center. No matter how frequent and reasoned the denial of this status by local politicians, the tourist board, and the chamber of commerce, Marseille did live up to its "Chicago on the Med" reputation. This did not mean that bullets were zinging through the streets or that citizens were being attacked in broad daylight. It did mean that *le milieu*, or underworld, and its *caïds*, or bosses, still occupied a traditional and important local role.

Prior to the growth of the worldwide narcotics trade in the mid-1960s, the Marseille gangs had long been involved in drug trafficking. *Brune*, or opium, from Indochina and the Near East, and hashish from North Africa had been the mainstays of this trade. But the *caïds* also ran the local rackets. Prostitution, protection, black market, theft, bank holdups, intimidation bombings, and paid assassinations were dependable money earners. The "bad boys" also invested heavily in nightclubs, bars, and restaurants.

There was usually one dominant gang at the top of the pile. The length of its dominance would depend on the skill of its top *caïd*, its sharing of different slices of crime with lesser gangs, and its skill and ruthlessness in ferreting out any challenge to its rule. Like the Mafia godfathers in the United States, the Corsican *caïds* of Marseille were normally older men who controlled their young, hot-blooded "soldiers" and maintained order on the streets. The living folklore of these gangsters was reflected in their colorful nicknames. A sampling of these includes: "White Haired Jo" or "Jo-Jo the Mandoline"; "Iron Arm Julot"; "Rat Face Nenesse"; "Francis the Rotten"; "One-Armed Paulo" and "Pretty Teeth Milo." The gold fillings I acquired over a considerable period in Marseille, the long-lasting work of my dentist and close friend Luc Valery, earned me, from my police friends, the moniker "Bouche d'Or" ("Mouth of Gold").

Unspoken, informal "understandings" with the police sometimes allowed the *caïds* to apply discipline within their own ranks or punish overly greedy criminal allies without too much official interference. The phrase *réglements de comptes*, or settling of accounts—meaning a gangland murder or shootout—remains a much-used description in the Marseille press. A glance at one page of local news in a Marseille daily under the head "A Chronical of a Murderous Summer" reveals a list of *réglements de comptes* that covered a June-to-October period during which 12 men were killed with heavy-caliber revolvers or sawed-off shotguns. Other reports on the same page are headed "Racket or Vengeance? Bar Bombed on the Cours Gouffe," "He Fires on Bar Owner," and "Canebiere: They Run Off with 4 Million... and Forget Five!"

The increased demand for heroin, particularly for the U.S. market, the long-established skill of the local "chemists" for refining opium into first-class heroin, and the city's geographic position combined to confirm Marseille as a crossroads of the international drug trade. This boom soon became a bonanza that upset the traditional crime balance in the city. Outside criminal elements were drawn like bees to honey. It was the California Gold Rush in a different place, a different time, with "white poison" replacing yellow nuggets.

The Sicilian Mafia became players, as did certain North African and Black African gangs. The well-established Corsican mobsters attempted to find a balance, seeking informal alliances and agreements that would avoid violence and not upset the trade. This did not always work. The Colt .45, the Magnum revolver, the sawed-off shotgun loaded with buckshot—known as "the widowmaker"—and the piano wire garrotte became the power tools of status quo or succession.

As Marseille's narcotics role became legendary, the Drug Enforcement Administration of the U.S. Department of Justice beefed up its office in the consulate general. Where before there had been one or two American "narcs" operating in Marseille, we now had four DEA special agents attached to the consulate. Although they were not legally involved in on-the-ground enforcement in France, they worked closely with their French counterparts and the Customs Service, sharing data, police intelligence, and tips. By the time I returned as consul general, an effective DEA office was well integrated into the French and international antidrug effort in Marseille.

My reintroduction to the local crime scene began with a detailed briefing from Fred Smith, the special agent in charge (SAIC) of the Marseille-based DEA team. Our first meeting marked the beginning of a close working relationship wherein we agreed that I'd be kept informed of everything I needed to know about the DEA operation. This involved access to most of their communications and periodic personal updates from Smith on ongoing cases.

This wasn't a question of prying into matters that didn't directly concern me. It was insurance against the worst-possible-case scenarios that could come from public disclosure of an operation that went wrong, unexpected injuries or fatalities, or bad blood between the DEA and their French counterparts. As principal officer, I didn't want to be caught with egg on my face. Happily, it was an easy working relationship. We often solidified Franco-American law enforcement links with lunches at Chez Étienne in the Panier district, a favored restaurant of the Marseille drug squad. The affable Étienne specialized in thin-crusted pizzas and crunchy, sauteed baby squid. In the underworld tradition of the Panier, it was only natural that local *caïds*, accompanied by some of their acolytes, were often customers in the same restaurant.

We were able to avoid the worst-case scenarios. In fact, the DEA agents working out of the consulate general became so close to the local French narcs that they sometimes had to be reminded that they were not fully operational in France. We had no need for a trigger-happy "Popeye Doyle" under our roof.

The isolated labs that produced the high-grade heroin were in small farmhouses or outbuildings scattered in the rough hill country behind Marseille and the rocky, pine-dotted fields near Aubagne and Aix-en-Provence. The chemists involved were masters of their trade and much in demand for their skills. To seek, locate, and "knock over" one of these production centers was a long-time project involving coordinating and sharing police intelligence from various sources; tracing the sale and movement of chemicals; using informants, telephone taps, and stake-outs; and participating in risky undercover work.

John R. Bartels, Jr., the administrator of DEA, visited Marseille during my tenure and saw for himself the needle-in-a-haystack aspect of the hidden labs. We drove to a pine forest near Aubagne, where the laboratory run by the notorious Cesari gang had recently been pumping out quality heroin destined for the United States. The small farmhouse with its sagging tile roof looked like any other unobtrusive structure in the area. Some time after John Bartels's visit I received the Drug Enforcement Administration Medallion as "a token of the appreciation and high esteem in which we hold you for your concern and warm support of our work and mission." Bartels had closed his covering letter by stating, "I regret not being able to personally present this award." The medallion had been sent to Marseille through the diplomatic pouch, and SAIC Fred Smith had passed it on. We celebrated with a draft beer in the corner café.

International terrorism in the early 1970s was becoming a true men-ace, largely because of interterrorist cooperation and the clandestine but real support provided by Iron Curtain intelligence organizations and certain Arab nations. The Abu Nidal Organization (Black September), which split from the Palestine Liberation Organization in 1974, had proclaimed the United States (and its overseas installations) among its principal enemies and targets. The Japanese Red Army Faction, considered one of the most dangerous terrorist groups, had carried out the 1972 massacre at Lod airport in Israel and two airline hijackings and was to attempt taking over the U.S. embassy in Kuala Lumpur. These and other terrorists were exchanging information, sharing weapons and explosives, and selecting targets throughout Europe.

All U.S. installations overseas had been warned of possible terrorist actions and were on the alert. Due to Marseille's position on the Mediterranean, its proximity to North Africa, its heterogeneous population, and the flow of traffic through its busy port and airport, the city was considered a tempting location for launching a terrorist action. The consulate general was obviously vulnerable, but we took what precautions we could. Our proximity to the préfecture and the préfecture de police was a comfort of sorts, but it soon faded when we considered the suicide actions often attempted by the more rabid terrorist groups.

I was particularly concerned with the security of the residence on the Corniche President Kennedy. My family was definitely living in a soft target. My first move was to install a rolling steel shutter over the entrance hall's large picture window, which looked out on the steep hill behind the residence—a perfect field of fire for a professional gunman. Additional security lights were installed and the main gate was firmly secured each night.

Although international terrorism was a reality, a paranoid fixation on the threat meant that the terrorists had already won half the battle. One reassuring element at this time was my acquaintance with Commissaire Divisionnaire Nguyen Van Loc, a Marseille-born Frenchman of Vietnamese ancestry and *barouder*, or "fighter," with a Commando section during the Algerian War. Loc, known locally as "Le Chinois," was the commander of the Marseille GIPN (Groupe d'Intervention Police National), the Intervention Group of the National Police, an elite 24-man unit divided into three teams, responsible for antigang and antiterrorist operations throughout southern France. The GIPN's 24-hour alert status could find them pitted against hostage takers, bank robbers, Muslim fundamentalists, Basque separatists, Corsican nationalists, or trigger-happy members of the left-wing Direct Action terrorist group. Their responsibility also extended to the protection of visiting VIPs and any consulates under threat of terrorist action.

I had met the incomparable Commissaire Loc for the first time during the Marseille stopover of James Keogh, the director of USIA. Keogh and his wife Verna were on their way to Morocco and had a few hours to kill at Marseille's Marignane airport between flights. While the

Keoghs and Simpsons relaxed in the airport's hospitality lounge, I'd had an opportunity to watch the smooth, unobtrusive technique of the GIPN. They were everywhere yet nowhere, always present but unobtrusive and self-effacing. The slight bulges of their Manurhin .357 Magnum revolvers were barely discernable under their jackets. I had seen special units in action during my three tours in Vietnam, and Loc's men were particularly impressive.

I was to encounter "Le Chinois" on several occasions and we became friends. Loc had a very direct—and politically incorrect—manner of dealing with hostage takers. On one occasion, with a member of his team threatened with execution by desperate bank robbers, the Commissaire entered the building, a .38-caliber derringer concealed in his armpit, to announce, "If you harm that man I'll put two slugs in your skull before you can aim in my direction." The gunmen surrendered.

One day, arriving home for lunch, I found a large Citroën belonging to the GIPN parked in our upper drive. Some of Loc's men were inspecting the property boundaries behind the residence. They were under orders to say nothing and they didn't. Later, Loc would only tell me that the alert had been justified but premature. This was frustrating and hardly reassuring, but it did indicate that his team was on the job. Checking further, I found that the GIPN had reacted to a terrorist alert passed to French authorities from an official American source! In the end it turned out to have been a false alarm.

My official, armored sedan was an additional counterterrorism measure. Its worth as a possible lifesaver had to be balanced against its awkward weight and the danger of a heavy door swinging shut on an arm or a leg. Early on, I decided to hire a former member of the Marseille police as my driver. I reviewed a number of applications and carried out a series of interviews, but my hiring ability was limited by a tight budget. Some of the applicants obviously thought I was seeking a full-time bodyguard. Others had definite ideas about limited working hours.

In the end, I chose someone who looked very good on paper: expert in first aid, skilled at evasive driving, long and honorable service in the police. In reality this paragon of enforcement virtues was not quite what I sought. He was short, slight, and a ringer for the French comedian Fernand Renaud. But time was running out, I needed a driver, he had a ready smile, and he was good with children. I later discovered that a few glasses of wine at a staff party were likely to put him in the mood for demonstrating his skill at tap dancing.

If most terrorist threats to American diplomatic and consular posts came from well-known international enemies of the United States, some of those who considered themselves our friends could send a cold shiver down your spine.

One morning I received a phone call from a veteran who had fought with the French Battalion in Korea. I'd met him at a commemoration ceremony some weeks before. He apologized for bothering me but insisted that I would be interested in meeting a friend of his who had just returned from the urban battlefield of Beirut. He didn't give me many details, but I took my proposed visitor to be a French Aid worker or possibly a young Frenchman who had done his military service as an overseas civilian *coopérant*. Beirut was a Middle East powder keg at the time, the United States was involved, and one never knew what bits and pieces of information could be important or parts of a larger picture.

The meeting turned out to be one of the most uncomfortable 15 minutes I have ever spent. My visitor was French, of medium height, and clean shaven with short-clipped blond hair. He was wearing a sport shirt that revealed tanned, muscled forearms. His pale eyes were steady and seemingly unblinking. If Quentin Tarantino had scripted my visitor into one of his scenarios, the critics would have cried "exaggeration!" I soon learned that the man prided himself on the title "mercenary," but it became obvious that the term "killer" might be more appropriate.

He had come to our meeting with a photo record of his deadly profession in much the same way a fashion model might bring an album of her work to an interview. It included photos of his "kills" taken with a telephoto lens from his sniping "hide" high in a gutted Beirut apartment block. Explaining that he had worked for both Muslims and Christians, he described in detail what arms and ammunition he'd used before discussing the technical problems that shadows and winds caused for a professional sniper.

Speedily turning the pages of his album, I felt the hairs rising on the back of my neck. I'd seen enough violence to last a lifetime, but I found the cold inhumanity of his presentation frightening. His targets had included Lebanese militiamen, PLO gunmen, civilian shoppers, men, women, and children. The final straw was a folded excerpt from *Paris Match* featuring colored shots of his "work" in Beirut.

When I rose to indicate our meeting had ended, he told me the object of his visit. Calmly gathering his material and completely at ease, he asked for my help in contacting the CIA. I told him that would be impossible and showed him out. When I returned to my desk I found a small card with a telephone number pushed under the desk blotter. I then tried to fathom what game he'd been playing. The possibilities ranged from pure dementia or a stillborn attempt to embarrass the U.S. government, to a straightforward but totally misled effort to sell his professional services. Whatever his objectives, I passed on appropriate warnings in the form of "something strange may come your way." Shortly thereafter I told his sponsor I wanted no further recommendations.

Cold War paranoia among Western diplomats could reach epic proportions. It could be labeled the "KGB under the bed" syndrome. Although this condition had to be controlled, it proved to be largely justified. The collapse of the Soviet regime and access to various Communist intelligence files has confirmed the widespread activities of the KGB and demonstrated that the fictional fantasies of spy novel writers were often close to the truth.

The high-walled Soviet consulate general located in the chic Perrier quarter of Marseille was a case in point. My counterpart, Consul General Yuri Konstantinovich Kolychev was a pleasant, rotund fellow with a seemingly bottomless supply of caviar and vodka. In 1971 he had been expelled from Britain for engaging in clandestine operations. The official consular list of Soviet staffers under Kolychev's direction came to 14, with a suspiciously high percentage of chauffeurs. This enumeration did *not* take into account official visitors or those assigned to temporary duty in the Marseille area.

I didn't begrudge Kolychev his large staff. There was certainly enough to keep them busy. Marseille was twinned with the Black Sea port of Odessa, the Soviets participated in the annual Marseille Trade Fair, and Russian cultural groups were constantly visiting Provence. On the more serious side, there were the movements of the U.S. 6th Fleet to monitor. Sudden departures of U.S. warships from French ports, signaled to Soviet intelligence-gathering trawlers, could confirm increased American involvement in the Middle East or other regions of the Mediterranean. Although the official Soviets kept a discreet distance from the French Communist Party, they monitored the local political scene with care. I could only surmise that Kolychev & Co. had been overjoyed at the electoral gains made by the party in the industrial belt around the Etang de Berre and at the former Socialist strong-hold of Arles.

The advent of a Communist mayor and city government in Arles promised problems. Arles had long been twinned with York, Pennsylvania, and their civic linkup had been one of the most effective in France. Annual student exchanges, cultural events, professional exchanges, and group visits had established lasting personal ties. Now we weren't sure how such a drastic political change might affect the Arles-York relationship.

Fortunately, aside from the occasional burst of standard dialectic from the *mairie*, the twinning was strong enough to weather the threatened political storm. The American visitors continued to arrive, and the Arlesians went off to Pennsylvania. One elderly, blue-rinse lady from York summed it up as we left the mayor's office after a civic reception. Pausing to glance over her shoulder at the stars and stripes hanging from the façade of the city hall, she gave me her views on the new mayor of Arles. "He may be a Communist," she said, "but he's such a nice man."

Consul General Kolychev, like other Soviet officials, was constantly quizzing me on the size of our American staff. He simply could not believe that we were only two. Finally, irritated at the repeated questioning, I informed him that we also had four "agents" working out of our consulate. I did not explain that I was referring to the special agents of the DEA.

On the occasion of the 58th anniversary of the October Revolution, Kolychev gave an outstanding reception at his residence cum consulate. The prefect sent his right-hand man; the president of the chamber of commerce was present along with the president of the port, a representative of the député-maire, the general commanding the 7th Military District, and the consular corps. A mix of civilian guests from the commercial, cultural, and media circles of Marseille completed the invitation list. There were hot pirozhki on toothpicks, slices of smoked sturgeon on toast, and generous portions of caviar to be washed down with iced vodka. The bar was manned by consulate "chauffeurs," whose military bearing and close-cropped skulls would not have looked out of place at a U.S. Marine Corps boot camp.

Halfway into the reception I became aware that a young, blue-eyed, well-dressed male member of the Soviet consular staff was paying particular attention to my wife. He was refilling her hors d'oeuvre plate as well as her vodka glass with particular insistence. It was such a blatant approach that Mary Alice winked while the Russian's back was turned to signal her awareness of what was going on. At this point Gerry Clode of the British consulate sidled up to me with a knowing smile on his face. "I think we've caught ourselves a 'raven,'" he murmured, referring to the male counterpart of the female "swallows" the Soviets employ for sexual entrapment.

We watched the young man's tactics for some time before Clode emitted a bored sigh. "Let me handle this," he suggested. I nodded my agreement.

"Young man," Clode addressed the clumsy Lothario, "do you speak English? Ah good! Then listen to me. You are wasting your time. This lady can drink you under the table at any time."

It was hardly a diplomatic turn of phrase and it took some time before Mary Alice saw its inherent humor. But it did have the desired effect. The raven folded his wings and scuttled off as if he had urgent business elsewhere.

Diplomatic social engagements can range from most pleasant to disastrous. My entry into the Eschansonnerie des Papes at Chateauneuf-de-Pape was one of the former. This ceremonial order of pink-nosed devotees to the hearty Cotes-du-Rhone were bon vivants par excellence and an evening spent with them in the surviving cellar dining room of the ruined chateau was a memorable experience. One of my fellow diners that night was General Gustav Fureau, the commander of the French Foreign Legion. Tall and bespectacled with the air of a serious professor, Fureau was the antithesis of the popular image of a Legion officer.

It was interesting to make contact again with the Legion after accompanying Legion units on operations in Tonkin during the Indochina War. When General Fureau discovered that I had spent some time with the Legion's 13th demi-Brigade at Dien Bien Phu, he insisted that I attend the Legion's annual celebration of the Battle of Camerone Hacienda. Since that fortuitous meeting at Chateauneuf-de-Pape in 1975 I've maintained close links with the contemporary Legion and recently published a book on its Parachute Regiment.

A 4th of July celebration at Saint Tropez might not have qualified as disastrous, but it came close. The event was held at the luxurious Hotel Byblos, and the guest list read like the Who's Who of the Riviera. I had been invited and asked to make the keynote speech. I decided to discuss the Provençal contribution to the French naval expedition sent to support the American War of Independence. The French fleet of 12 ships of the line and five frigates had sailed from Toulon on April 13,

1778, and I guessed, correctly, that there would be plentiful background material available in the local archives. One of the ships, *le Marseillois* (74 guns) had been financed and contributed by the Marseille chamber of commerce.

The attendance was a rich mix of designer dresses, expensive jewelry, white dinner jackets, black ties, and deep tans. Champagne corks were still popping when I rose to speak. Having had experience with the short attention span of after-dinner audiences, I was determined to keep the presentation short. I had decided to approach France's role in our Revolutionary War from a different angle. For too long, I explained, we had honored the noblemen and commanders of high rank, including the Comte d'Estaing and the Comte de Grasse. Although these noblemen remained worthy of our respect and gratitude, it was now time to honor the thousands of humble Provençaux: sailors, gunners, soldiers, cooks, supply personnel, and armorers who made up the expeditionary force. Men from Marseille, Toulon, and Nice, many of whom were destined never to see France again.

Well—I had not adequately analyzed my audience. Asking that gathering to put aside the nobility to consider the fate of the common man was the equivalent of reading from Karl Marx at a papal audience. It would be charitable to describe the applause following my conclusion as desultory. I soothed my parched throat with a brimming glass of Dom Perignon and consoled myself with the thought that if any of the long-departed crewmen from *le Marseillois*, *le Languedoc*, or *le Cesar* could have heard my words, *they* would have approved.

14

Leaving the Ranks

The mistral that had blown hard for three days was subsiding and the morning sun had just appeared over the jagged mountains of the Sainte Baume. In a deep valley near Signes the first rays of sun had triggered the repetitive buzzing of cicadas. Small green grasshoppers leaped out of the dry grass and a high-flying jet crayoned a golden contrail across the blue sky.

I'd come to this lost valley during the hot summer of 1976 to attend a special ceremony. Ceremonies commemorating the World War II highlights of the Allied landings and the liberation of Marseille were usually held on a wide parapet of Fort Saint Nicolas, high above Marseille's Vieux Port. These functions, attended by local officials and the consular corps, were militarily efficient, timed to perfection, and bordering on the unemotional.

The ceremony at the charnier de Signes (charnel house of Signes), commemorating members of the Résistance captured, tortured, and summarily executed by the Germans, was simple yet deeply impressive. I had arrived early, parked, and walked to the small cemetery. A convoy of cars then wound down the dirt road, leaving a pall of yellow dust behind them. I shook hands with the newly arrived military and civilian officials and watched the Résistance veterans unload flagstaffs and wreaths from their cars. Most of the men were elderly or middle-aged. They wore dark suits, and their medals clinked together as they walked to the cemetery. Some of them had berets pulled forward over their brows. Others used canes or walking sticks and moved with difficulty. There was one petite, gray-haired woman among them. She wore a tailored suit with the twisted barbed wire emblem of the wartime concentration camps on its lapel. The Signe memorial represented a microcosm of the Résistance experience, one that included heroism, betrayal, entrapment, torture, and death.

In July 1944, the Germans and the collaborationist Vichy Milice, tipped off to a meeting of nine leaders of the Basses Alpes Committee of Résistance in the small town of d'Oraison, had set an elaborate trap. Members of the Milice, posing as Résistants from the neighboring Hautes Alpes, staged a fake battle with the Germans in and around d'Oraison on the day of the meeting. When the "defeated" Germans withdrew, taking their "dead and wounded" with them, the Résistance leaders came out of hiding to fraternize with the "victors." Later, as the two groups conferred in a local restaurant "guarded" by the false Résistants, the strong force of Germans—including the miraculously recovered dead and wounded—returned, surrounded the building, and captured the nine leaders.

After three days and nights of torture and beatings at Gestapo headquarters on the rue Paradis in Marseille, the dying captives were driven to Signes in a truck. There they were dumped into a common grave that already held the remains of 39 Résistance fighters previously tortured by the Gestapo. Sand found in the noses and lungs of many of those interred at Signes indicated that they had been buried alive. Someone aware of secret Résistance planning must have been the informer, but, to this day and to my knowledge, the informer's identity has never been revealed. It is difficult to establish definitive truth when most of the witnesses are dead.

The ceremony at Signes was marked by a respectful silence. No clash of brass or rattle of drums. The orations were brief. Even the bugle sounding *Aux Morts*, the French equivalent of taps, seemed muted. There were tears but no overt sobs, just the hiss of the dying mistral high in the tall cyprus and pine. If the Résistance can be called a family, this was definitely a family affair. Nevertheless, the warmth of the postceremony welcome I received from the former Résistance members assured me that I was not considered an outsider. I returned to Marseille with a new respect for the *real* Résistance and those French men and women who had died so horribly 32 years earlier.

Ambassadorial visits could be a headache. Some ambassadors (or their wives) could be demanding, their special assistants often acted like nervous courtiers, and the strain an official cortege puts on a small post can result in semicontrolled chaos. The classic visit to Marseille usually included a formal dinner at the prefecture, a call on the député-maire, a visit to the University of Aix-Marseille and a meeting with the American students there, an informal luncheon with speeches as a guest of the organization France–États Unis, a meeting with the local media, and a walk through the consulate general to meet the staff. Additions to the program would depend on an ambassador's time and particular interests. An ambassador's wife, although she participated in certain official functions, was able to choose her own schedule. It could include a tour of an art museum; a meeting with local professional women; or a visit to a school, hospital, or market. A less ambitious program could include standard tourism: a visit to the Chateau d'If or the basilica of Notre Dame de la Garde, the church that dominates the city, topped by the gilded statue of the Virgin—*la bonne mère*.

Ambassadorial visits were usually short in duration but busy. As in gearing up for a presidential arrival, the preparations were the hardest. Invitation lists, security, transport, menus, timing, speech texts and remarks, media interviews, rest periods—all these were part of the mix that would hopefully produce a successful visit.

During a previous tour in Marseille with USIS I'd welcomed Ambassador Bohlen to rue Saint Jacques for a meeting with local journalists and accompanied him during his call on the rector of the University of Aix-Marseille. That visit had been a cake walk, largely because of Bohlen's professionalism as a veteran diplomat and his relaxed personal manner.

In 1976 I prepared for the visit of Ambassador Kenneth Rush with some trepidation. A successful businessman, Rush had previously held a number of important government posts in both the State and Defense Departments before being appointed ambassador to France by President Gerald Ford. He'd served as a counselor to the president, charged with coordinating national and international economic policy, as ambassador to the German Federal Republic in 1969, and as a deputy secretary of state. My concern about Ambassador Rush's visit centered primarily on his encounter with Député-Maire Defferre.

Defferre had not held back on his criticisms of U.S. foreign policy over the previous months. I was not looking forward to leading Ambassador Rush, a former president of both a bank and a chemical company, into the lion's den of Marseille's foremost Socialist. Nervous calls from the embassy trying to chart in advance the possible direction of a

Rush-Defferre conversation only added to my foreboding. The fact that Defferre controlled the political content of his influential newspapers made me doubly wary.

When I accompanied the ambassador into Defferre's office, it was obvious that my concern had been unjustified. The hardnosed militant Socialist and the successful capitalist and expert on international economics hit it off well from the first handshake. The ambassador's calm delivery was a perfect counterpoint to Defferre's rapid-fire questions. Rush, who had been one of the chief American negotiators of the quadripartite accords on Berlin, was a shrewd judge of politicians. Defferre, who had received ambassadors from many nations in his office, was noted for his quick, often critical, assessment of their worth. The fact that the ambassador left the *Mairie* smiling and that the député-maire put in a rare personal appearance at an exhibit of American photographs opened by the ambassador the next day made my job a lot easier. With Nguyen Van Loc and his GIPN team ensuring the ambassador's safety, I had no real worries regarding security.

Other nongovernmental visits were easier to handle. Pierre Salinger of ABC, my old friend from San Francisco newspaper days and an unofficial "Mr. America" in France, agreed to speak at a dinner of the Marseille Rotary Club. As President Kennedy's former press secretary, the cigar-chomping Salinger was much in demand as a speaker and respected by the French media. His presence on innumerable television talk shows and TV political discussions was always a breath of fresh air. He was direct and often blunt in explaining U.S. policies, cutting through the fuzzy cant and prejudice of pompous French intellectuals with a natural ease that threw them off balance. I arranged a press luncheon at the residence to introduce Salinger to a group of Marseille editors. It was an informal, shirtsleeve affair with abundant food and wine. There were plentiful humorous journalism anecdotes shared over the armagnac and coffee. Some editors were late for their first deadline. It was almost like being back in the city room.

The bombshell hit as we approached the end of my second year in Marseille as consul general. Somewhere in the Department of State a decision had been made to classify Marseille as an economic/commercial reporting post. In personal terms this meant my plans for a tour of two years followed by home leave and then two more years was out the window. I was notified that an FSO specializing in economic matters would replace me at the end of my first two years. This was an unexpected, unwelcome development. Most troubling was the disruptive effect it would have on the children's schooling.

No stranger to the importance of lobbying within government, I fired off some telegrams and worked the telephone. After several days I knew that State would *not* change its stand on Marseille. My sources in Washington informed me that, in addition to the push to make Marseille an economic reporting post to please the Department of Commerce, the State Department was miffed because USIA had not offered an equal number of overseas positions to State's Foreign Service Officers. Fortunately, the ambassador, the deputy chief of mission, and USIA requested that my cut-off date be extended for six months, thus allowing the children to finish their school term and their father to obtain a suitable onward assignment.

The jolt of this sudden change did have one practical result. It prompted me to think seriously about an early retirement. This possibility had crossed my mind in Algeria during the episode of the "Christmas Bombing." Now the thought returned with increased relevance, although my six-month grace period would allow adequate decision time. I had published five novels. Like most writers, I harbored the unrealistic dream of eventually living off my literary product.

Meanwhile, I had to find a new posting, and they were not thick on the ground. In the end, it was Bill Payeff who threw me a lifeline. He was to be assigned as counselor of embassy for public affairs in Paris, he was looking for a deputy, and he wanted to know whether I was interested. The only problem appeared to be the time gap of four months between my departure from Marseille and my tentative arrival in Paris.

Payeff came up with the answer. He had been offered a short stint as a diplomat in residence at the University of South Carolina's Institute of International Studies. Unable to accept because of his Washington commitments, he arranged to have me fill the temporary slot, a perfect solution to my timing problem.

We had never been to the Deep South before. Columbia, South Carolina, with the Stars and Bars flying from its state house and the impact points of Yankee cannonballs marked by bronze stars bolted into its walls, was indeed a new experience. We lived in a small apartment adjacent to the campus, and I returned to academia for the four month period. I lectured on the Far East and France, supervised seminars on foreign policy and diplomacy, advised graduate students on aspects of their research papers, and lunched periodically at the Faculty Club. I found the students serious, questioning, and open to new ideas.

But I was also surprised to learn how little these students of international affairs knew about their own nation's diplomatic structures and the realities of life in the Foreign Service. Off campus, I spoke on the French Communist Party at a senior officer's seminar at the Fort Jackson Infantry Center and appeared on local TV and radio.

I had an easy, joking relationship with Richard L. "Dixie" Walker, the institute's director, a Chinese speaker and specialist on East Asia who was soon to serve as U.S. ambassador to South Korea. I also renewed my friendship with Paul Kattenburg, a professor at the institute, an expert on Indochina and former State Department officer whose career had been blunted for telling the unpalatable truth about Vietnam.

Perhaps the most difficult readjustment to be made in Columbia related to the local cuisine. Everything that swam, flew, or padded on four legs seemed to end up in the deep-fry pot—except the grits. I never did understand why certain restaurants could serve hard liquor with meals but not wine. But these were minor complaints. All in all, I was lucky to have found this temporary billet and grateful to the South Carolinians for their easy hospitality and friendship.

As my residency at the university came to a close, the personnel office in Washington asked Dick Walker to fill out the standard officer evaluation report covering my time at his institute. He performed this task and dutifully sent the completed form to Washington. If anything, it overstated my contribution to the institute's program. Then, always the prankster, he filled out a second report for my benefit. These are some of his "rating remarks."

POSITION DESCRIPTION: Basically two—Chauffeur to Heathwood school and Pipe Cleaning.

WORK REQUIREMENTS AND PRIORITIES: None—which made the task all the more difficult. Simpson's usual question was "how can I do nothing and still not be occupied with it?"

DISCUSSION OF WORK PERFORMANCE: What work? What performance?

MANAGERIAL ABILITY: He did manage to learn how to unlock his office door and occasionally managed even to get into the room."

I returned to Paris in the summer of 1977 and immediately took up my work as deputy public affairs officer, supervising a staff of 14

Americans and 66 French nationals. The USIS operation—with the exception of the press attaché's office—was still housed in the embassy annex that had once been the historic Hôtel Tallyrand. The Simpson family moved into a government-leased apartment on the rue de la Tour Maubourg, not far from the Seine. Raymond Marcellin, President Giscard d'Estaing's minister of the interior and the nation's "top cop," occupied the apartment above us. This automatically guaranteed a 24-hour police guard on the building. Kate and Maggie entered a nearby French lycée, Shawn was completing her graduate degree at the University of Aix-Marseille, and Lisa was about to begin her study of medicine at Trinity College, Dublin.

All seemed well in the best of all possible worlds, and yet it wasn't. I had never cared for administrative work and suddenly it took up most of my day. I was immediately faced with the reorganization of ICA France and the restructuring of its programs. Under the Carter administration, USIA had become ICA, the International Communication Agency, a name more fitting a worldwide telephone company than an overseas arm of government.

My previous impression of the Paris embassy as a huge diplomatic factory was now compounded. It seemed even larger and the dull staff meetings even longer. Representation allowances had been cut drastically, and the days of the long bistro lunches with French editorialists were over. Rather than join some of my colleagues for sandwiches in the embassy lounge, where ongoing business was often the topic of conversation, I welcomed a brisk walk to le Rubis, near the Marché St. Honoré. It was a small, traditional wine bar where bankers rubbed shoulders with workers as they enjoyed tasty *plats du jour, saucisson* sandwiches on country bread, and Beaujolais straight from vineyard proprietors. Standing at the zinc-topped bar of le Rubis I closed my mind to business and felt I was truly back in Paris.

Arthur A. Hartman, the new career ambassador to France, had served in Paris with the Economic Cooperation Administration in 1948 when I had been part of the bearded, ex-GI bohemia of the Left Bank. The Hartmans were eager for USIS to take a more active role in Parisian cultural affairs, and their invitation lists for social events at the residence were filled with the French cultural elite and their American counterparts. Despite my Parisian art training and secondary career as a novelist, I had never served as a cultural officer and was unenthusiastic about USIS cultural programming. In the end Bill Payeff arranged for the assignment of a specialist to act as the ambassador's cultural major-domo.

To complete what I came to label the "Paris Embassy Blues," my third tour there was marked by two major events: a visit to France by President Jimmy Carter and the arrival of an ICA inspection team.

The Carter entourage included another example of that strange genus, the obnoxious White House advance man and weight-thrower. Fortunately, Bill Payeff had asked Ed Harper, a veteran USIS officer, to fly in from Madrid to back up our press attaché during the presidential visit. Harper, whom I had known in Nigeria as an effective flour sales-man, had also been a semipro boxer and did not take kindly to young White House political appointees who threw their weight around. In fact, during a previous visit of Secretary of State Cyrus Vance to Madrid, Harper had warned one of the advance men to stop interfering with the planning or suffer a broken jaw. Harper's appearance in Paris had a definite calming effect on that particular visitor. Later, during the president's speech to a select audience gathered in the Palais des Congrès, a large conference center at La Porte Maillot, the advance man managed to get locked out of the hall by French security personnel. "Disaster," he'd murmured in despair, slumping near the closed door.

The Carter speech was not particularly impressive. The high-water trousers and visibly short socks he was wearing served to perpetuate the myth of the country bumpkin. Fortunately, the president's visit to the Normandy landing beaches with President Giscard d'Estaing was a positive diplomatic and public relations move. It stressed continued Franco-American ties, washed away some of the Gaullist bitterness, and received heavy and positive media coverage.

The inspection of ICA Paris was another administrative nightmare. It was the standard paper chase followed by individual interviews, staff meetings, and required social events. As I had experienced other inspections and had led the inspection team to Zaire, the procedure was not a new experience for me. But coordinating the presentations of each section, ensuring that the inspectors obtained the documents they required, and arranging for them to speak privately with all the staff and other embassy sections reminded me of how much I'd appre-ciated working on a smaller scale at a smaller post. No skeletons were found in our closets, but, as always, the inspectors submitted a num-ber of recommendations that had to be addressed within a specific time limit. The task of ensuring compliance landed on my desk. Once again, the tempting image of retirement hovered on the edge of my consciousness.

One of the best methods of decompression after a hard week at "the factory" was our Saturday morning visit to the marché on the rue Cler. This bustling outdoor market and the food shops along the same street, with their colors and scents, were a salute to the variety and seriousness of French gastronomy. Stands filled with red radishes and ripe tomatoes, yellow and green peppers, oranges and tangerines, carrots and cabbages, strawberries and purple grapes were manned by raspy-voiced vendors vying for shopper's attention by offering a taste of their product.

A cheese shop with a sidewalk display offered Cantal and Brie, Camembert and Fourme, Gruyere, Munster, Tomme de Savoie and innumerable goat cheeses, both hard and soft, formed in circles, pyramids, and blocks. The authoritative odor of the display tempted any cheese fancier to enter the shop's interior where many more varieties were on offer.

The boucherie was hung with meat: aging sides and cuts of beef; whole lambs; meticulously cut chops, steaks, and roasts; and trays of liver, tripe, and tongue. Wild game adorned the shop's façade in the winter. Wild boar, hare, teal, pheasant, grouse, snipe, and deer were on display, dripping fresh blood on the newly fallen snow.

The charcuterie offered terrines of paté, ready-cooked dishes, rolled ham, truffled poultry, *boudin noir*, galantine of rabbit, *saucisson*, head cheese, mortadella, smoked ham and sausages, veal pies, and *foie gras* in all its forms.

Walking home, we would pause outside the shop of Petrossian, the famed purveyor of smoked salmon, to eye the tins of expensive caviar and watch the employees cutting thin, pink slices of salmon with long, razor-sharp knives. Pausing for an apéritif at a neighborhood café, I would glance up the rue de la Tour Maubourg toward the Hôtel des Invalides and ponder an incongruous but very French reality, namely, that Napoleon's tomb, the French government's principal clandestine (underground) telephone tapping facility, and a major outdoor food market were all in easy walking distance of each other.

"How many assignments have you had in France?" The question was posed early in 1979 by John E. Reinhardt, the director of ICA, as he was leaving our apartment following an informal luncheon in his honor. He was on an official visit to Paris, checking on our operations and conferring with Ambassador Hartman.

"Six," I replied, after some hurried finger counting. "Branch PAO in Marseille; assistant press and publications officer in Paris; BPAO Marseille again; information officer, Paris; consul general, Marseille; and deputy country public affairs officer, Paris.

"Six!" Reinhardt repeated, obviously dumbfounded. "We'll have to see about that."

That comment had an ominous ring, and I hastened to remind him that I'd done my time in hardship posts, including four years in Vietnam, two in Nigeria, and two in Algeria. Mary Alice had heard this exchange. Once the director had departed, she sighed and commented, "There goes Paris!" I disagreed.

Reinhardt said nothing more about the subject during his stay, and I thought it was a dead issue. As it turned out, Mary Alice was right and I was wrong. Some weeks later I received a call from a friend in the agency's personnel office informing me that a telegram was being drafted authorizing my direct transfer to Kinshasa, Zaire, as counselor of public affairs and chief of the ICA operation.

The well-meaning caller wanted to prepare me for the receipt of the telegram. He also wanted to present this direct transfer in the best possible light. He underlined the positive: Kinshasa was one of the agency's largest posts in one of Africa's most important nations; the assignment would definitely mean a promotion; and someone with my experience was needed there. My caller was, after all, working in personnel.

I put down the telephone, rose from my desk in the Hôtel Tallyrand, and walked to the window. The view included the Tuileries Gardens, part of the Place de la Concorde, and the busy rue de Rivoli, almost the same vista I'd enjoyed during my tour as information officer. If this was the way the agency now treated its senior officers, I wanted no part of it. Then my eyes fixed on the small memorial plaques fixed to the wall of the Tuileries across the street. They marked the spot where a French tank had taken a direct hit during the liberation of Paris. All of its crew had died after fighting their way into the French capital. My problem suddenly seemed comparatively minor.

When I broke the news that evening, Mary Alice was not surprised. We had a long conversation while Kate and Maggie remained in their rooms doing their homework. The decision-making scale was heavily weighted against accepting the Kinshasa assignment. The size of the ICA residence on the banks of the Congo River would never balance the real problem of uprooting two teenagers and transplanting them into what then promised to be a politically unstable and perhaps violent environment.

The Kinshasa telegram acted as a catalyst, reviving all my past daydreams of an early retirement. We finally agreed that if I was going to retire early and write, it would be better to do it then, at 54, than later. The next day I informed the agency that, rather than arrive in Kinshasa in a few weeks' time, I was applying for voluntary retirement within the same time frame. After one last attempt to convince me that I was making a mistake, personnel began processing my retirement, and I left the ranks for good on June 29, 1979. It had been a great life and I wouldn't have traded my Foreign Service experiences for any other career.

Index

About the Author

Howard R. Simpson's varied career in the Foreign Service ranged from his role as a decorated USIA war correspondent during the Franco-Vietminh War to that of U.S. consul general in Marseille, from official delegate to the Cannes Film Festival to advisor to the president of the Naval War College. Other assignments took him to Nigeria, Australia, and Algeria. Now a novelist and writer on defense matters, Simpson has published eleven novels, including *Someone Else's War*, and four works of nonfiction, including *The Paratroopers of the French Foreign Legion*. His writing has appeared in *Harper's*, *Commonweal*, the *International Herald Tribune*, *Newsday*, *Military Review*, *Army*, and other publications. He lives outside Washington, D.C.